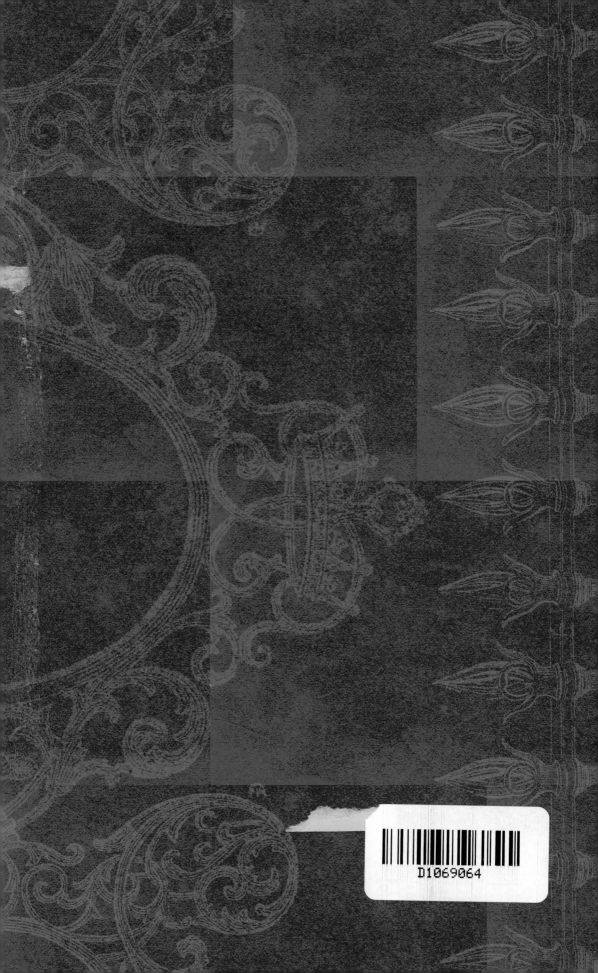

D1069064

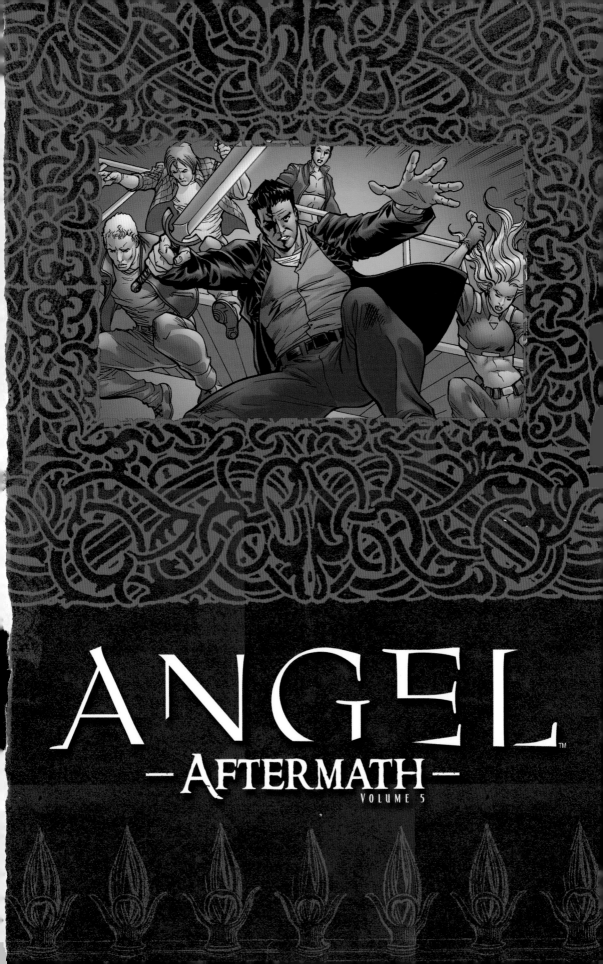

ANGEL

-AFTERMATH-

VOLUME 5

WRITTEN BY KELLEY ARMSTRONG

ORIGINAL SERIES EDITS BY CHRIS RYALL & MARIAH HUEHNER
COLLECTION EDITS BY MARIAH HUEHNER & JUSTIN EISINGER
COLLECTION DESIGN BY NEIL UYETAKE
COLLECTION COVER BY NICK RUNGE

IDW Publishing
Operations:
Ted Adams, Chief Executive Officer
Greg Goldstein, Chief Operating Officer
Matthew Ruzicka, CPA, Chief Financial Officer
Alan Payne, VP of Sales
Lorelei Bunjes, Dir. of Digital Services
AnnaMaria White, Marketing & PR Manager
Marci Hubbard, Executive Assistant
Alonzo Simon, Shipping Manager
Angela Loggins, Staff Accountant
Editorial:
Chris Ryall, Publisher/Editor-in-Chief
Scott Dunbier, Editor, Special Projects
Andy Schmidt, Senior Editor
Justin Eisinger, Editor
Kris Oprisko, Editor/Foreign Lic.
Denton J. Tipton, Editor
Tom Waltz, Editor
Mariah Huehner, Associate Editor
Carlos Guzman, Editorial Assistant
Design:
Robbie Robbins, EVP/Sr. Graphic Artist
Neil Uyetake, Art Director
Chris Mowry, Graphic Artist
Amauri Osorio, Graphic Artist
Gilberto Lazcano, Production Assistant

ISBN: 978-1-60010-516-6

12 11 10 09   1 2 3 4

www.IDWPUBLISHING.com

Angel created by Joss Whedon and David Greenwalt.
Special thanks to our Watcher, Joss Whedon, and Fox Worldwide Publishing's
Debbie Olshan for their invaluable assistance.

The Hell Moment. A sliver of time when all of L.A. got sucked into the stuff of nightmares. All because Angel decided not to let Evil Incorporated (Wolfram & Hart) pull his strings anymore. Everything appeared normal to anyone outside of L.A. … or at least as normal as L.A. has ever seemed to those outside it. Inside, however, it was the end of days. And Angel, as punishment, was made human and weak.

Doing what he could, despite his handicap, Angel hides himself from his allies and goes about trying to right what's gone horribly wrong. Meanwhile, Illyria is shifting in time again, going slowly insane, and becoming Fred whenever it's least convenient. Spike sticks with her, while Lorne tries to keep order, and Connor, Nina, Gwen, and Kate band together to fight the hordes. Oh, and Wesley is a ghost liaison to the Senior Partners.

But it's Gunn who has made the most radical turn, literally, as a crazed vampire who believes he still has a soul and is destined to become "the" vamp of the Shanshu Prophecy. Manipulated by Wolfram & Hart, he eventually kills the Fred-persona once and for all, causing Illyria to come out in her true and massive demon form, in an effort to end it all. She is taken down by the memories of Fred from Wesley and Spike, projected into her from Betta George.

Desperate and deluded, Gunn makes one final attempt to assert control, and kills Connor—the one thing that finally allows Angel to see a way out. Goading Gunn into combat, Angel sacrifices himself for his son, for his friends, and for the city he loves.

But of course, Wolfram & Hart can't have that. Pulling Angel out of his timeline, they reset to the moment in the alley… the very moment before everything went to Hell. Angel and his friends make short work of their enemies, blasting the army of W&H away with the combined wrath of Illyria and the dragon. Angel then finds Gunn, badly wounded, near death, and attempts to take him back to Wolfram & Hart… only to find that all trace of the building and its inhabitants are gone… almost like they never existed at all.

At the hospital with Gunn, Angel is reunited with Connor. Some very manly tears are shed.

Yet, something seems off. And that's when Angel realizes…everyone *remembers*. Everyone knows what he did, how he saved them, and what he sacrificed to get them out. He's famous. No more anonymity, no more lurking in the shadows. He's the vampire with a destiny… now what?

chapter

One

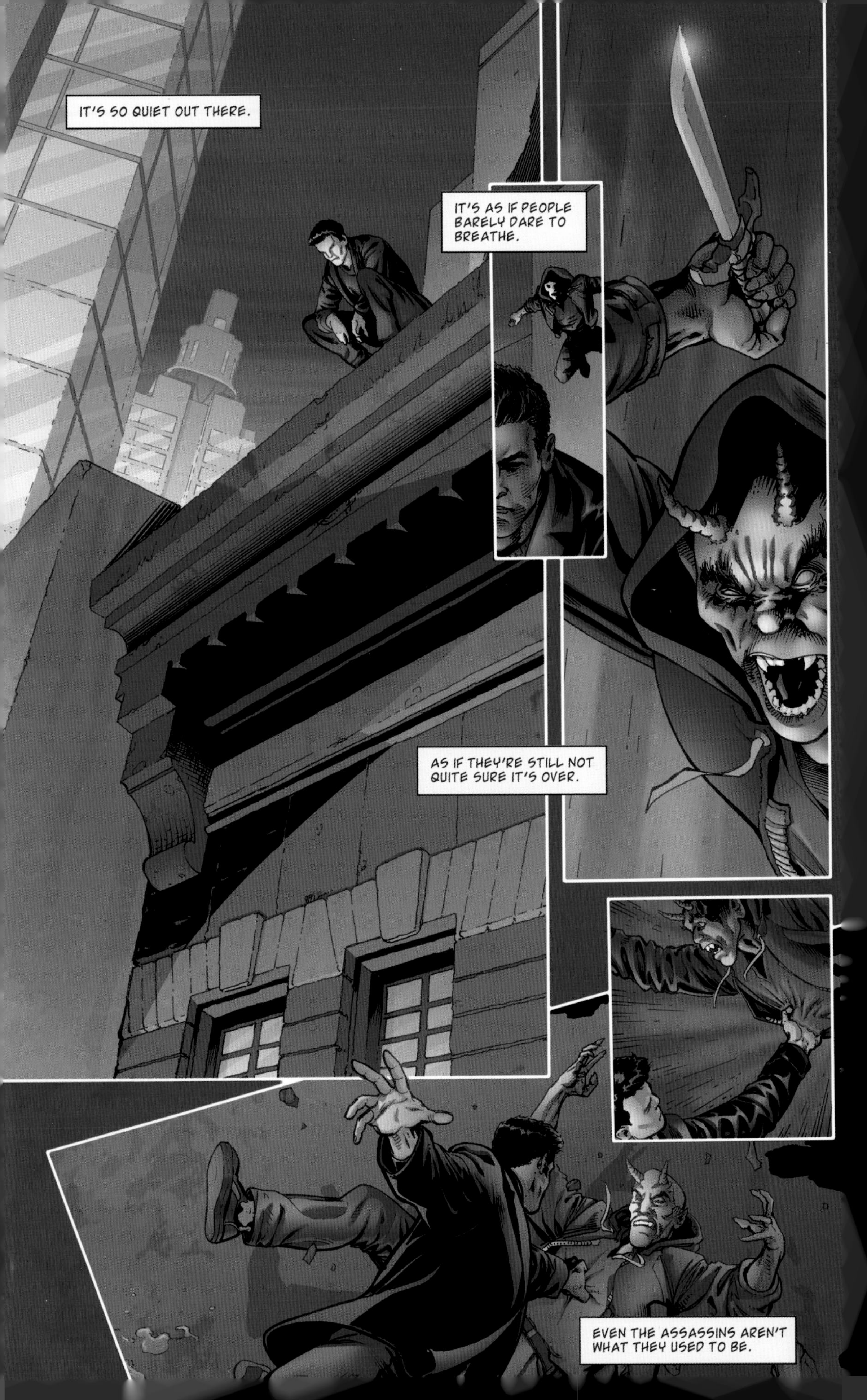
IT'S SO QUIET OUT THERE.
IT'S AS IF PEOPLE BARELY DARE TO BREATHE.
AS IF THEY'RE STILL NOT QUITE SURE IT'S OVER.
EVEN THE ASSASSINS AREN'T WHAT THEY USED TO BE.

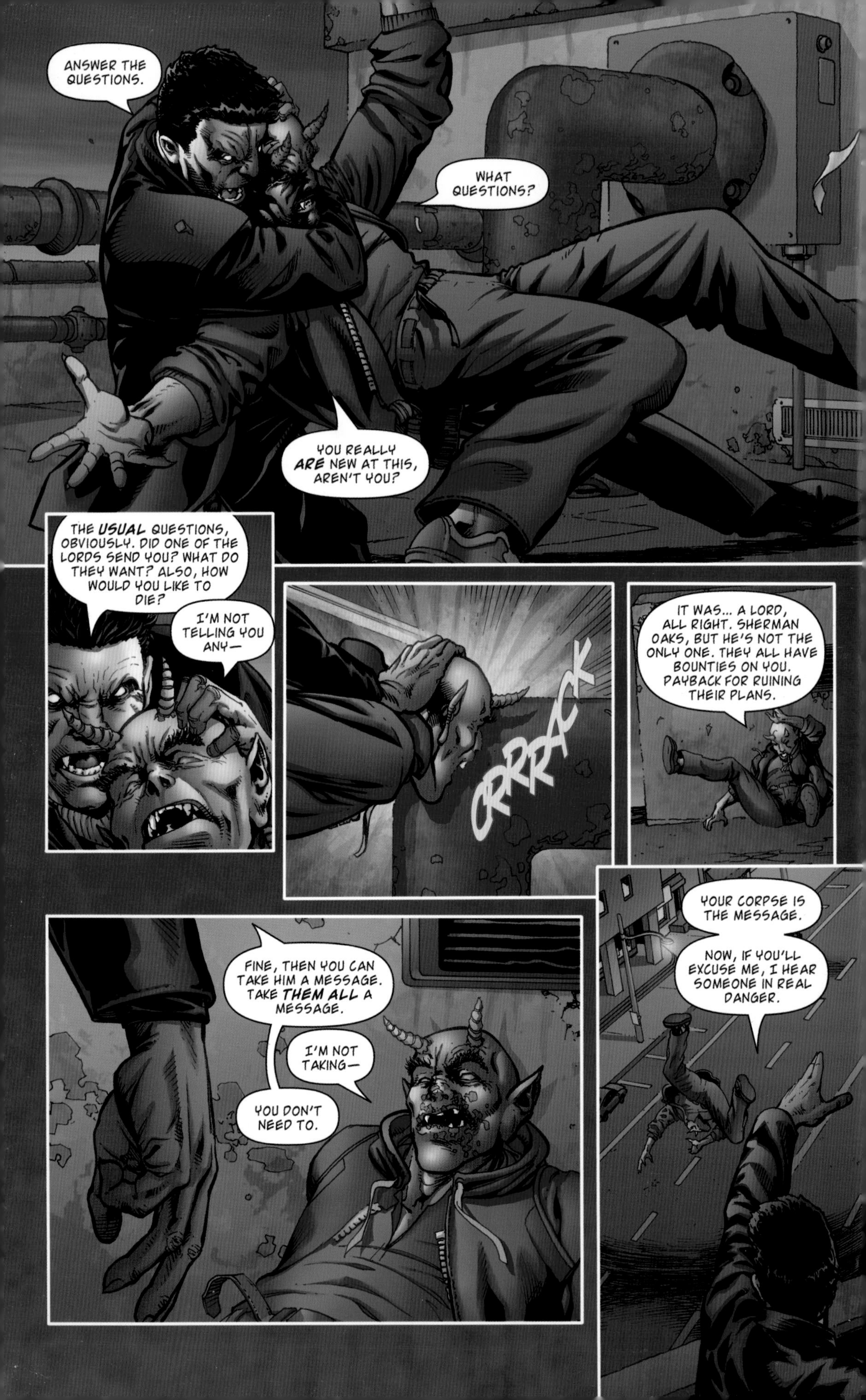

ANSWER THE QUESTIONS.
WHAT QUESTIONS?
YOU REALLY ARE NEW AT THIS, AREN'T YOU?
THE USUAL QUESTIONS, OBVIOUSLY. DID ONE OF THE LORDS SEND YOU? WHAT DO THEY WANT? ALSO, HOW WOULD YOU LIKE TO DIE?
I'M NOT TELLING YOU ANY—
CRRRACK
IT WAS... A LORD, ALL RIGHT. SHERMAN OAKS, BUT HE'S NOT THE ONLY ONE. THEY ALL HAVE BOUNTIES ON YOU. PAYBACK FOR RUINING THEIR PLANS.
FINE, THEN YOU CAN TAKE HIM A MESSAGE. TAKE THEM ALL A MESSAGE.
I'M NOT TAKING—
YOU DON'T NEED TO.
YOUR CORPSE IS THE MESSAGE.
NOW, IF YOU'LL EXCUSE ME, I HEAR SOMEONE IN REAL DANGER.

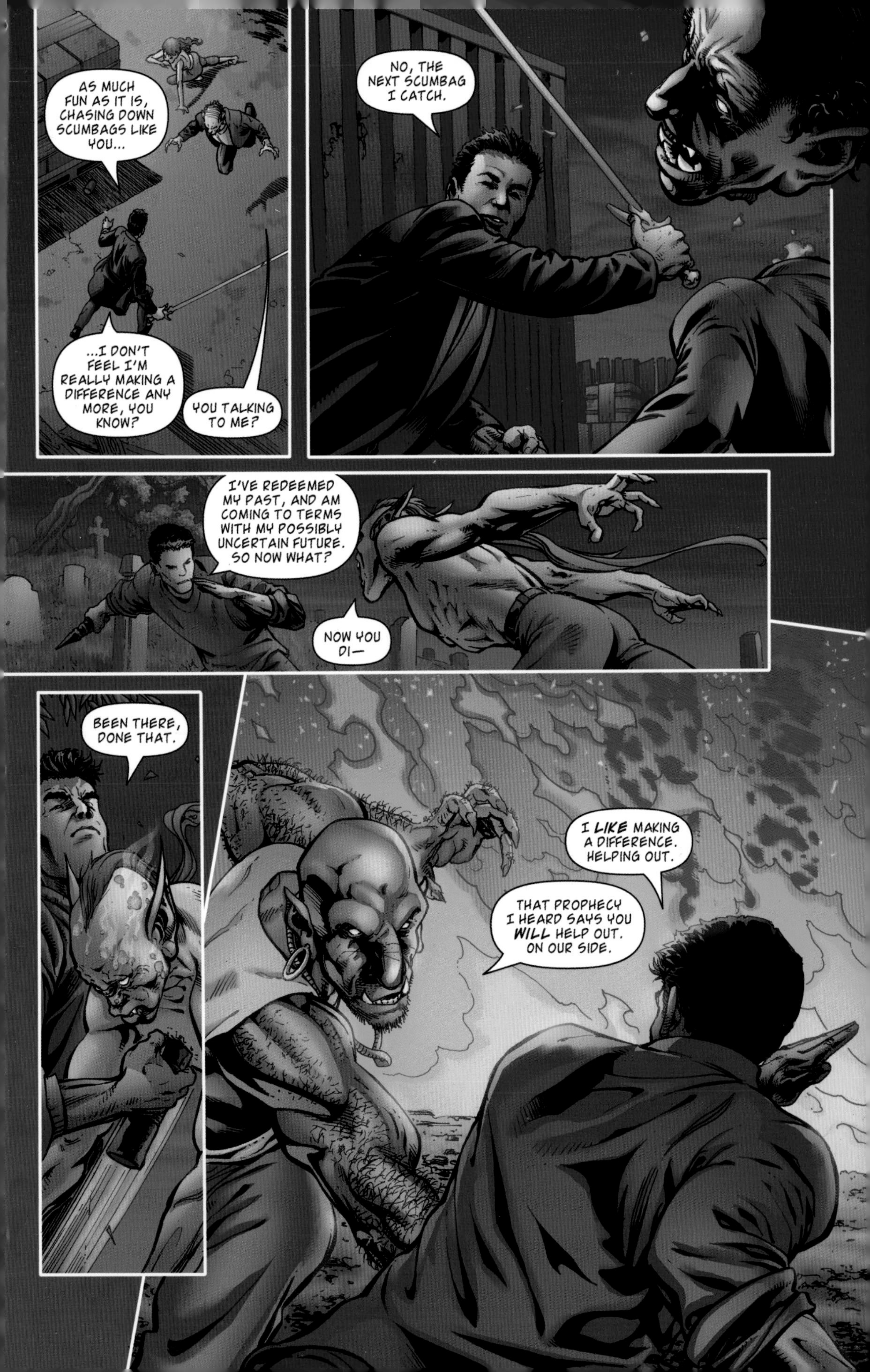
AS MUCH FUN AS IT IS, CHASING DOWN SCUMBAGS LIKE YOU...
...I DON'T FEEL I'M REALLY MAKING A DIFFERENCE ANY MORE, YOU KNOW?
YOU TALKING TO ME?
NO, THE NEXT SCUMBAG I CATCH.
I'VE REDEEMED MY PAST, AND AM COMING TO TERMS WITH MY POSSIBLY UNCERTAIN FUTURE. SO NOW WHAT?
NOW YOU DI—
BEEN THERE, DONE THAT.
I LIKE MAKING A DIFFERENCE. HELPING OUT.
THAT PROPHECY I HEARD SAYS YOU WILL HELP OUT. ON OUR SIDE.

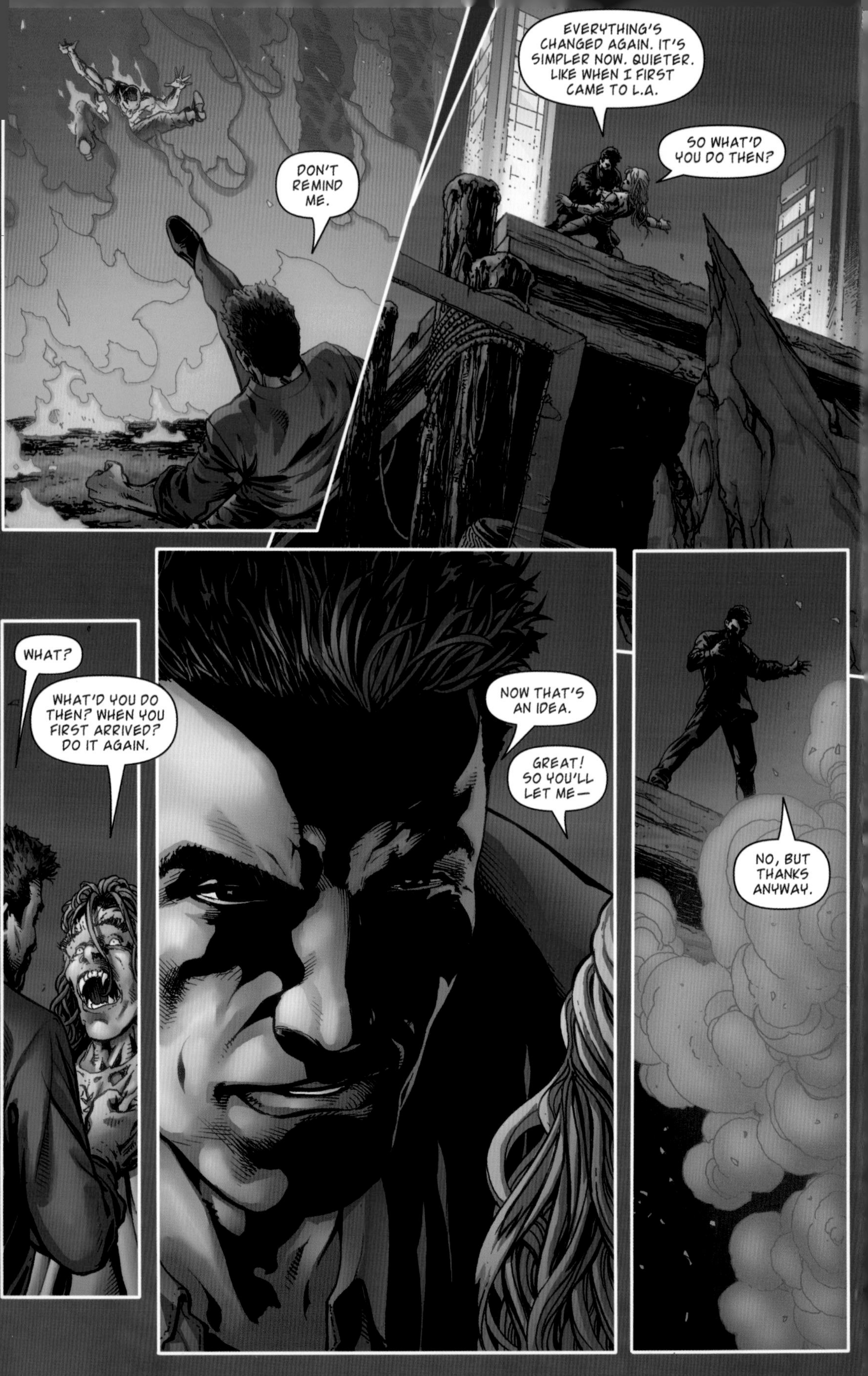
DON'T REMIND ME.
EVERYTHING'S CHANGED AGAIN. IT'S SIMPLER NOW. QUIETER. LIKE WHEN I FIRST CAME TO L.A.
SO WHAT'D YOU DO THEN?
WHAT?
WHAT'D YOU DO THEN? WHEN YOU FIRST ARRIVED? DO IT AGAIN.
NOW THAT'S AN IDEA.
GREAT! SO YOU'LL LET ME—
NO, BUT THANKS ANYWAY.

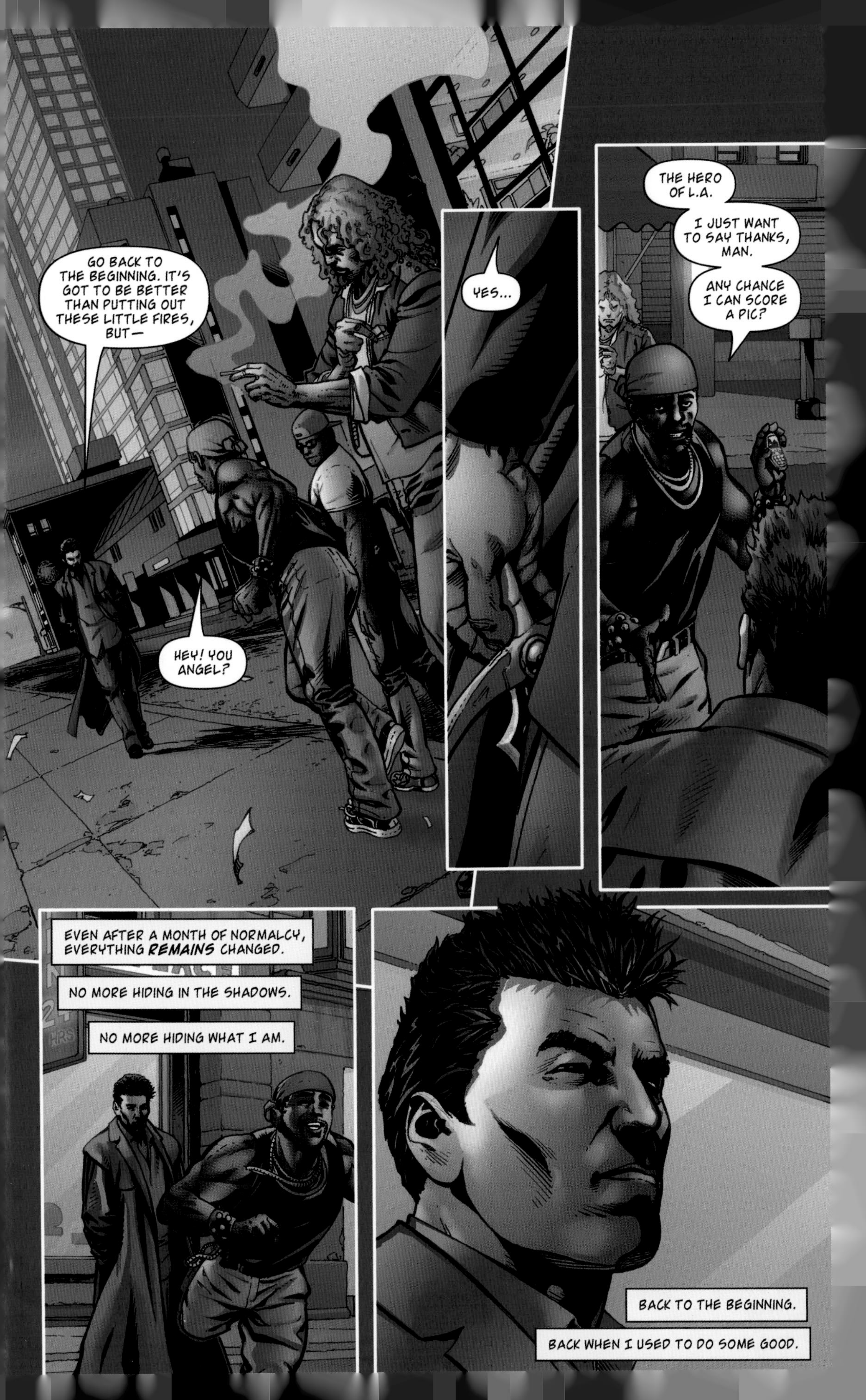
GO BACK TO THE BEGINNING. IT'S GOT TO BE BETTER THAN PUTTING OUT THESE LITTLE FIRES, BUT—
HEY! YOU ANGEL?
YES...
THE HERO OF L.A.
I JUST WANT TO SAY THANKS, MAN.
ANY CHANCE I CAN SCORE A PIC?
EVEN AFTER A MONTH OF NORMALCY, EVERYTHING REMAINS CHANGED.
NO MORE HIDING IN THE SHADOWS.
NO MORE HIDING WHAT I AM.
BACK TO THE BEGINNING.
BACK WHEN I USED TO DO SOME GOOD.

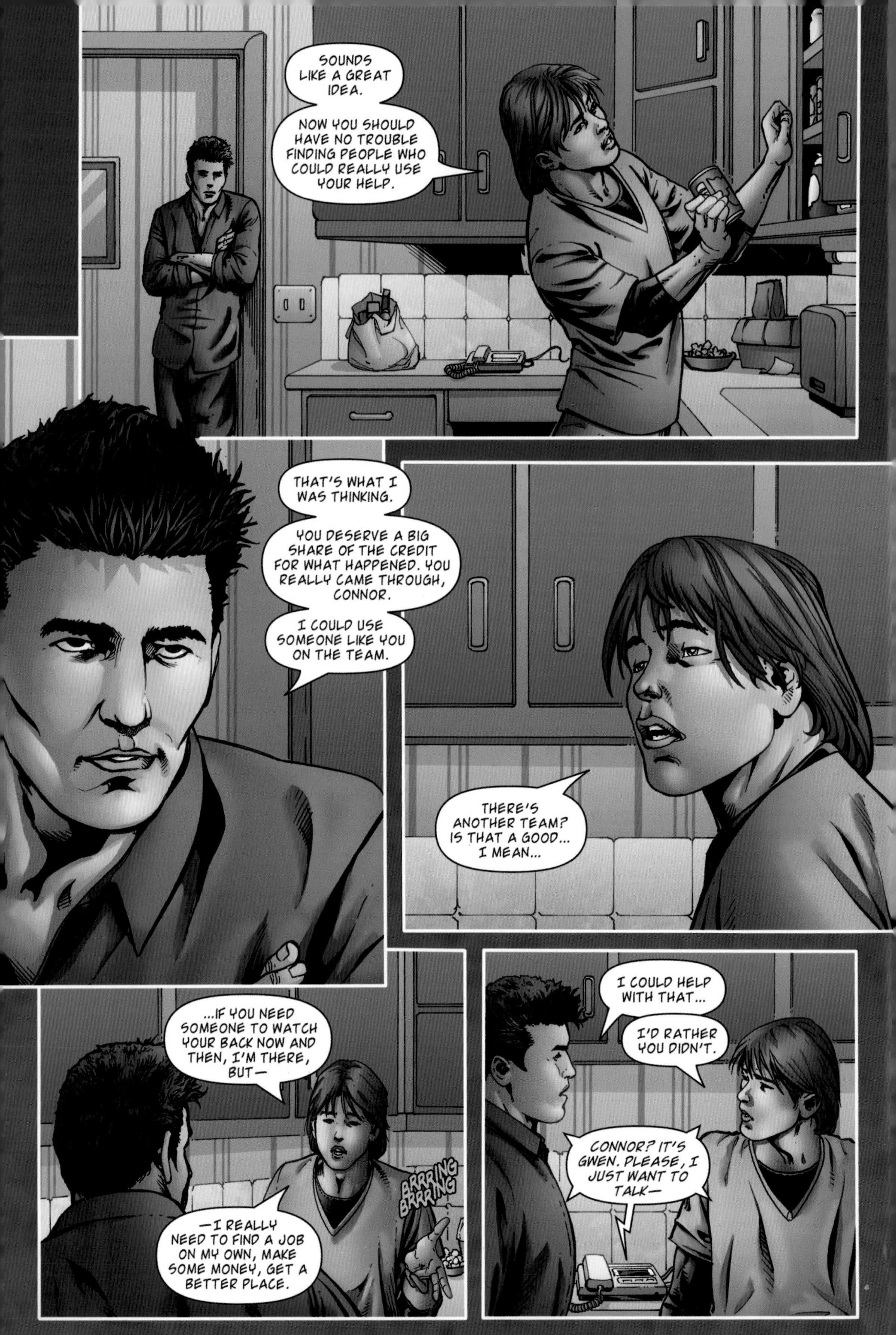
SOUNDS LIKE A GREAT IDEA.
NOW YOU SHOULD HAVE NO TROUBLE FINDING PEOPLE WHO COULD REALLY USE YOUR HELP.
THAT'S WHAT I WAS THINKING.
YOU DESERVE A BIG SHARE OF THE CREDIT FOR WHAT HAPPENED. YOU REALLY CAME THROUGH, CONNOR.
I COULD USE SOMEONE LIKE YOU ON THE TEAM.
THERE'S ANOTHER TEAM? IS THAT A GOOD... I MEAN...
...IF YOU NEED SOMEONE TO WATCH YOUR BACK NOW AND THEN, I'M THERE, BUT—
—I REALLY NEED TO FIND A JOB ON MY OWN, MAKE SOME MONEY, GET A BETTER PLACE.
BRRRING BRRRING
I COULD HELP WITH THAT...
I'D RATHER YOU DIDN'T.
CONNOR? IT'S GWEN. PLEASE, I JUST WANT TO TALK—

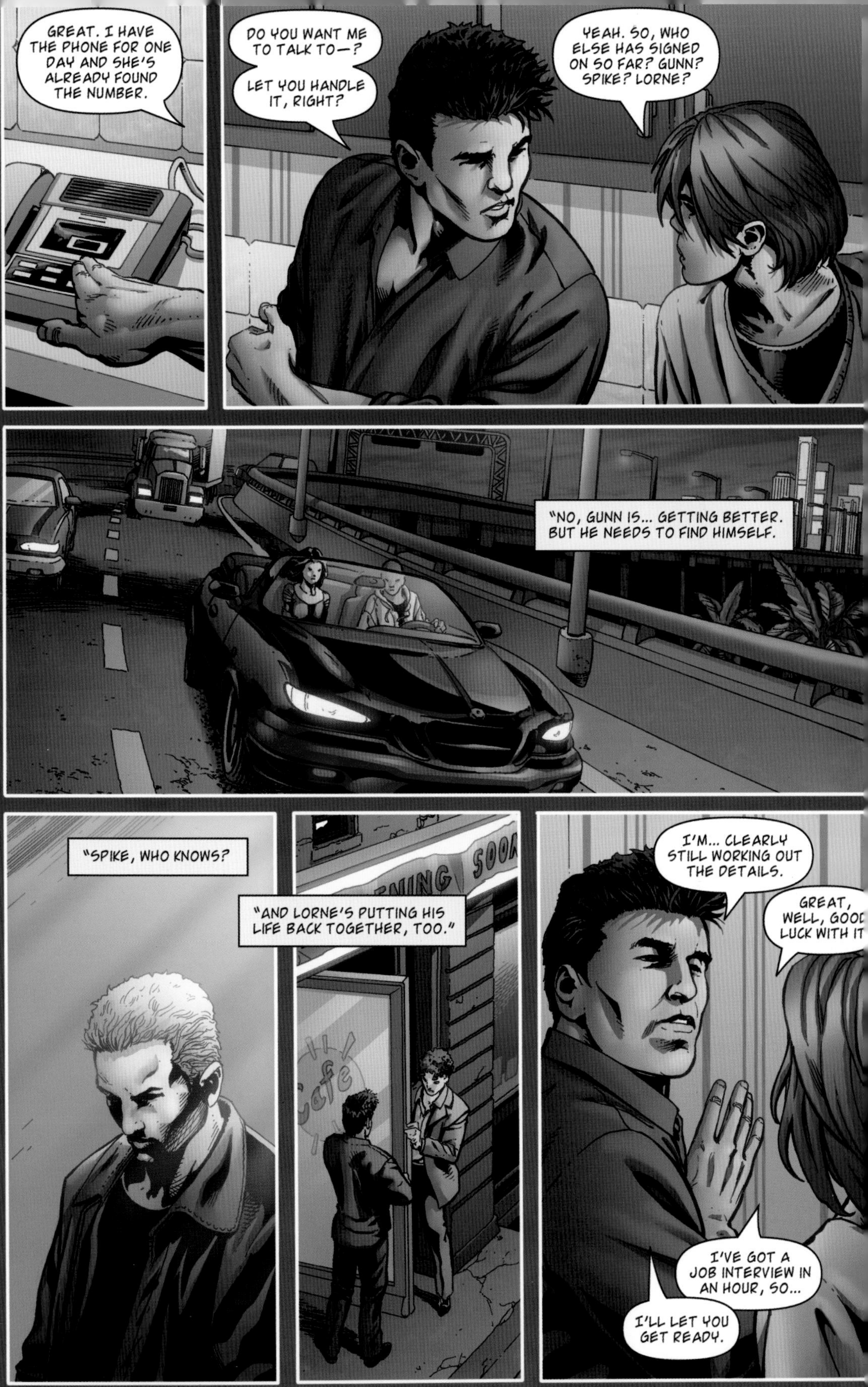
GREAT. I HAVE THE PHONE FOR ONE DAY AND SHE'S ALREADY FOUND THE NUMBER.
DO YOU WANT ME TO TALK TO—?
LET YOU HANDLE IT, RIGHT?
YEAH. SO, WHO ELSE HAS SIGNED ON SO FAR? GUNN? SPIKE? LORNE?
"NO, GUNN IS... GETTING BETTER. BUT HE NEEDS TO FIND HIMSELF.
"SPIKE, WHO KNOWS?
"AND LORNE'S PUTTING HIS LIFE BACK TOGETHER, TOO."
I'M... CLEARLY STILL WORKING OUT THE DETAILS.
GREAT, WELL, GOOD LUCK WITH IT
I'VE GOT A JOB INTERVIEW IN AN HOUR, SO...
I'LL LET YOU GET READY.

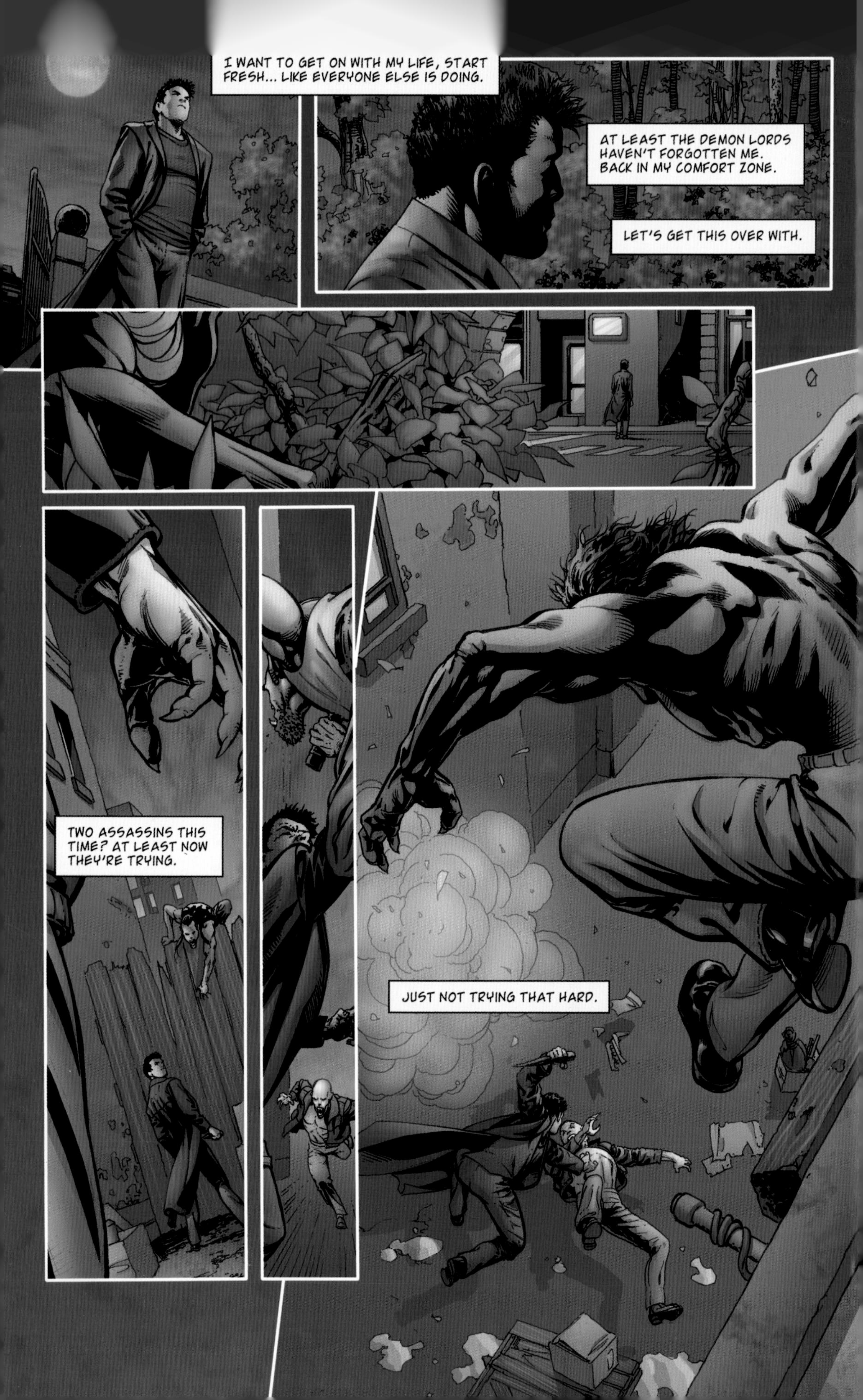
I WANT TO GET ON WITH MY LIFE, START FRESH... LIKE EVERYONE ELSE IS DOING.
AT LEAST THE DEMON LORDS HAVEN'T FORGOTTEN ME. BACK IN MY COMFORT ZONE.
LET'S GET THIS OVER WITH.
TWO ASSASSINS THIS TIME? AT LEAST NOW THEY'RE TRYING.
JUST NOT TRYING THAT HARD.

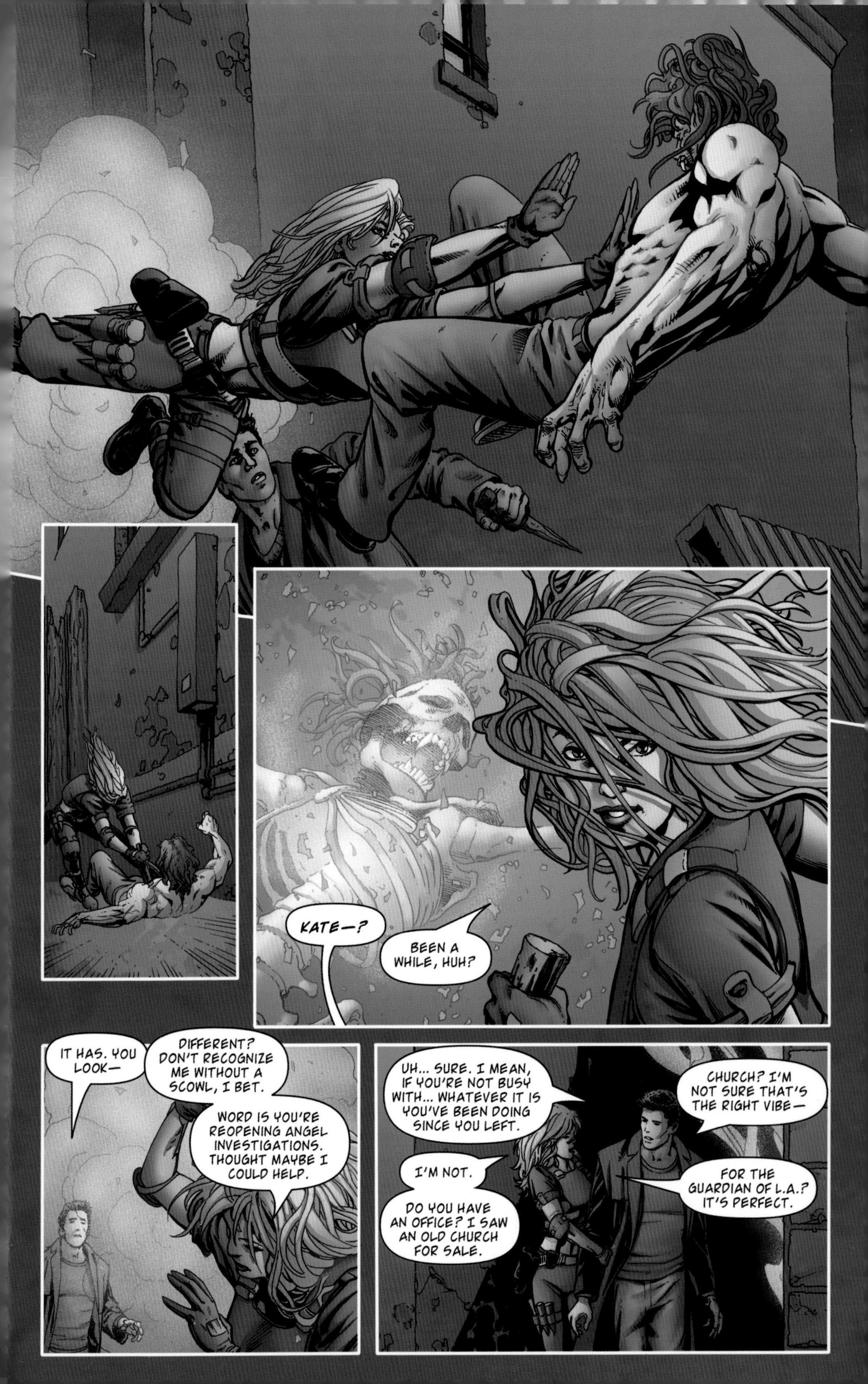
KATE—?
BEEN A WHILE, HUH?
IT HAS. YOU LOOK—
DIFFERENT? DON'T RECOGNIZE ME WITHOUT A SCOWL, I BET.
WORD IS YOU'RE REOPENING ANGEL INVESTIGATIONS. THOUGHT MAYBE I COULD HELP.
UH... SURE. I MEAN, IF YOU'RE NOT BUSY WITH... WHATEVER IT IS YOU'VE BEEN DOING SINCE YOU LEFT.
I'M NOT.
DO YOU HAVE AN OFFICE? I SAW AN OLD CHURCH FOR SALE.
CHURCH? I'M NOT SURE THAT'S THE RIGHT VIBE—
FOR THE GUARDIAN OF L.A.? IT'S PERFECT.

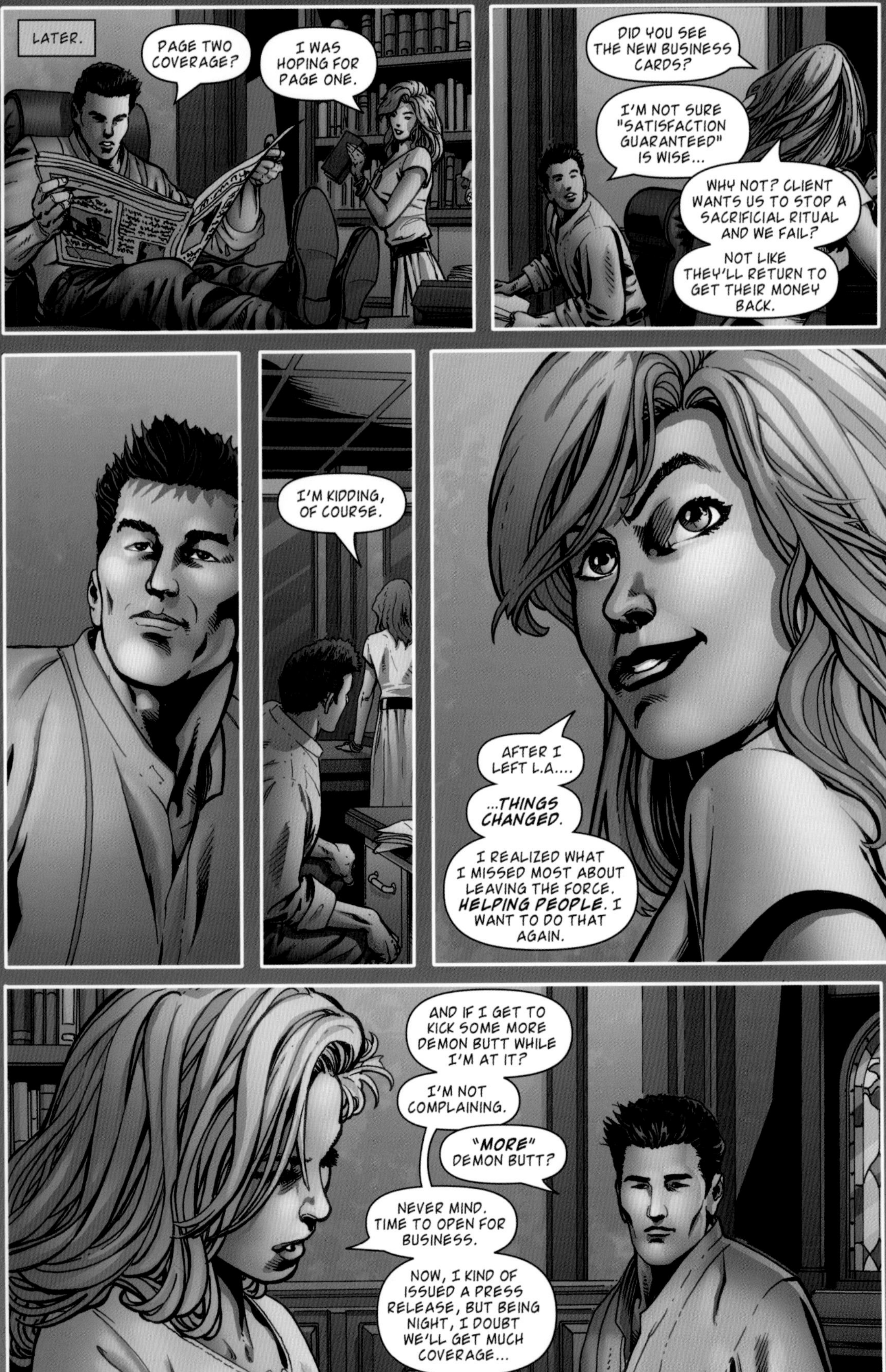
LATER.
PAGE TWO COVERAGE?
I WAS HOPING FOR PAGE ONE.
DID YOU SEE THE NEW BUSINESS CARDS?
I'M NOT SURE "SATISFACTION GUARANTEED" IS WISE...
WHY NOT? CLIENT WANTS US TO STOP A SACRIFICIAL RITUAL AND WE FAIL?
NOT LIKE THEY'LL RETURN TO GET THEIR MONEY BACK.
I'M KIDDING, OF COURSE.
AFTER I LEFT L.A....
...THINGS CHANGED.
I REALIZED WHAT I MISSED MOST ABOUT LEAVING THE FORCE. HELPING PEOPLE. I WANT TO DO THAT AGAIN.
AND IF I GET TO KICK SOME MORE DEMON BUTT WHILE I'M AT IT?
I'M NOT COMPLAINING.
"MORE" DEMON BUTT?
NEVER MIND. TIME TO OPEN FOR BUSINESS.
NOW, I KIND OF ISSUED A PRESS RELEASE, BUT BEING NIGHT, I DOUBT WE'LL GET MUCH COVERAGE...

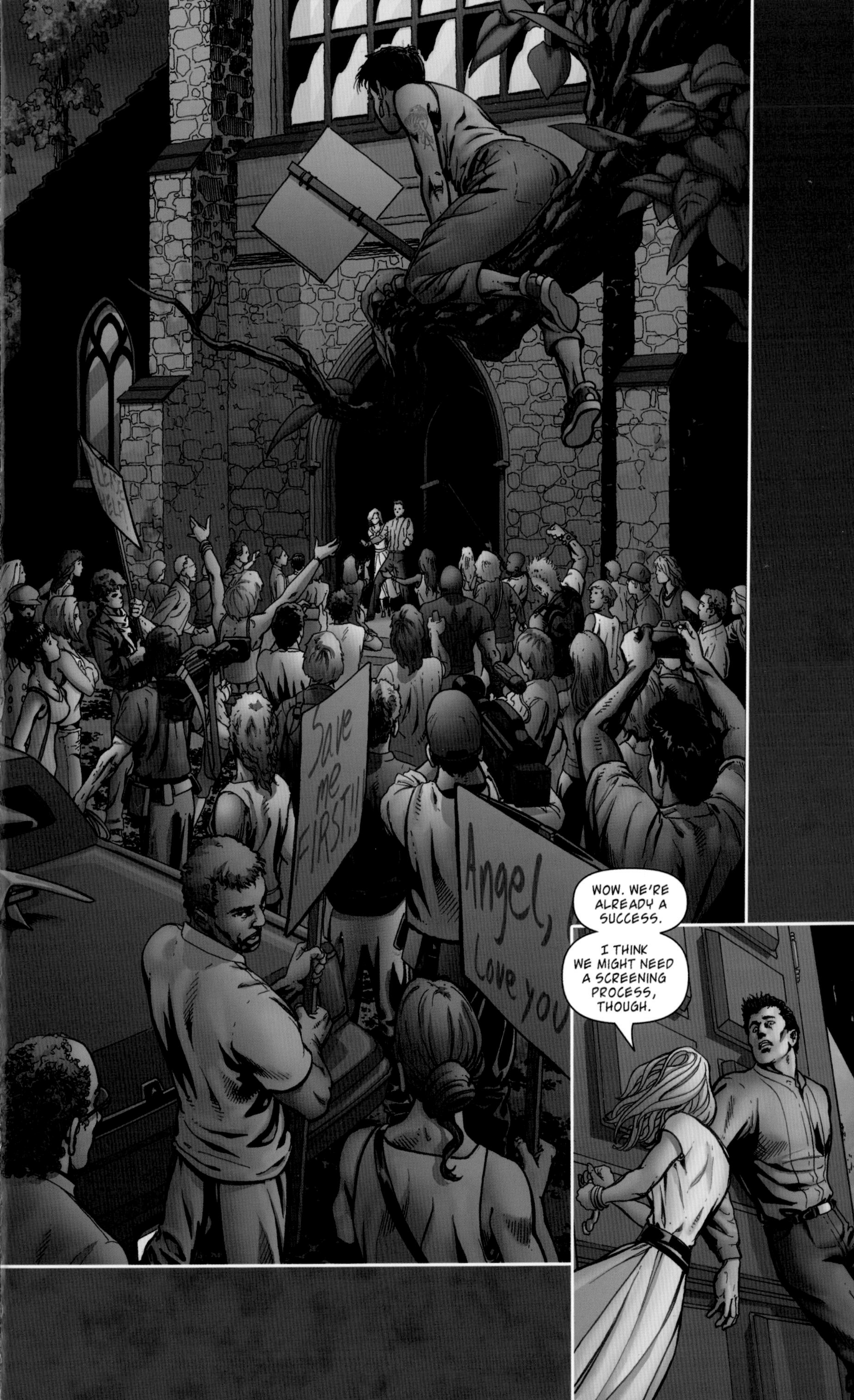

Save me FIRST!!
Angel,
Love you
WOW. WE'RE ALREADY A SUCCESS.
I THINK WE MIGHT NEED A SCREENING PROCESS, THOUGH.

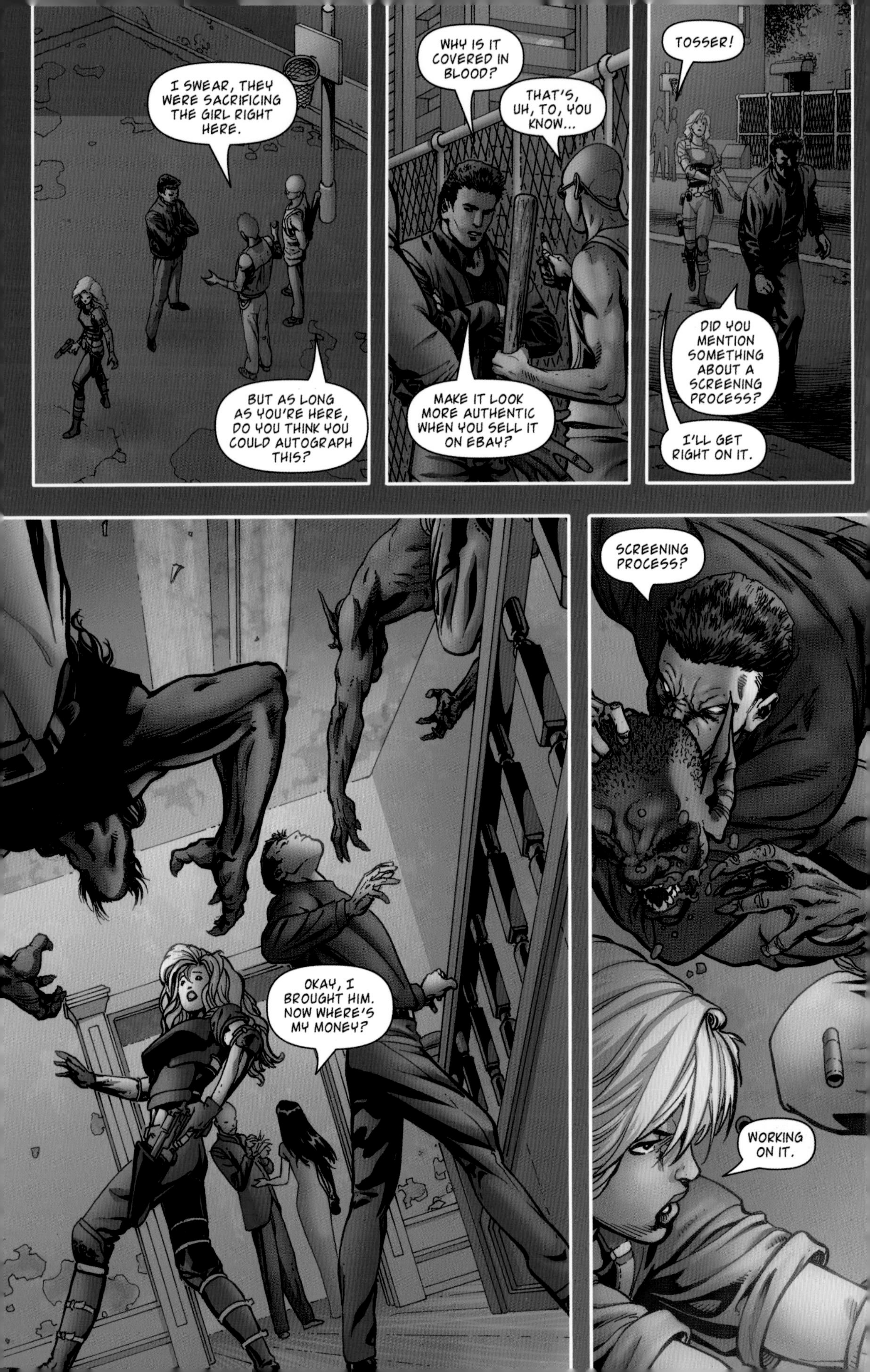
I SWEAR, THEY WERE SACRIFICING THE GIRL RIGHT HERE.
BUT AS LONG AS YOU'RE HERE, DO YOU THINK YOU COULD AUTOGRAPH THIS?
WHY IS IT COVERED IN BLOOD?
THAT'S, UH, TO, YOU KNOW...
MAKE IT LOOK MORE AUTHENTIC WHEN YOU SELL IT ON EBAY?
TOSSER!
DID YOU MENTION SOMETHING ABOUT A SCREENING PROCESS?
I'LL GET RIGHT ON IT.
OKAY, I BROUGHT HIM. NOW WHERE'S MY MONEY?
SCREENING PROCESS?
WORKING ON IT.

AT LEAST THERE WERE DEMONS THIS TIME.

AND SOMEONE WAS IN DANGER.

I DON'T COUNT.

GOOD THING OUR CHURCH COMES WITH A CONVENIENTLY LOCATED TUNNEL.

A SURPRISING NUMBER OF PLACES IN L.A. DO.

AH, GOOD, YOU'RE BACK.

THAT WON'T BE NECESSARY.

BUT IF IT MAKES YOU MORE COMFORTABLE, PLEASE TAKE IT OUT.

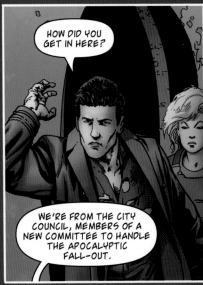

HOW DID YOU GET IN HERE?

WE'RE FROM THE CITY COUNCIL, MEMBERS OF A NEW COMMITTEE TO HANDLE THE APOCALYPTIC FALL-OUT.

I DON'T KNOW WHERE YOU'VE BEEN, BUT THAT APOCALYPSE? AVOIDED. BY HIM.

TRUE, THE NAME IS RATHER MISLEADING.

TYPICAL MUNICIPAL BUREAUCRACY.

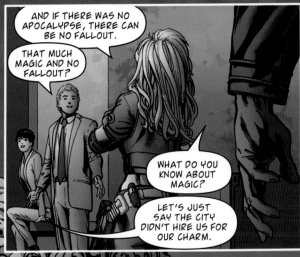

AND IF THERE WAS NO APOCALYPSE, THERE CAN BE NO FALLOUT.

THAT MUCH MAGIC AND NO FALLOUT?

WHAT DO YOU KNOW ABOUT MAGIC?

LET'S JUST SAY THE CITY DIDN'T HIRE US FOR OUR CHARM.

THEY DIDN'T KNOWINGLY HIRE US AT ALL.

TRUE... BUT THAT'S ANOTHER STORY.

THE POINT IS, YOU MADE A VERY BIG MESS, ANGEL.

AND WE'D LIKE YOU TO CLEAN IT UP.

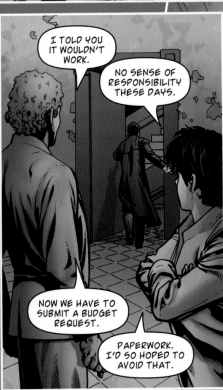

I TOLD YOU IT WOULDN'T WORK.

NO SENSE OF RESPONSIBILITY THESE DAYS.

NOW WE HAVE TO SUBMIT A BUDGET REQUEST.

PAPERWORK. I'D SO HOPED TO AVOID THAT.

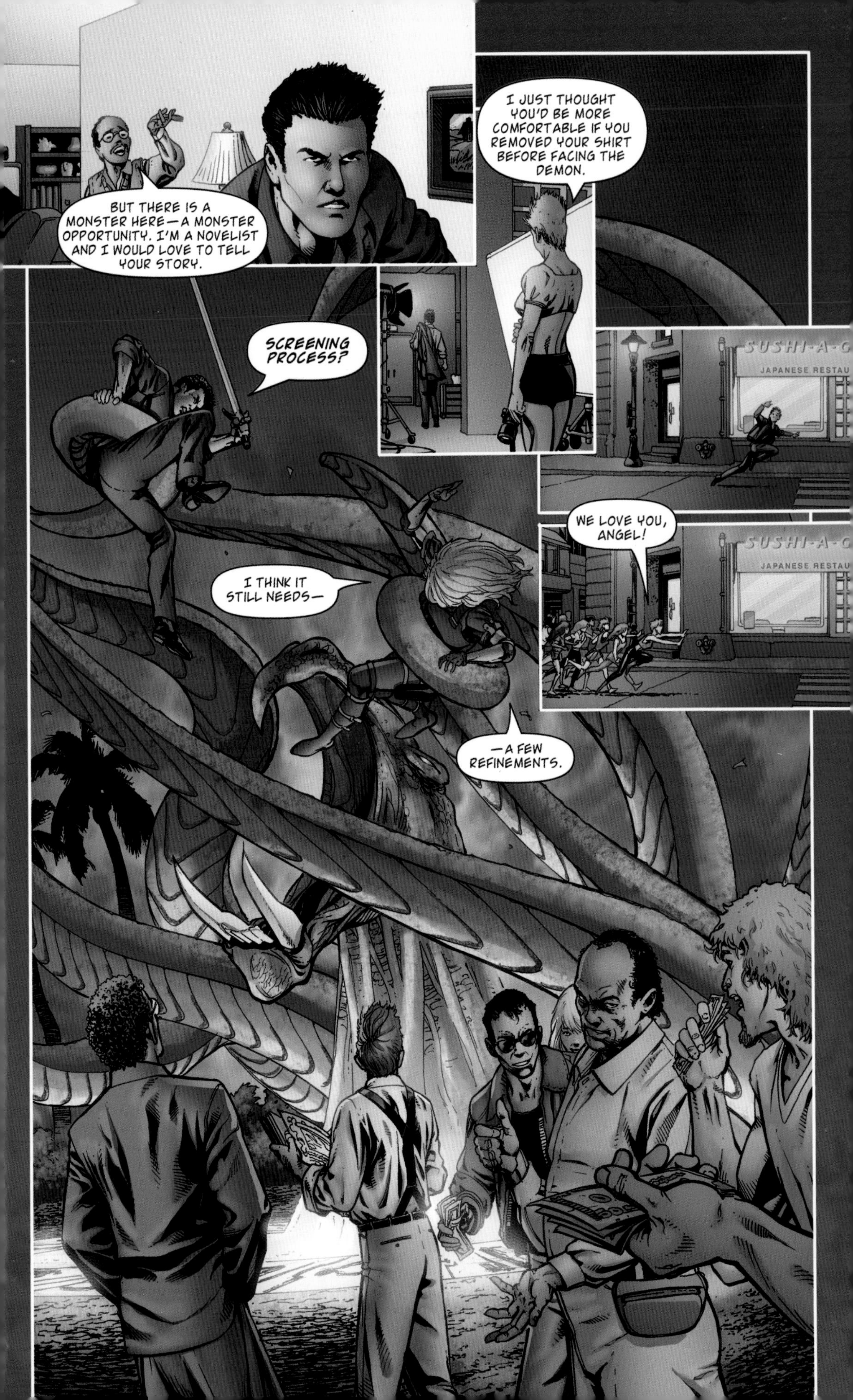
BUT THERE IS A MONSTER HERE—A MONSTER OPPORTUNITY. I'M A NOVELIST AND I WOULD LOVE TO TELL YOUR STORY.
I JUST THOUGHT YOU'D BE MORE COMFORTABLE IF YOU REMOVED YOUR SHIRT BEFORE FACING THE DEMON.
SCREENING PROCESS?
JAPANESE RESTAU
WE LOVE YOU, ANGEL!
JAPANESE RESTAU
I THINK IT STILL NEEDS—
—A FEW REFINEMENTS.

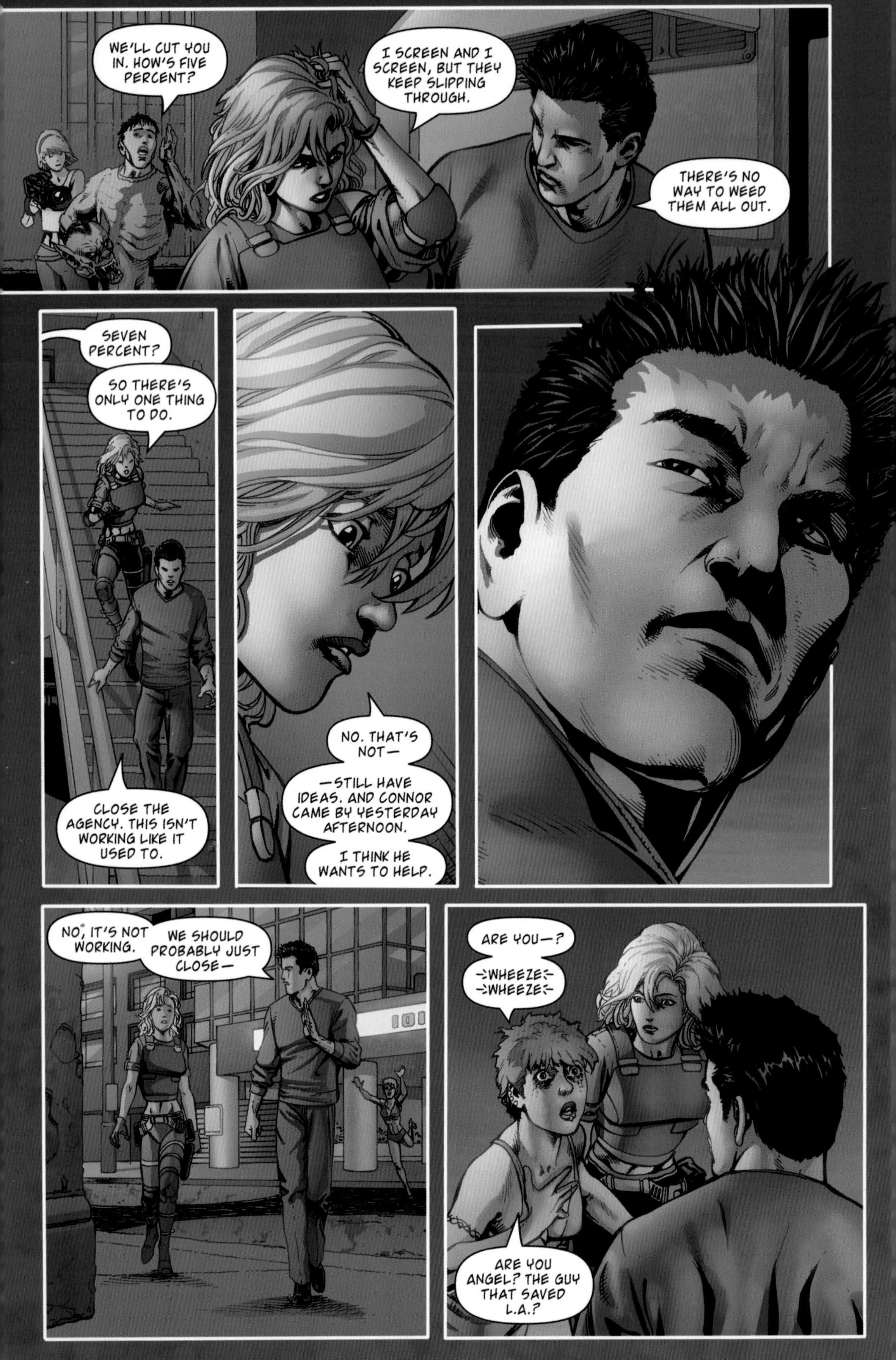
WE'LL CUT YOU IN. HOW'S FIVE PERCENT?
I SCREEN AND I SCREEN, BUT THEY KEEP SLIPPING THROUGH.
THERE'S NO WAY TO WEED THEM ALL OUT.
SEVEN PERCENT?
SO THERE'S ONLY ONE THING TO DO.
CLOSE THE AGENCY. THIS ISN'T WORKING LIKE IT USED TO.
NO. THAT'S NOT—
—STILL HAVE IDEAS. AND CONNOR CAME BY YESTERDAY AFTERNOON.
I THINK HE WANTS TO HELP.
NO, IT'S NOT WORKING.
WE SHOULD PROBABLY JUST CLOSE—
ARE YOU—?
-WHEEZE-
-WHEEZE-
ARE YOU ANGEL? THE GUY THAT SAVED L.A.?

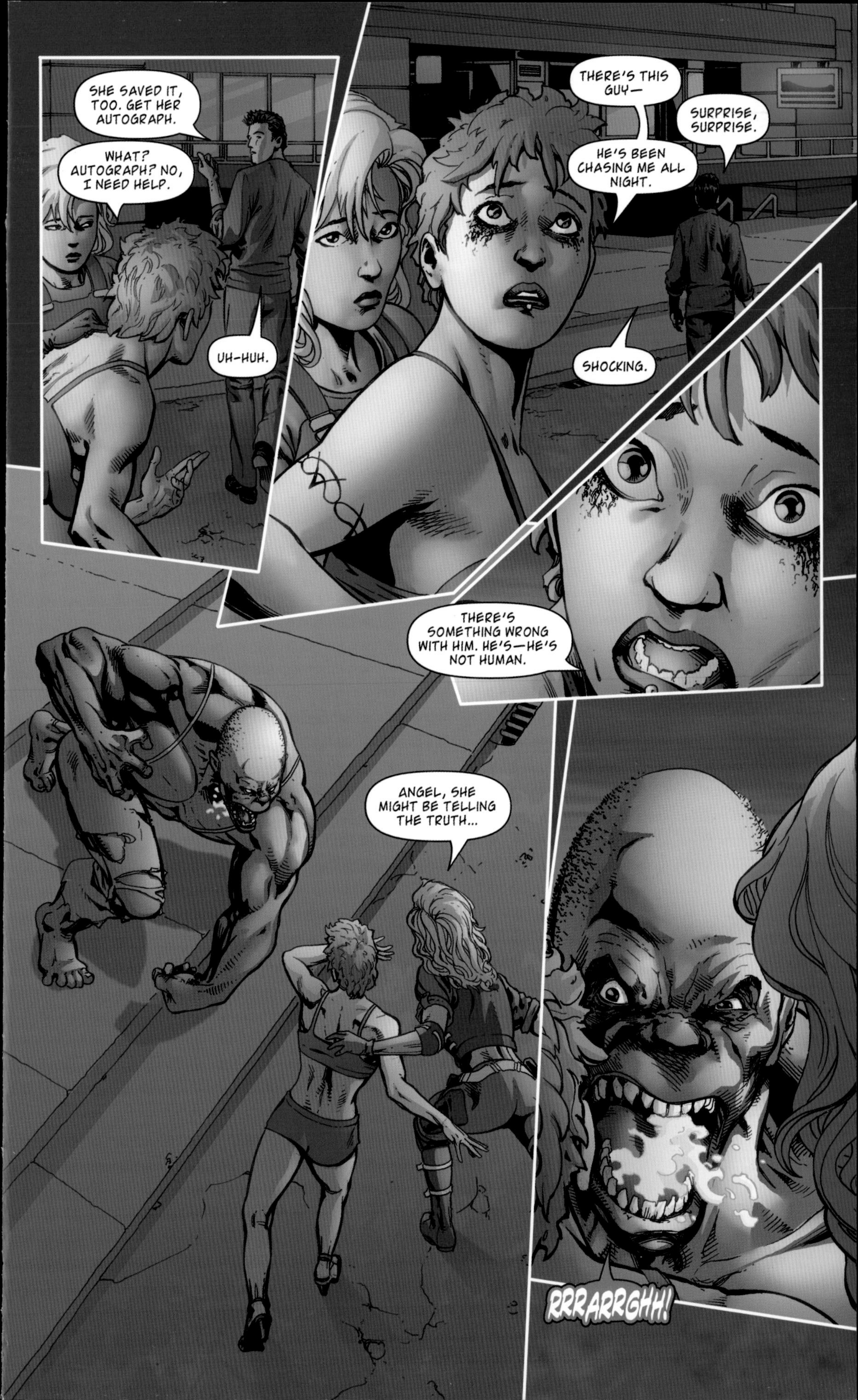
SHE SAVED IT, TOO. GET HER AUTOGRAPH.
WHAT? AUTOGRAPH? NO, I NEED HELP.
UH-HUH.
THERE'S THIS GUY—
HE'S BEEN CHASING ME ALL NIGHT.
SURPRISE, SURPRISE.
SHOCKING.
THERE'S SOMETHING WRONG WITH HIM. HE'S—HE'S NOT HUMAN.
ANGEL, SHE MIGHT BE TELLING THE TRUTH...
RRRARRGHH!

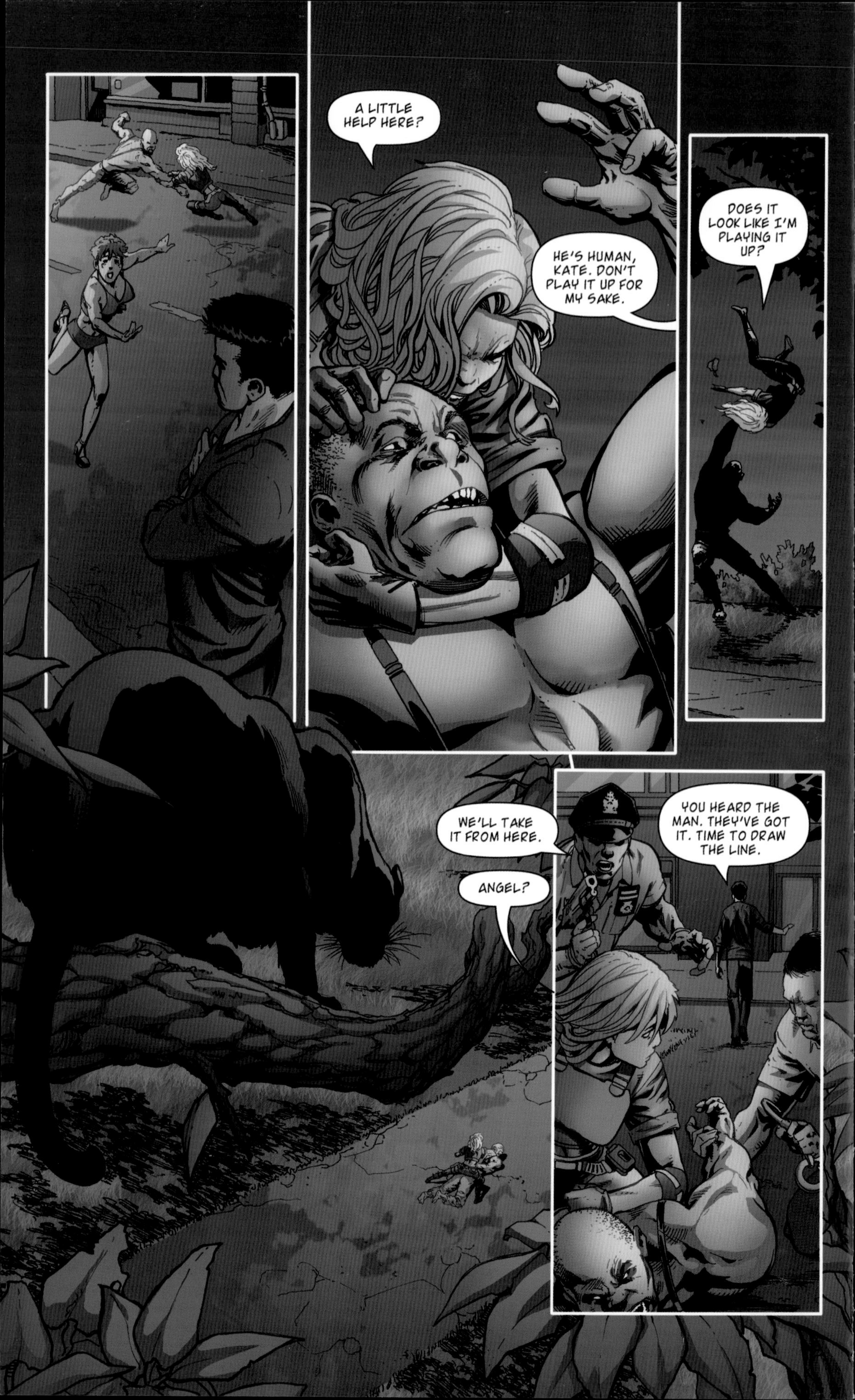
A LITTLE HELP HERE?
HE'S HUMAN, KATE. DON'T PLAY IT UP FOR MY SAKE.
DOES IT LOOK LIKE I'M PLAYING IT UP?
WE'LL TAKE IT FROM HERE.
ANGEL?
YOU HEARD THE MAN. THEY'VE GOT IT. TIME TO DRAW THE LINE.

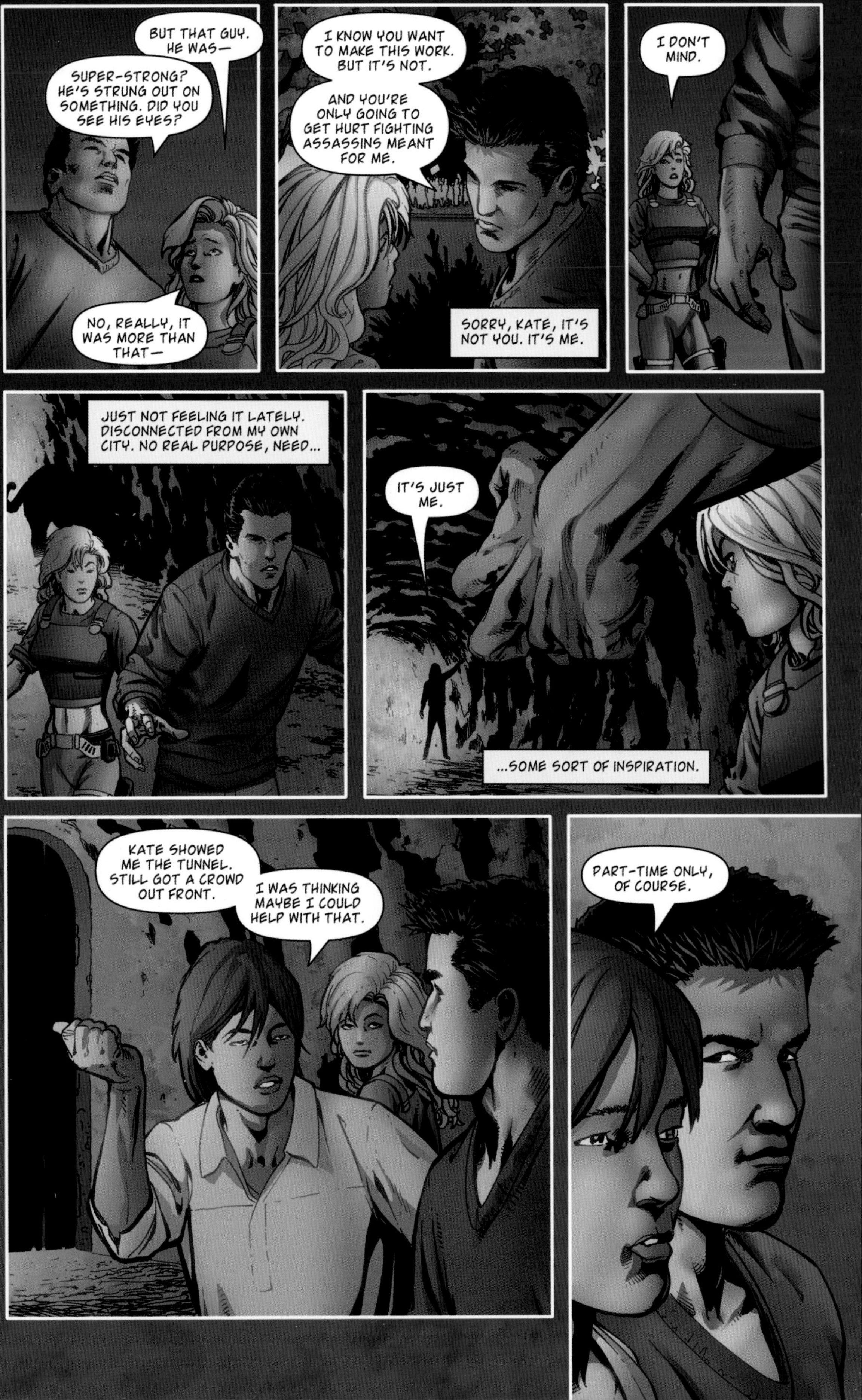
BUT THAT GUY. HE WAS—
SUPER-STRONG? HE'S STRUNG OUT ON SOMETHING. DID YOU SEE HIS EYES?
NO, REALLY, IT WAS MORE THAN THAT—
I KNOW YOU WANT TO MAKE THIS WORK. BUT IT'S NOT.
AND YOU'RE ONLY GOING TO GET HURT FIGHTING ASSASSINS MEANT FOR ME.
SORRY, KATE, IT'S NOT YOU. IT'S ME.
I DON'T MIND.
JUST NOT FEELING IT LATELY. DISCONNECTED FROM MY OWN CITY. NO REAL PURPOSE, NEED...
IT'S JUST ME.
...SOME SORT OF INSPIRATION.
KATE SHOWED ME THE TUNNEL. STILL GOT A CROWD OUT FRONT.
I WAS THINKING MAYBE I COULD HELP WITH THAT.
PART-TIME ONLY, OF COURSE.

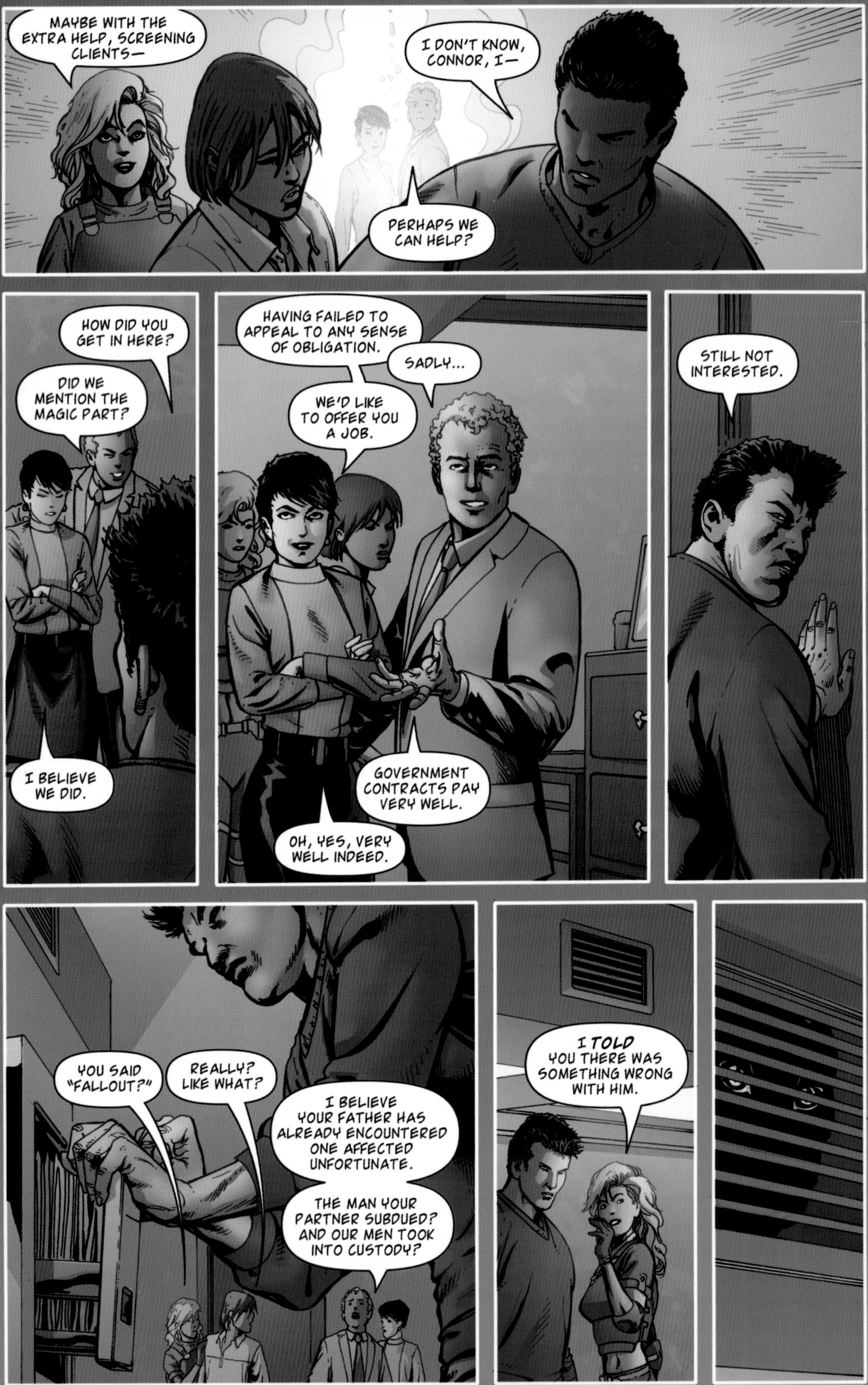
MAYBE WITH THE EXTRA HELP, SCREENING CLIENTS—
I DON'T KNOW, CONNOR, I—
PERHAPS WE CAN HELP?
HOW DID YOU GET IN HERE?
DID WE MENTION THE MAGIC PART?
I BELIEVE WE DID.
HAVING FAILED TO APPEAL TO ANY SENSE OF OBLIGATION.
SADLY...
WE'D LIKE TO OFFER YOU A JOB.
GOVERNMENT CONTRACTS PAY VERY WELL.
OH, YES, VERY WELL INDEED.
STILL NOT INTERESTED.
YOU SAID "FALLOUT?"
REALLY? LIKE WHAT?
I BELIEVE YOUR FATHER HAS ALREADY ENCOUNTERED ONE AFFECTED UNFORTUNATE.
THE MAN YOUR PARTNER SUBDUED? AND OUR MEN TOOK INTO CUSTODY?
I TOLD YOU THERE WAS SOMETHING WRONG WITH HIM.

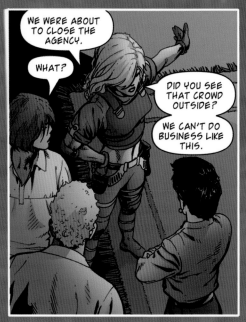

WE WERE ABOUT TO CLOSE THE AGENCY.

WHAT?

DID YOU SEE THAT CROWD OUTSIDE?

WE CAN'T DO BUSINESS LIKE THIS.

CONSIDER THEM CLEARED.

AND WE'LL ASSIGN AN OFFICER ROUND-THE-CLOCK.

THEY AREN'T JUST HERE. THEY FOLLOW US ON CASES.

THE SAVIOR OF L.A. NEEDS A BODYGUARD?

I WAS THINKING MORE OF A CITY ORDINANCE.

I WANT AN ORDINANCE MAKING IT ILLEGAL TO INTERFERE WITH ANGEL OR HIS WORK.

A CITY-WIDE RESTRAINING ORDER?

HIGHLY IRREGULAR.

HE SAVED THE CITY FROM HELL. MAKE AN EXCEPTION.

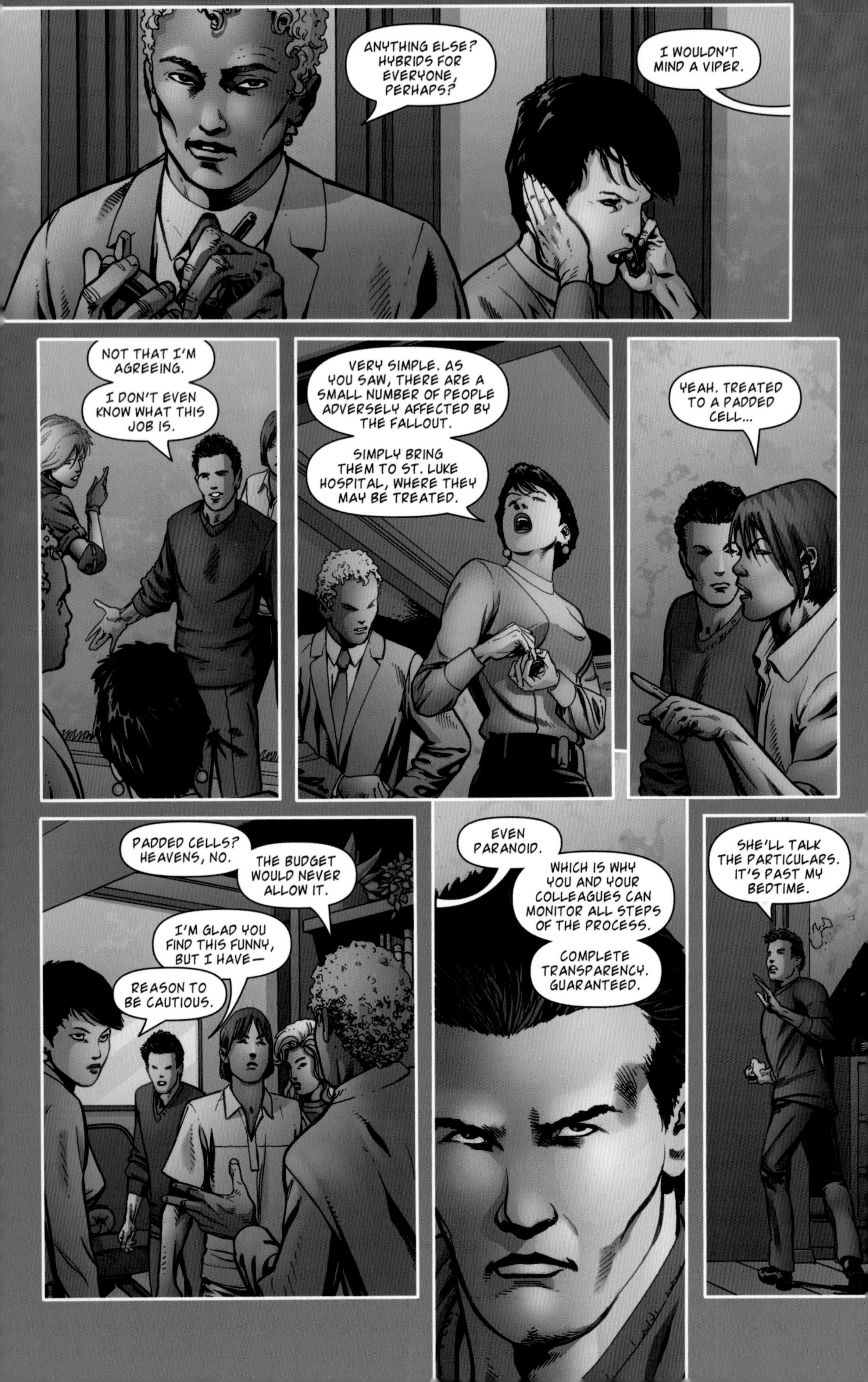
ANYTHING ELSE? HYBRIDS FOR EVERYONE, PERHAPS?
I WOULDN'T MIND A VIPER.
NOT THAT I'M AGREEING.
I DON'T EVEN KNOW WHAT THIS JOB IS.
VERY SIMPLE. AS YOU SAW, THERE ARE A SMALL NUMBER OF PEOPLE ADVERSELY AFFECTED BY THE FALLOUT.
SIMPLY BRING THEM TO ST. LUKE HOSPITAL, WHERE THEY MAY BE TREATED.
YEAH. TREATED TO A PADDED CELL...
PADDED CELLS? HEAVENS, NO.
THE BUDGET WOULD NEVER ALLOW IT.
I'M GLAD YOU FIND THIS FUNNY, BUT I HAVE—
REASON TO BE CAUTIOUS.
EVEN PARANOID.
WHICH IS WHY YOU AND YOUR COLLEAGUES CAN MONITOR ALL STEPS OF THE PROCESS.
COMPLETE TRANSPARENCY. GUARANTEED.
SHE'LL TALK THE PARTICULARS. IT'S PAST MY BEDTIME.

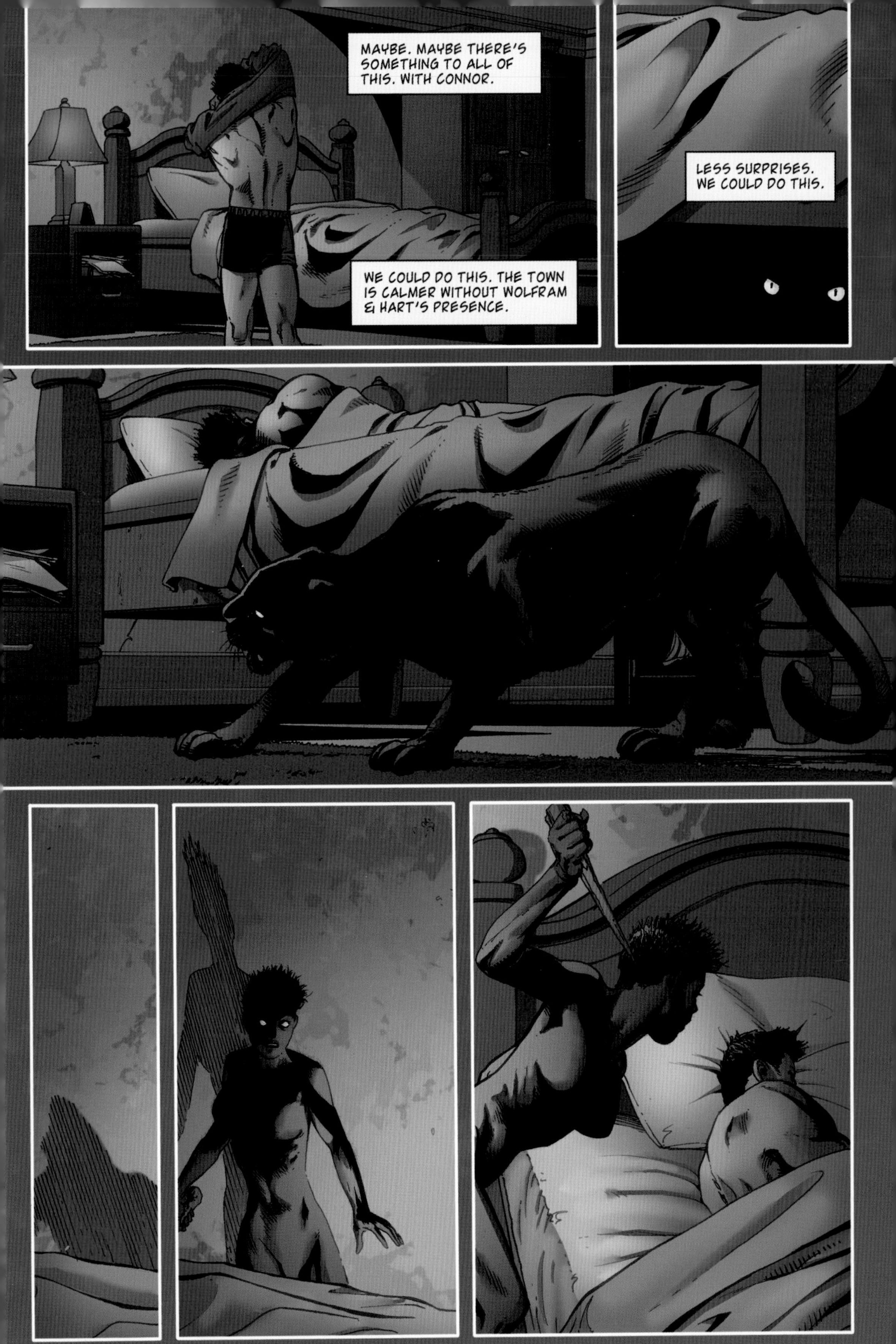
MAYBE. MAYBE THERE'S SOMETHING TO ALL OF THIS. WITH CONNOR.
WE COULD DO THIS. THE TOWN IS CALMER WITHOUT WOLFRAM & HART'S PRESENCE.
LESS SURPRISES. WE COULD DO THIS.

chapter
two

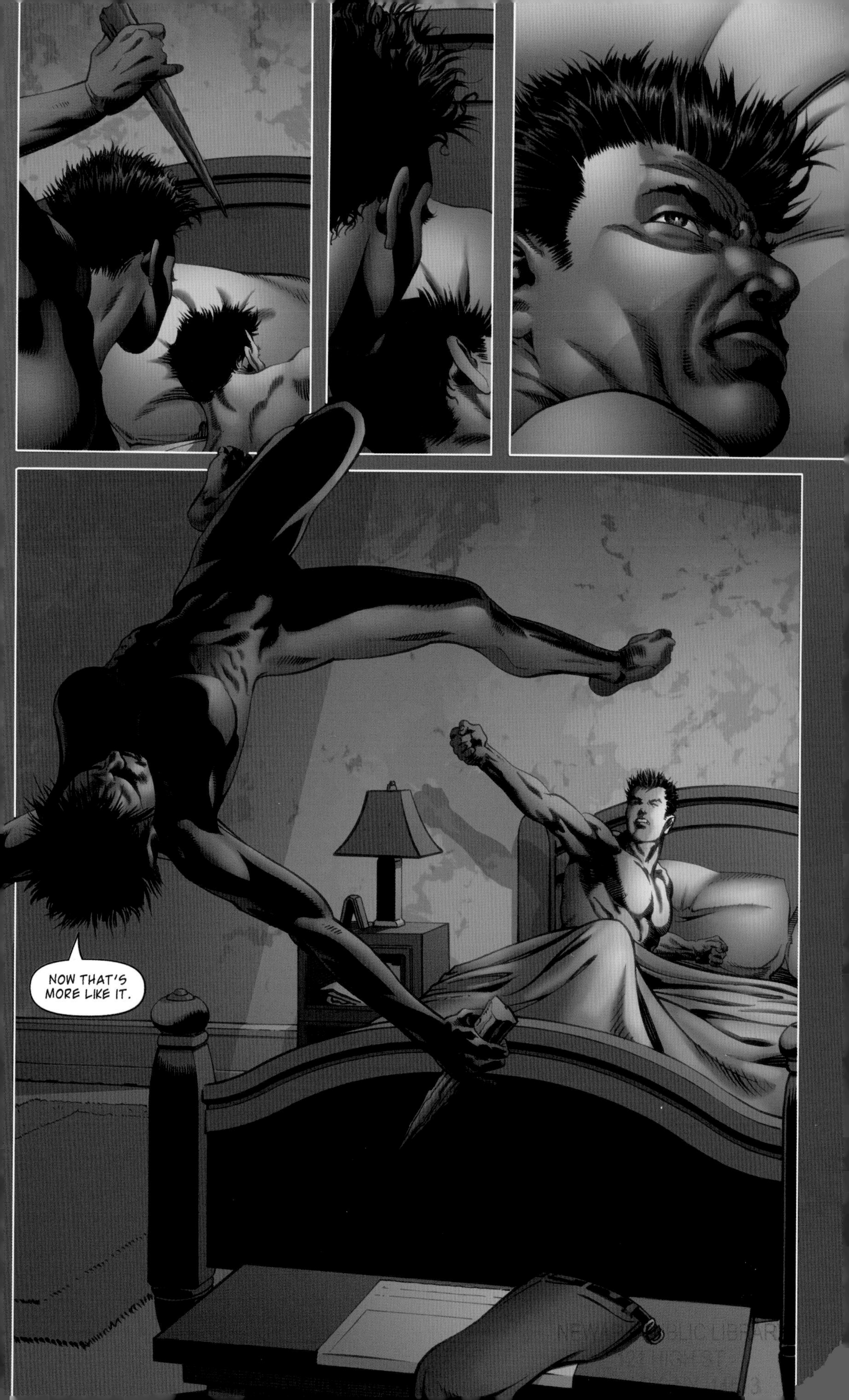
NOW THAT'S MORE LIKE IT.

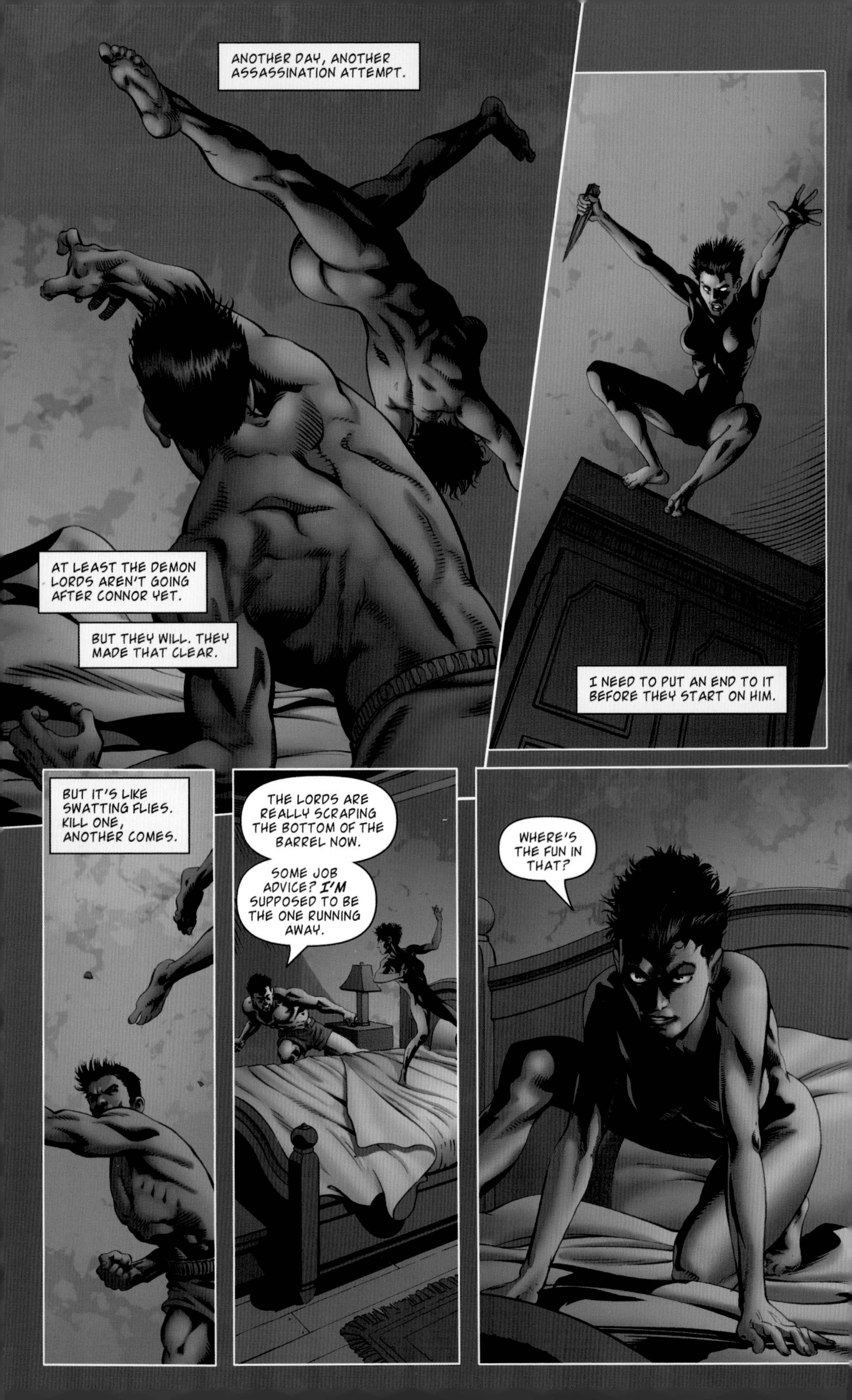
ANOTHER DAY, ANOTHER ASSASSINATION ATTEMPT.
AT LEAST THE DEMON LORDS AREN'T GOING AFTER CONNOR YET.
BUT THEY WILL. THEY MADE THAT CLEAR.
I NEED TO PUT AN END TO IT BEFORE THEY START ON HIM.
BUT IT'S LIKE SWATTING FLIES. KILL ONE, ANOTHER COMES.
THE LORDS ARE REALLY SCRAPING THE BOTTOM OF THE BARREL NOW.
SOME JOB ADVICE? I'M SUPPOSED TO BE THE ONE RUNNING AWAY.
WHERE'S THE FUN IN THAT?

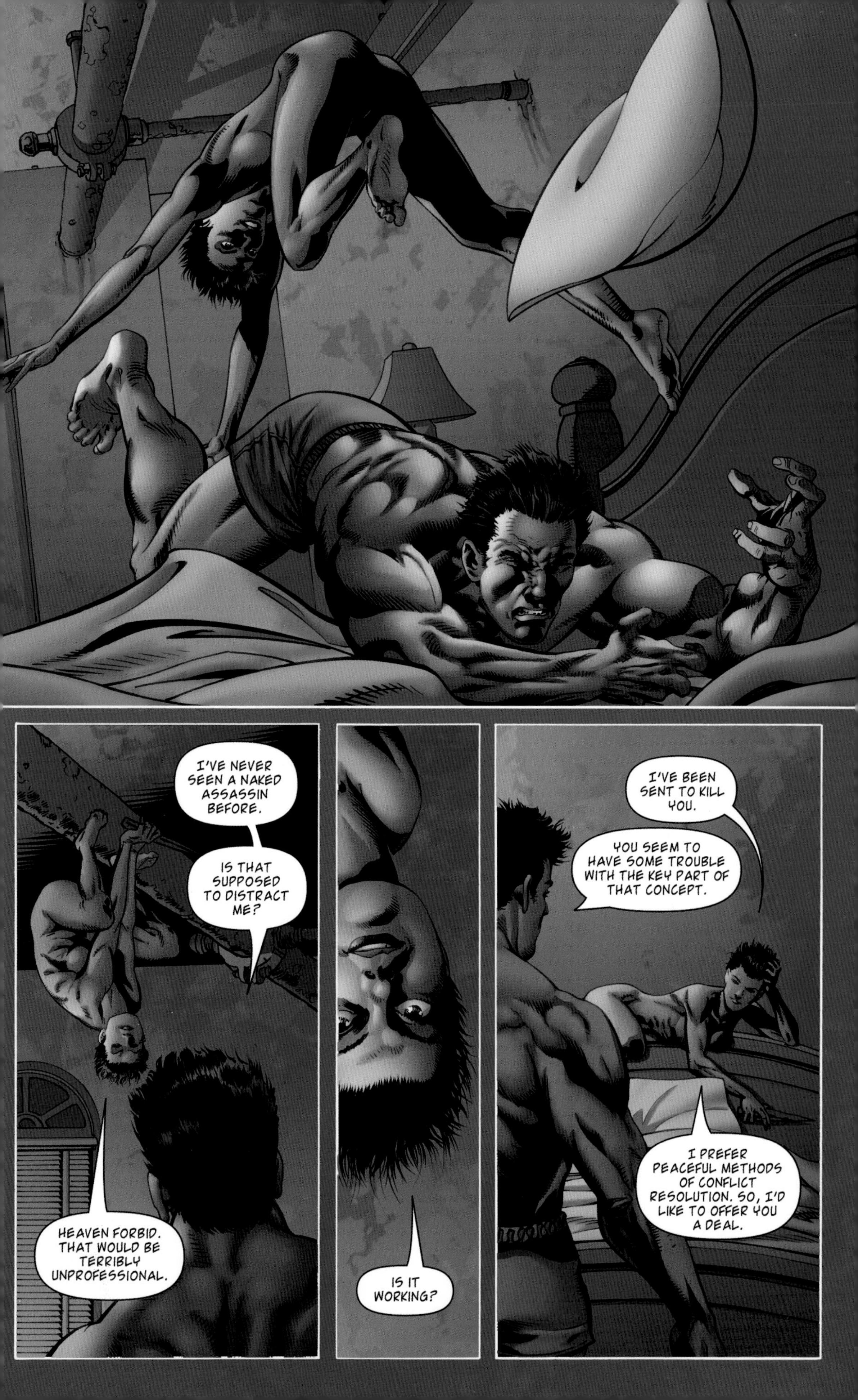
I'VE NEVER SEEN A NAKED ASSASSIN BEFORE.
IS THAT SUPPOSED TO DISTRACT ME?
HEAVEN FORBID. THAT WOULD BE TERRIBLY UNPROFESSIONAL.
IS IT WORKING?
I'VE BEEN SENT TO KILL YOU.
YOU SEEM TO HAVE SOME TROUBLE WITH THE KEY PART OF THAT CONCEPT.
I PREFER PEACEFUL METHODS OF CONFLICT RESOLUTION. SO, I'D LIKE TO OFFER YOU A DEAL.

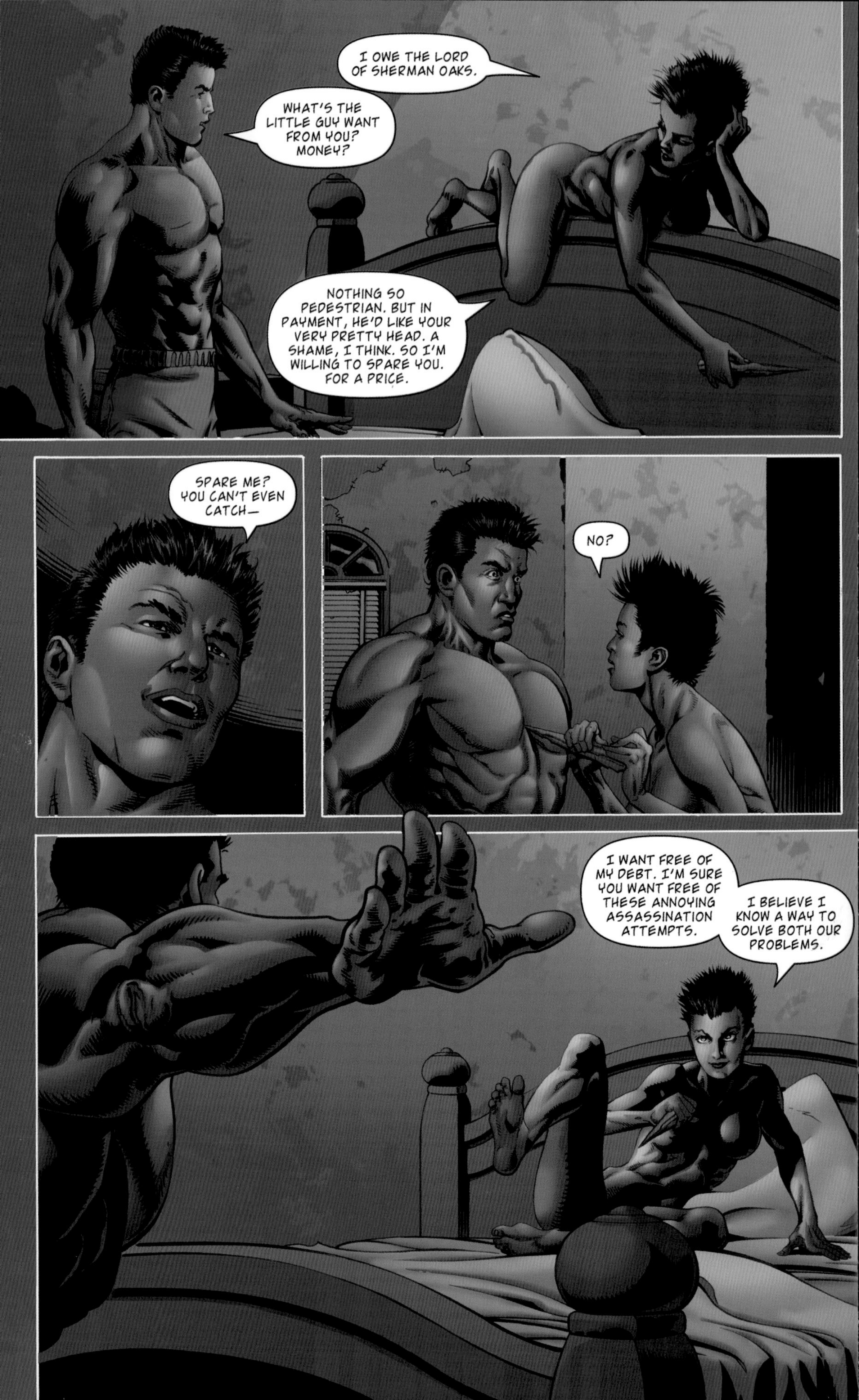
I OWE THE LORD OF SHERMAN OAKS.
WHAT'S THE LITTLE GUY WANT FROM YOU? MONEY?
NOTHING SO PEDESTRIAN. BUT IN PAYMENT, HE'D LIKE YOUR VERY PRETTY HEAD. A SHAME, I THINK. SO I'M WILLING TO SPARE YOU. FOR A PRICE.
SPARE ME? YOU CAN'T EVEN CATCH—
NO?
I WANT FREE OF MY DEBT. I'M SURE YOU WANT FREE OF THESE ANNOYING ASSASSINATION ATTEMPTS.
I BELIEVE I KNOW A WAY TO SOLVE BOTH OUR PROBLEMS.

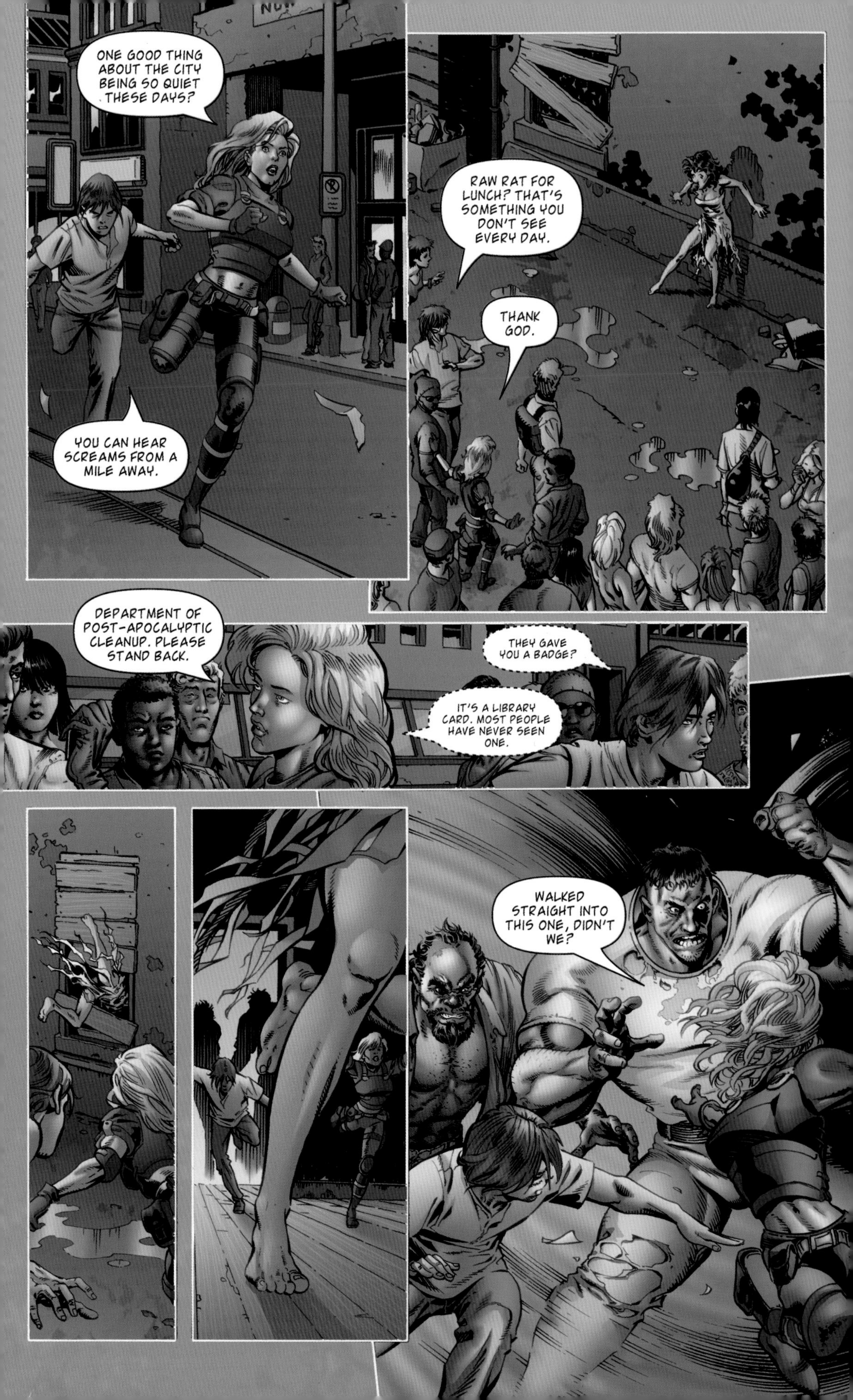

ONE GOOD THING ABOUT THE CITY BEING SO QUIET THESE DAYS?
YOU CAN HEAR SCREAMS FROM A MILE AWAY.
RAW RAT FOR LUNCH? THAT'S SOMETHING YOU DON'T SEE EVERY DAY.
THANK GOD.
DEPARTMENT OF POST-APOCALYPTIC CLEANUP. PLEASE STAND BACK.
THEY GAVE YOU A BADGE?
IT'S A LIBRARY CARD. MOST PEOPLE HAVE NEVER SEEN ONE.
WALKED STRAIGHT INTO THIS ONE, DIDN'T WE?

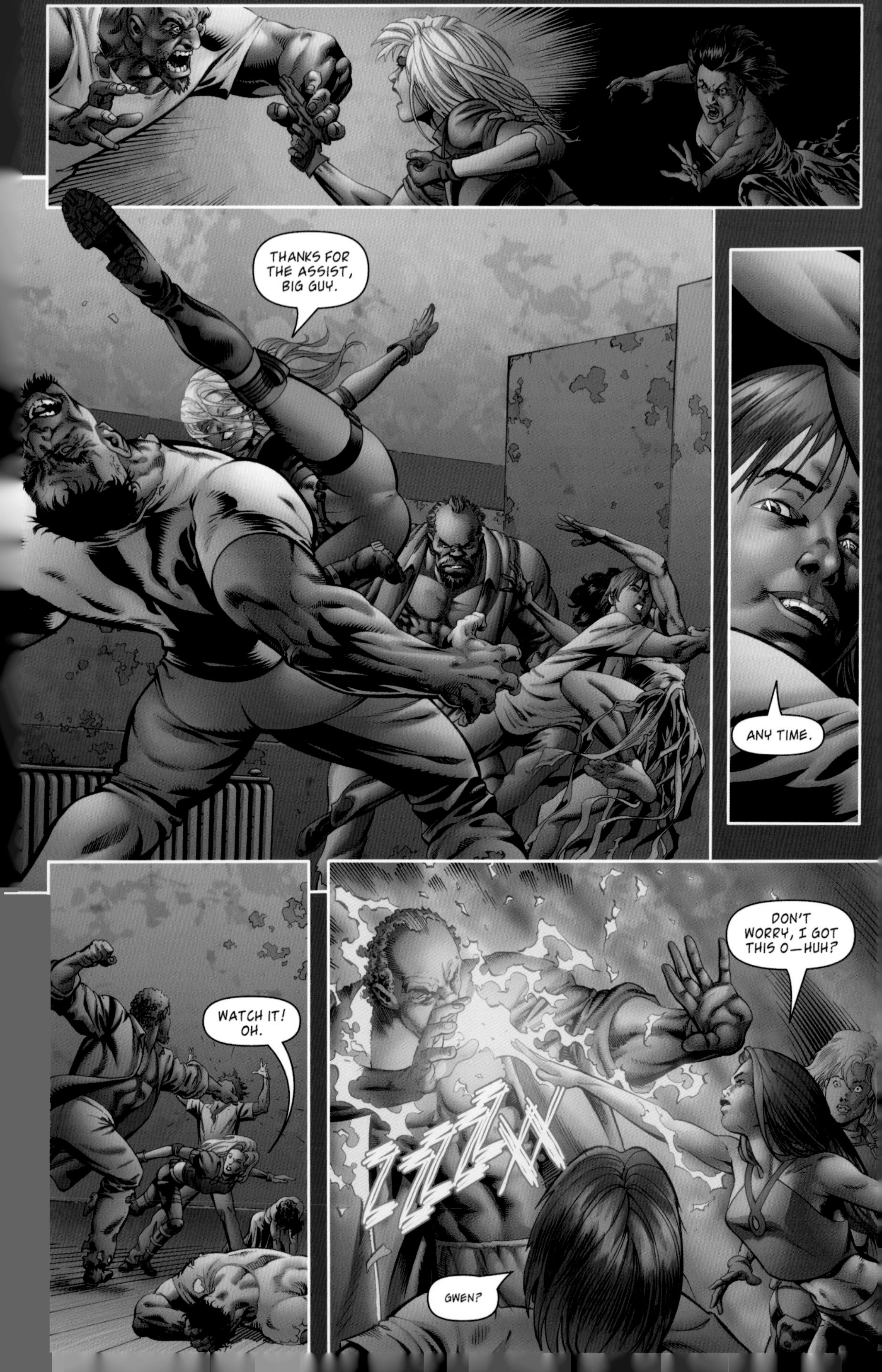
THANKS FOR THE ASSIST, BIG GUY.
ANY TIME.
WATCH IT! OH.
DON'T WORRY, I GOT THIS O—HUH?
ZZZZXX
GWEN?

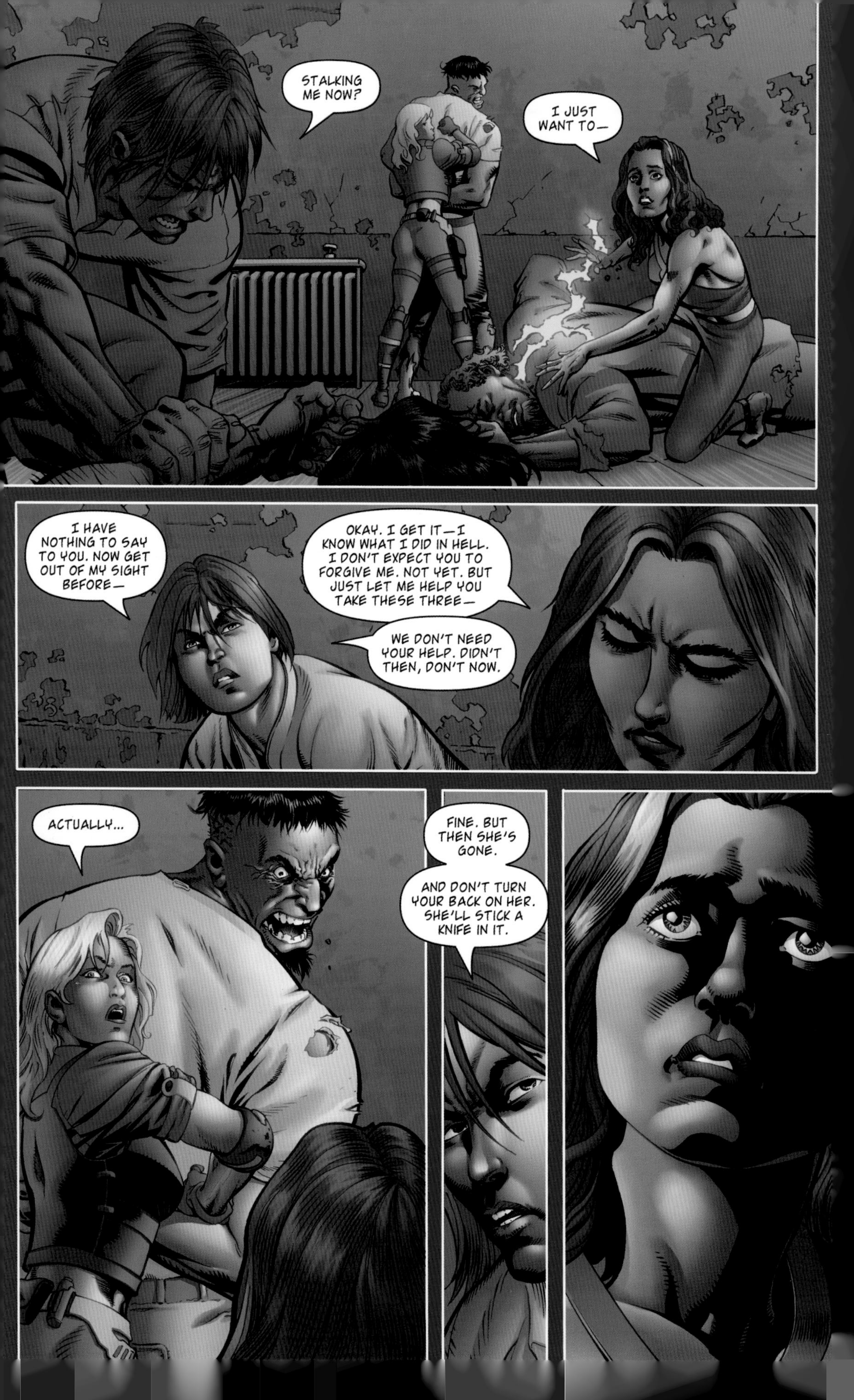
STALKING ME NOW?
I JUST WANT TO—
I HAVE NOTHING TO SAY TO YOU. NOW GET OUT OF MY SIGHT BEFORE—
OKAY. I GET IT—I KNOW WHAT I DID IN HELL. I DON'T EXPECT YOU TO FORGIVE ME. NOT YET. BUT JUST LET ME HELP YOU TAKE THESE THREE—
WE DON'T NEED YOUR HELP. DIDN'T THEN, DON'T NOW.
ACTUALLY...
FINE. BUT THEN SHE'S GONE.
AND DON'T TURN YOUR BACK ON HER. SHE'LL STICK A KNIFE IN IT.

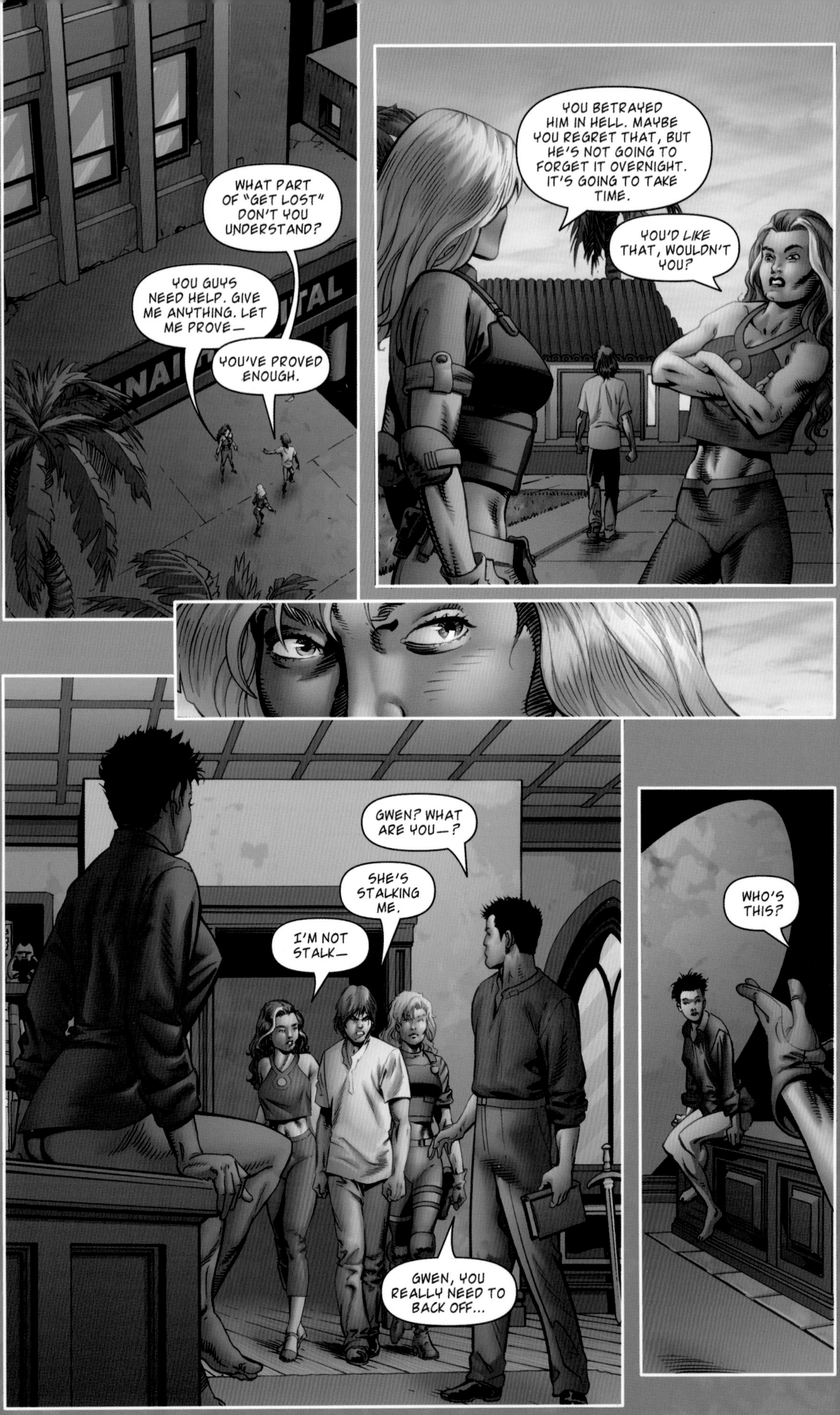
WHAT PART OF "GET LOST" DON'T YOU UNDERSTAND?
YOU GUYS NEED HELP. GIVE ME ANYTHING. LET ME PROVE—
YOU'VE PROVED ENOUGH.
YOU BETRAYED HIM IN HELL. MAYBE YOU REGRET THAT, BUT HE'S NOT GOING TO FORGET IT OVERNIGHT. IT'S GOING TO TAKE TIME.
YOU'D LIKE THAT, WOULDN'T YOU?
GWEN? WHAT ARE YOU—?
SHE'S STALKING ME.
I'M NOT STALK—
GWEN, YOU REALLY NEED TO BACK OFF...
WHO'S THIS?

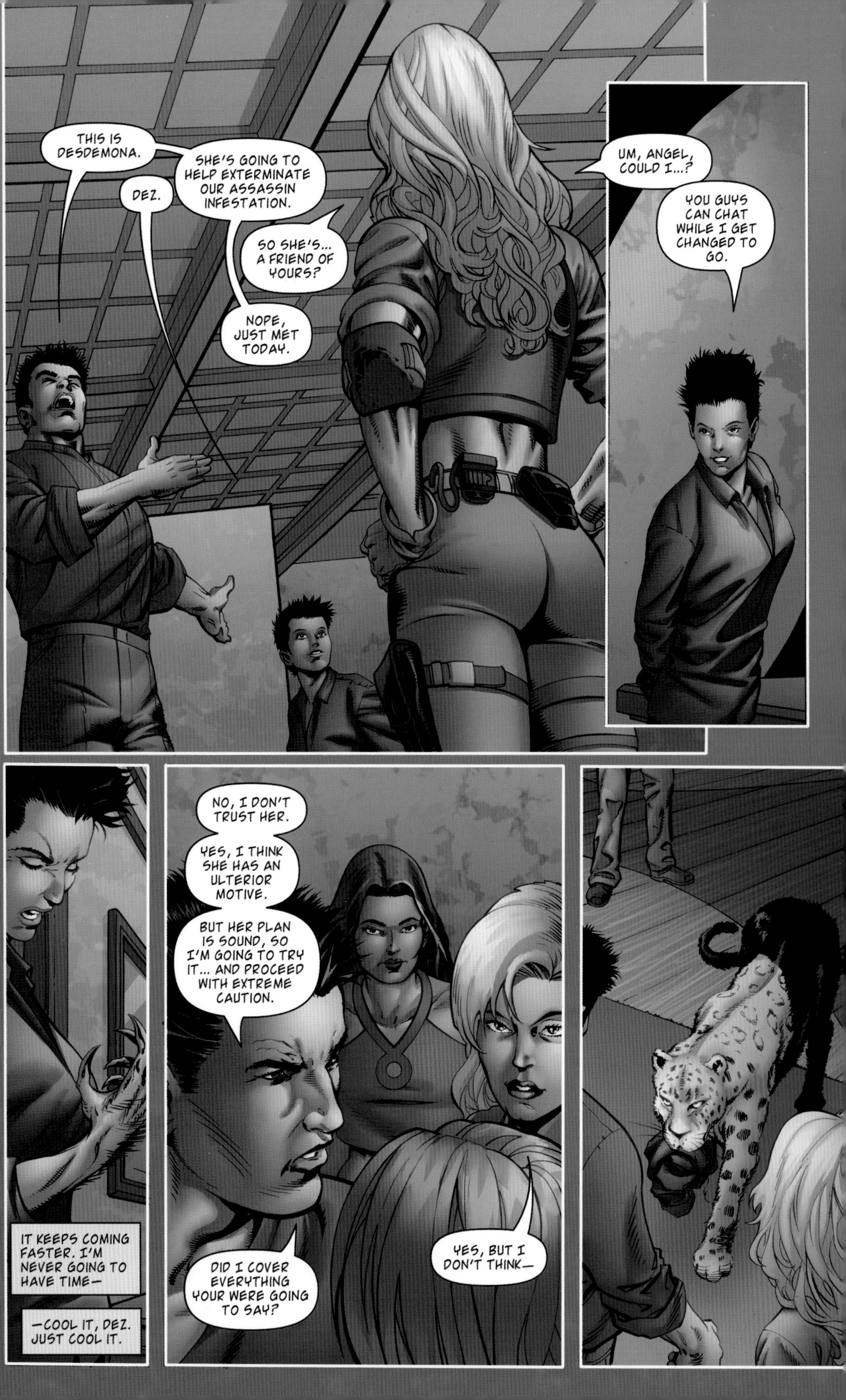
THIS IS DESDEMONA.
DEZ.
SHE'S GOING TO HELP EXTERMINATE OUR ASSASSIN INFESTATION.
SO SHE'S... A FRIEND OF YOURS?
NOPE, JUST MET TODAY.
UM, ANGEL, COULD I...?
YOU GUYS CAN CHAT WHILE I GET CHANGED TO GO.
IT KEEPS COMING FASTER. I'M NEVER GOING TO HAVE TIME—
—COOL IT, DEZ. JUST COOL IT.
NO, I DON'T TRUST HER.
YES, I THINK SHE HAS AN ULTERIOR MOTIVE.
BUT HER PLAN IS SOUND, SO I'M GOING TO TRY IT... AND PROCEED WITH EXTREME CAUTION.
DID I COVER EVERYTHING YOUR WERE GOING TO SAY?
YES, BUT I DON'T THINK—

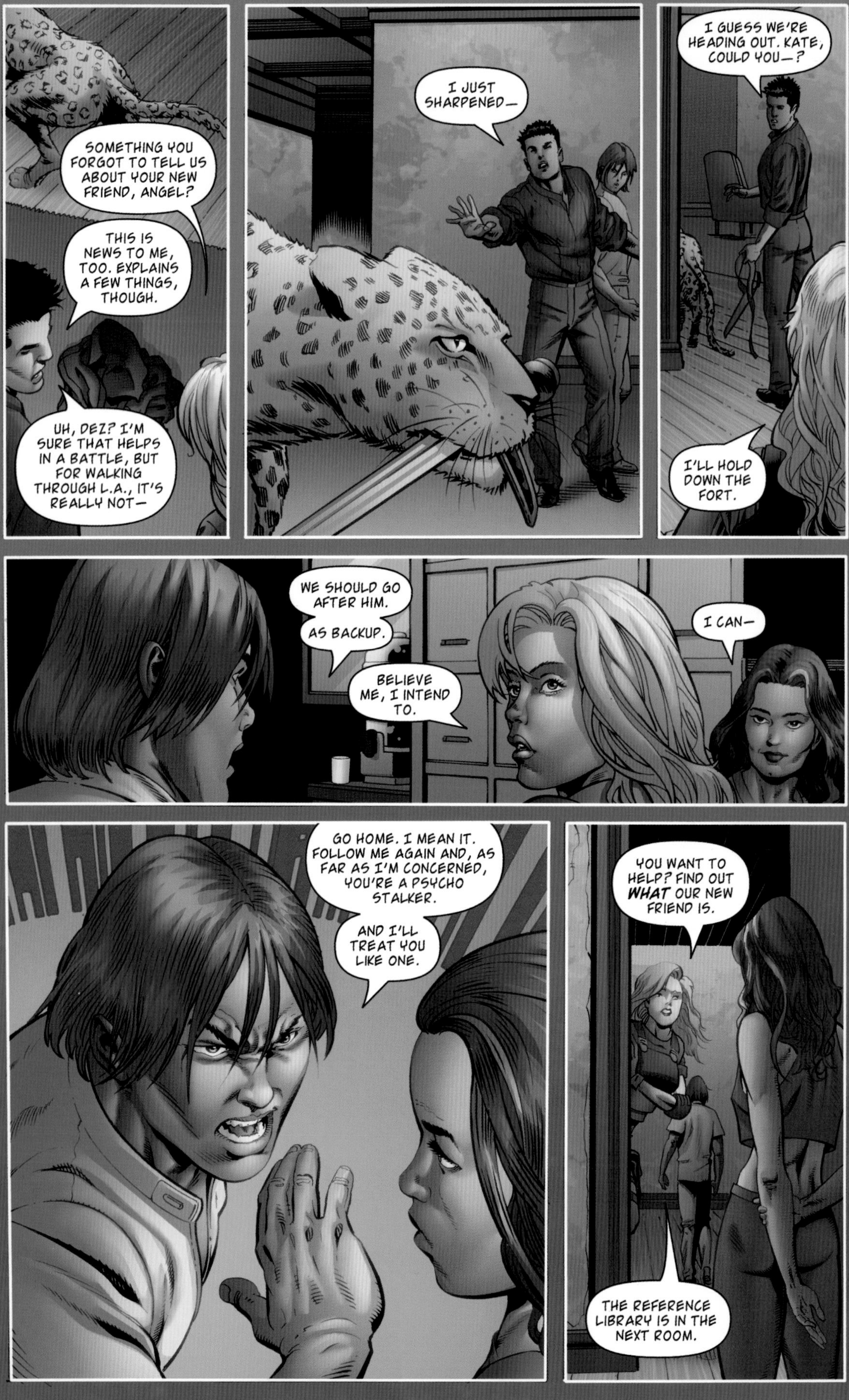
SOMETHING YOU FORGOT TO TELL US ABOUT YOUR NEW FRIEND, ANGEL?
THIS IS NEWS TO ME, TOO. EXPLAINS A FEW THINGS, THOUGH.
UH, DEZ? I'M SURE THAT HELPS IN A BATTLE, BUT FOR WALKING THROUGH L.A., IT'S REALLY NOT—
I JUST SHARPENED—
I GUESS WE'RE HEADING OUT. KATE, COULD YOU—?
I'LL HOLD DOWN THE FORT.
WE SHOULD GO AFTER HIM.
AS BACKUP.
BELIEVE ME, I INTEND TO.
I CAN—
GO HOME. I MEAN IT. FOLLOW ME AGAIN AND, AS FAR AS I'M CONCERNED, YOU'RE A PSYCHO STALKER.
AND I'LL TREAT YOU LIKE ONE.
YOU WANT TO HELP? FIND OUT ***WHAT*** OUR NEW FRIEND IS.
THE REFERENCE LIBRARY IS IN THE NEXT ROOM.

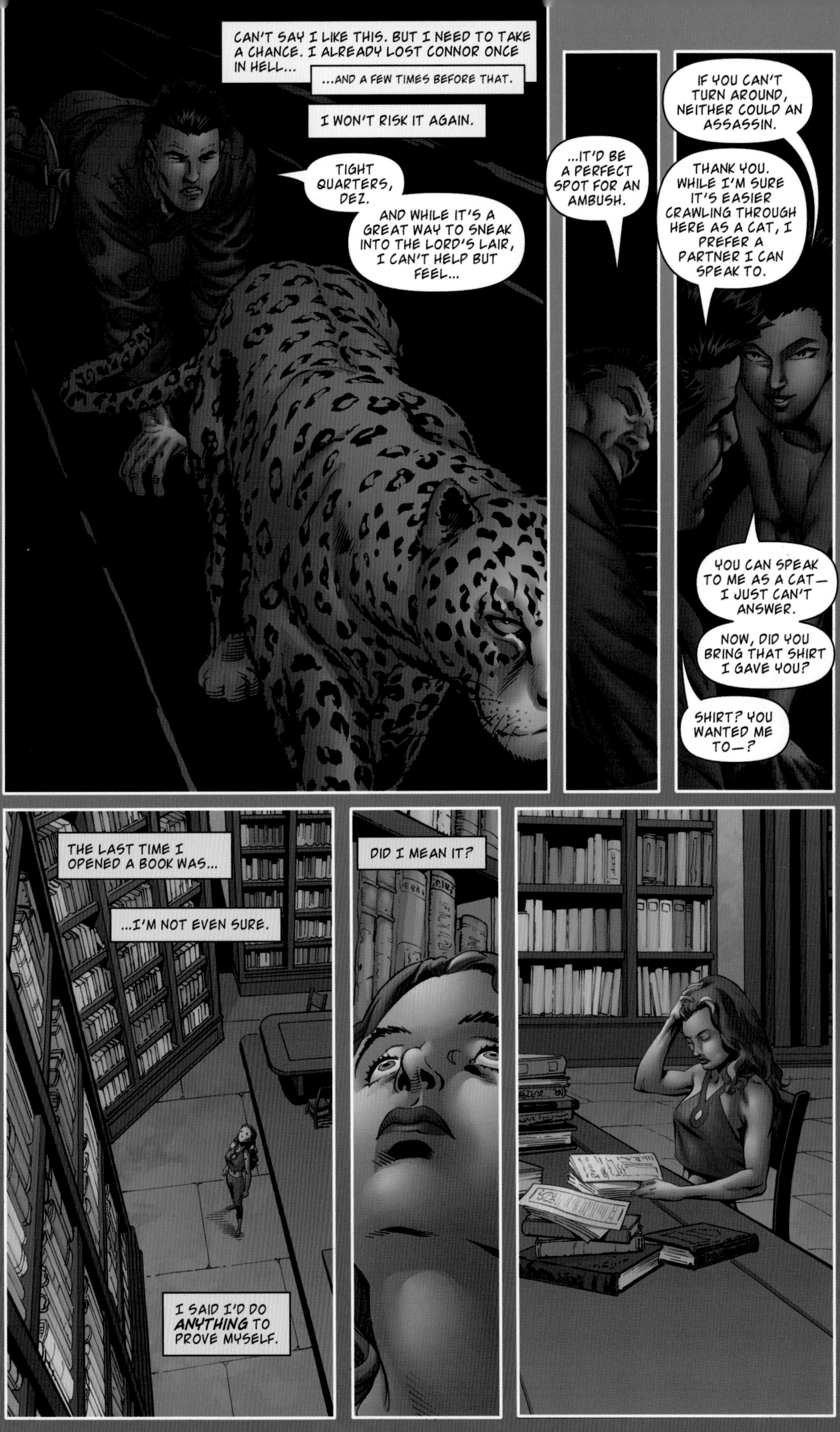

CAN'T SAY I LIKE THIS. BUT I NEED TO TAKE A CHANCE. I ALREADY LOST CONNOR ONCE IN HELL...
...AND A FEW TIMES BEFORE THAT.
I WON'T RISK IT AGAIN.
TIGHT QUARTERS, DEZ.
AND WHILE IT'S A GREAT WAY TO SNEAK INTO THE LORD'S LAIR, I CAN'T HELP BUT FEEL...
...IT'D BE A PERFECT SPOT FOR AN AMBUSH.
IF YOU CAN'T TURN AROUND, NEITHER COULD AN ASSASSIN.
THANK YOU. WHILE I'M SURE IT'S EASIER CRAWLING THROUGH HERE AS A CAT, I PREFER A PARTNER I CAN SPEAK TO.
YOU CAN SPEAK TO ME AS A CAT— I JUST CAN'T ANSWER.
NOW, DID YOU BRING THAT SHIRT I GAVE YOU?
SHIRT? YOU WANTED ME TO—?
THE LAST TIME I OPENED A BOOK WAS...
...I'M NOT EVEN SURE.
I SAID I'D DO ANYTHING TO PROVE MYSELF.
DID I MEAN IT?

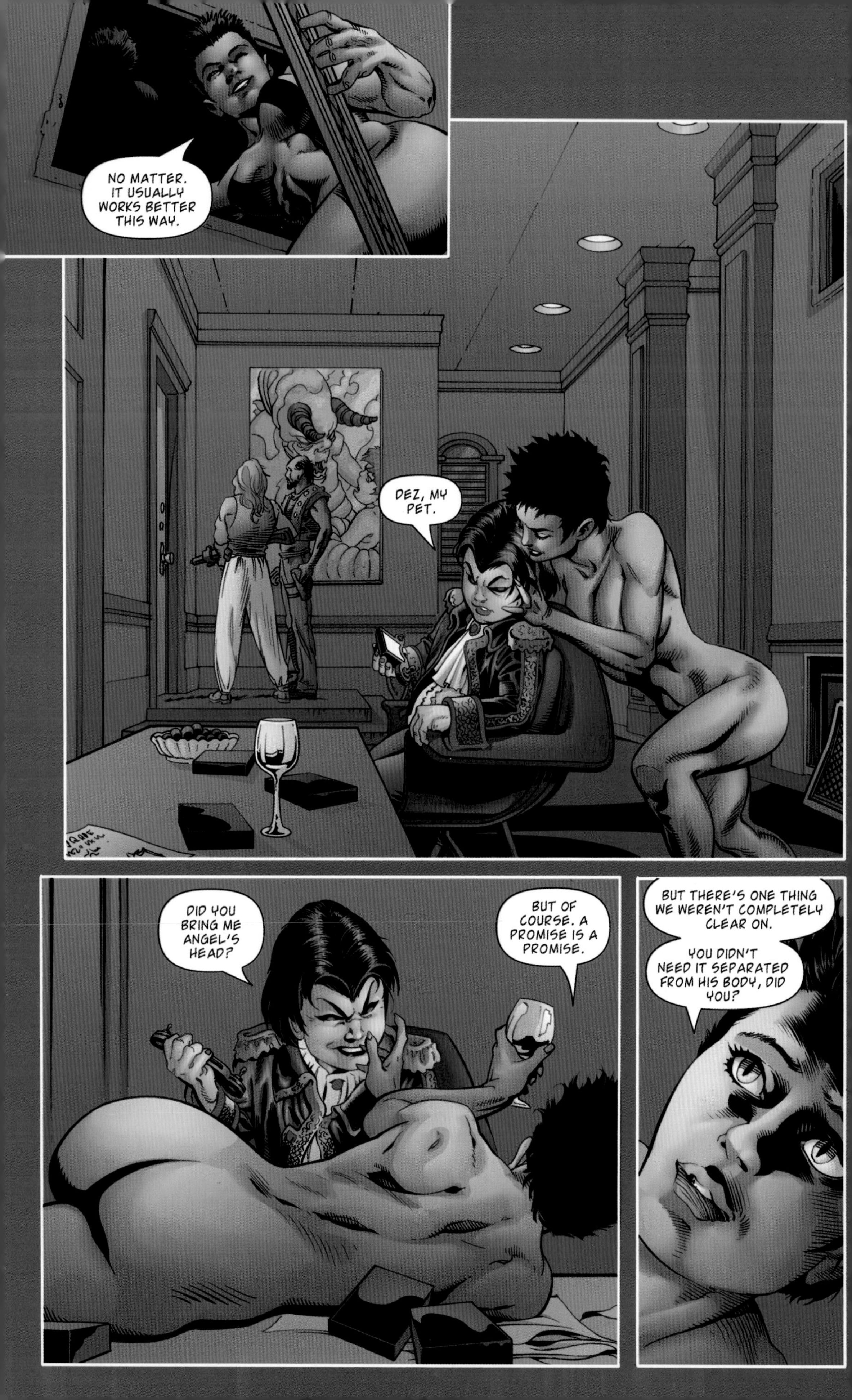
NO MATTER. IT USUALLY WORKS BETTER THIS WAY.
DEZ, MY PET.
DID YOU BRING ME ANGEL'S HEAD?
BUT OF COURSE. A PROMISE IS A PROMISE.
BUT THERE'S ONE THING WE WEREN'T COMPLETELY CLEAR ON.
YOU DIDN'T NEED IT SEPARATED FROM HIS BODY, DID YOU?

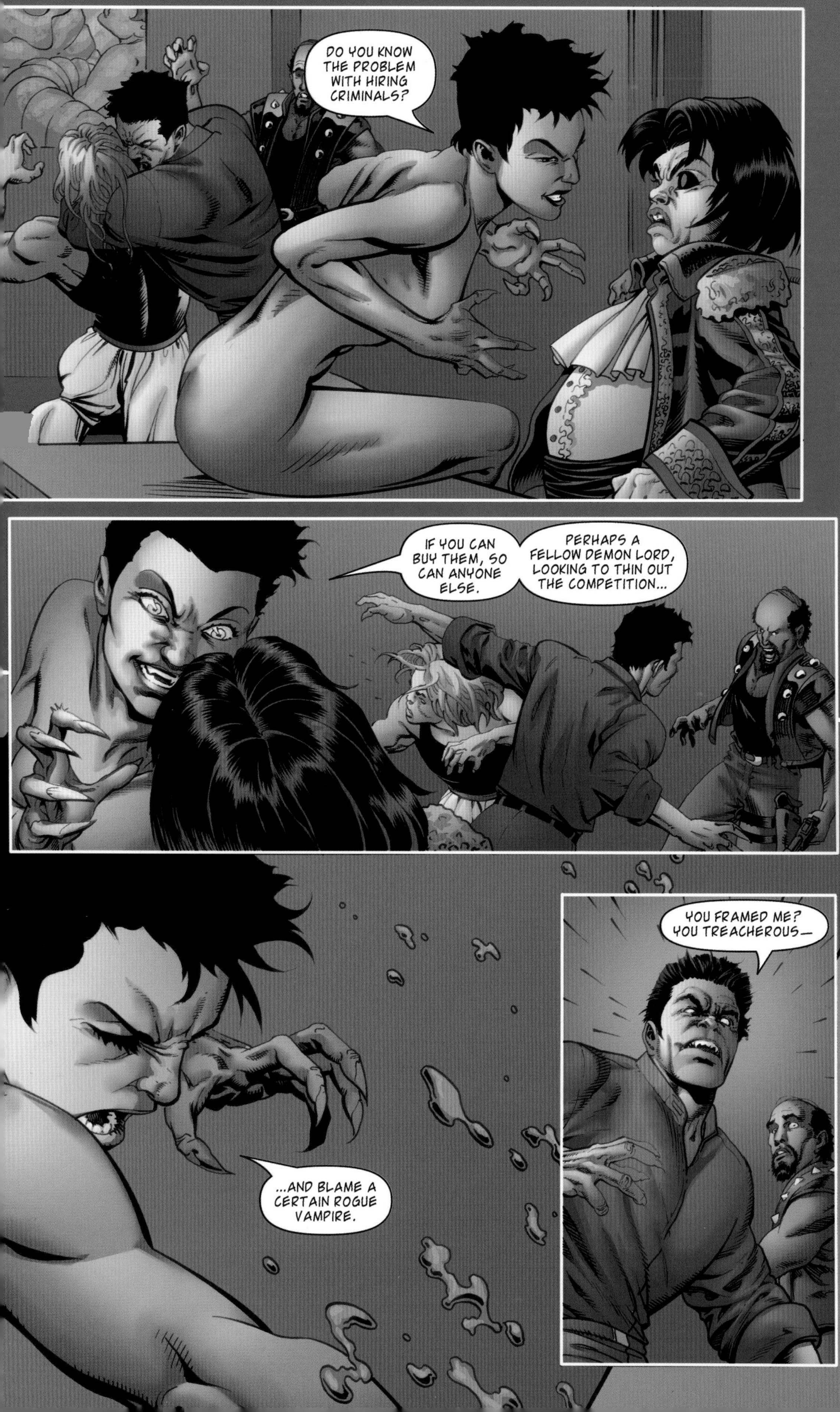

DO YOU KNOW THE PROBLEM WITH HIRING CRIMINALS?
IF YOU CAN BUY THEM, SO CAN ANYONE ELSE.
PERHAPS A FELLOW DEMON LORD, LOOKING TO THIN OUT THE COMPETITION...
...AND BLAME A CERTAIN ROGUE VAMPIRE.
YOU FRAMED ME? YOU TREACHEROUS—

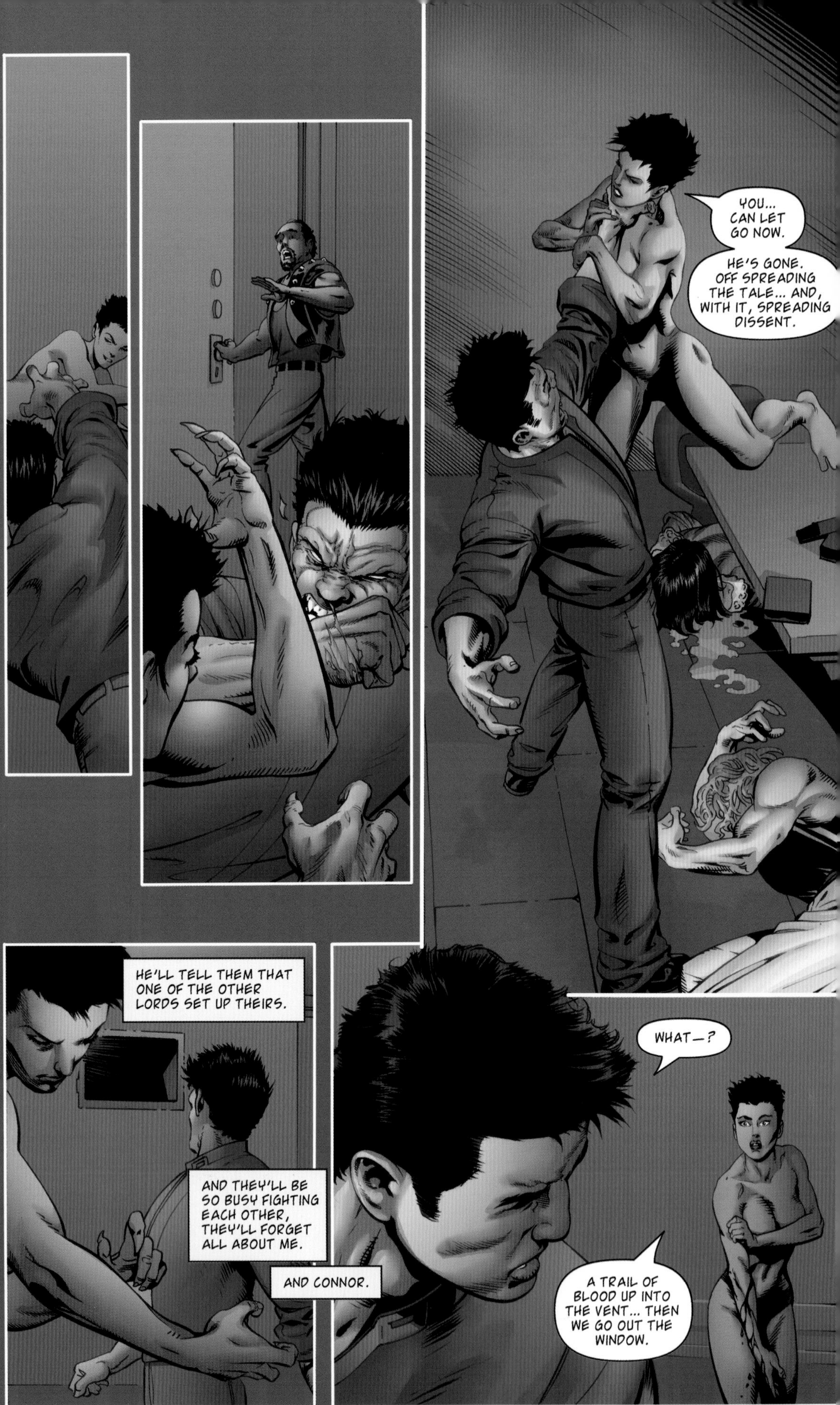
YOU... CAN LET GO NOW.
HE'S GONE. OFF SPREADING THE TALE... AND, WITH IT, SPREADING DISSENT.
HE'LL TELL THEM THAT ONE OF THE OTHER LORDS SET UP THEIRS.
AND THEY'LL BE SO BUSY FIGHTING EACH OTHER, THEY'LL FORGET ALL ABOUT ME.
AND CONNOR.
WHAT—?
A TRAIL OF BLOOD UP INTO THE VENT... THEN WE GO OUT THE WINDOW.

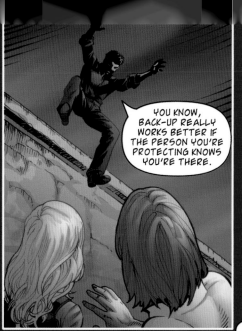

YOU KNOW, BACK-UP REALLY WORKS BETTER IF THE PERSON YOU'RE PROTECTING KNOWS YOU'RE THERE.

SPEAKING OF BACK-UP, WHERE'S YOUR KITTY FRIEND?

WE SPLIT UP. SHE SEEMS TO LIKE TAKING THE HIGH ROAD...

COOL.

SHE GOT ANGEL TO DO HER DIRTY WORK FOR HER. NOTHING COOL ABOUT THAT.

NO, DEZ DID ALL HER OWN STUNTS. AND SPEAKING OF STUNTS...

...NEXT TIME YOU WANT TO COVER MY BACK—JUST SAY SO, OKAY?

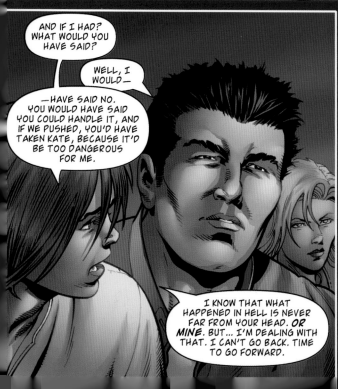

AND IF I HAD? WHAT WOULD YOU HAVE SAID?

WELL, I WOULD—

—HAVE SAID NO. YOU WOULD HAVE SAID YOU COULD HANDLE IT, AND IF WE PUSHED, YOU'D HAVE TAKEN KATE, BECAUSE IT'D BE TOO DANGEROUS FOR ME.

I KNOW THAT WHAT HAPPENED IN HELL IS NEVER FAR FROM YOUR HEAD. *OR MINE*. BUT... I'M DEALING WITH THAT. I CAN'T GO BACK. TIME TO GO FORWARD.

I'M SORRY FOR THAT.

BUT YOU'RE RIGHT.

TIME TO GO FORWARD.

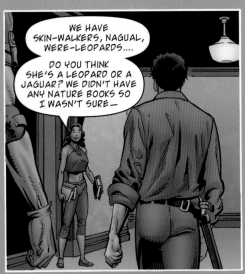

WE HAVE SKIN-WALKERS, NAGUAL, WERE-LEOPARDS....

DO YOU THINK SHE'S A LEOPARD OR A JAGUAR? WE DIDN'T HAVE ANY NATURE BOOKS SO I WASN'T SURE—

WHERE IS SHE? LOSING THE FUR COAT?

I DON'T KNOW. SHE WAS FOLLOWING. BUT I HAVEN'T SEEN HER SINCE...

SHE TOOK OFF A MILE BACK. FOR GOOD IF WE'RE LUCKY. SHE GOT WHAT SHE WANTED.

SO I GUESS YOU DON'T NEED...

JUST LEAVE IT ON THE DESK.

WE SHOULD GET SOME HUNTING IN BEFORE DAWN. GOT A CONTRACT TO FILL.

I COULD HELP. I COULD—

I COULD... DO MORE RESEARCH.

I DON'T THINK—

THESE GUYS WE'RE HUNTING. SEE IF YOU CAN FIND ANY PRECEDENT.

FINE. DO THAT THEN.

THANKS.

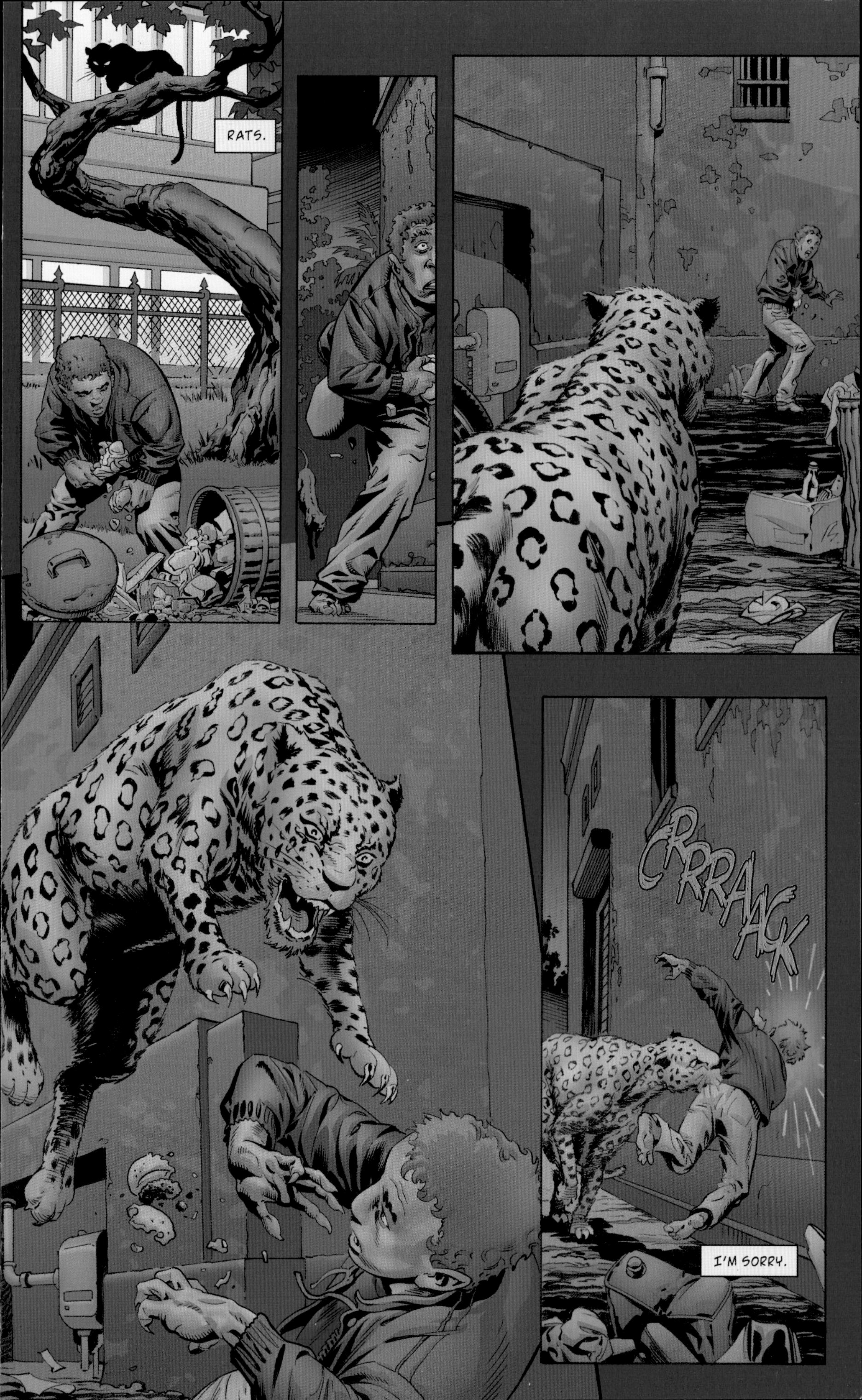
RATS.
CRRRAACK
I'M SORRY.

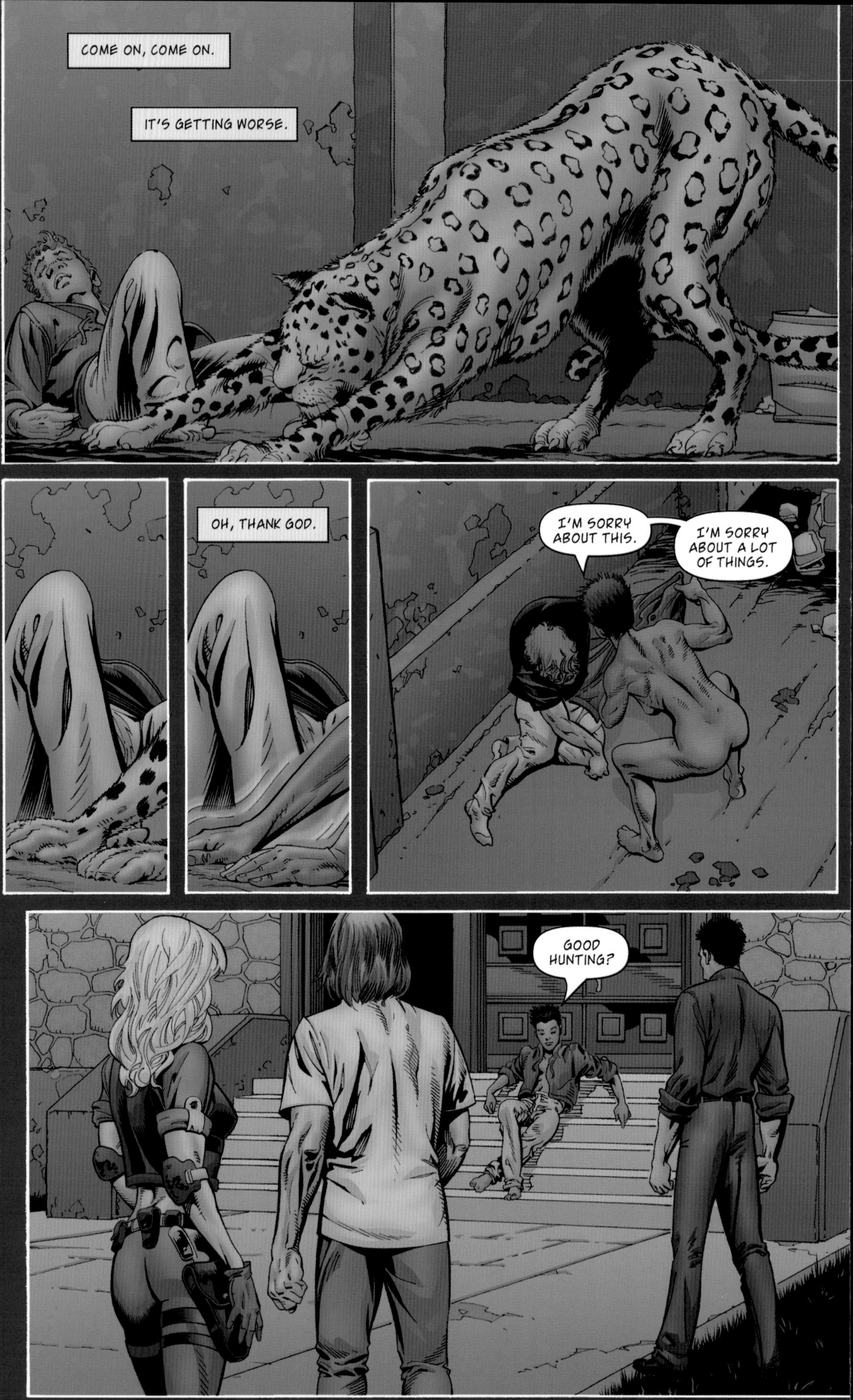
COME ON, COME ON.
IT'S GETTING WORSE.
OH, THANK GOD.
I'M SORRY ABOUT THIS.
I'M SORRY ABOUT A LOT OF THINGS.
GOOD HUNTING?

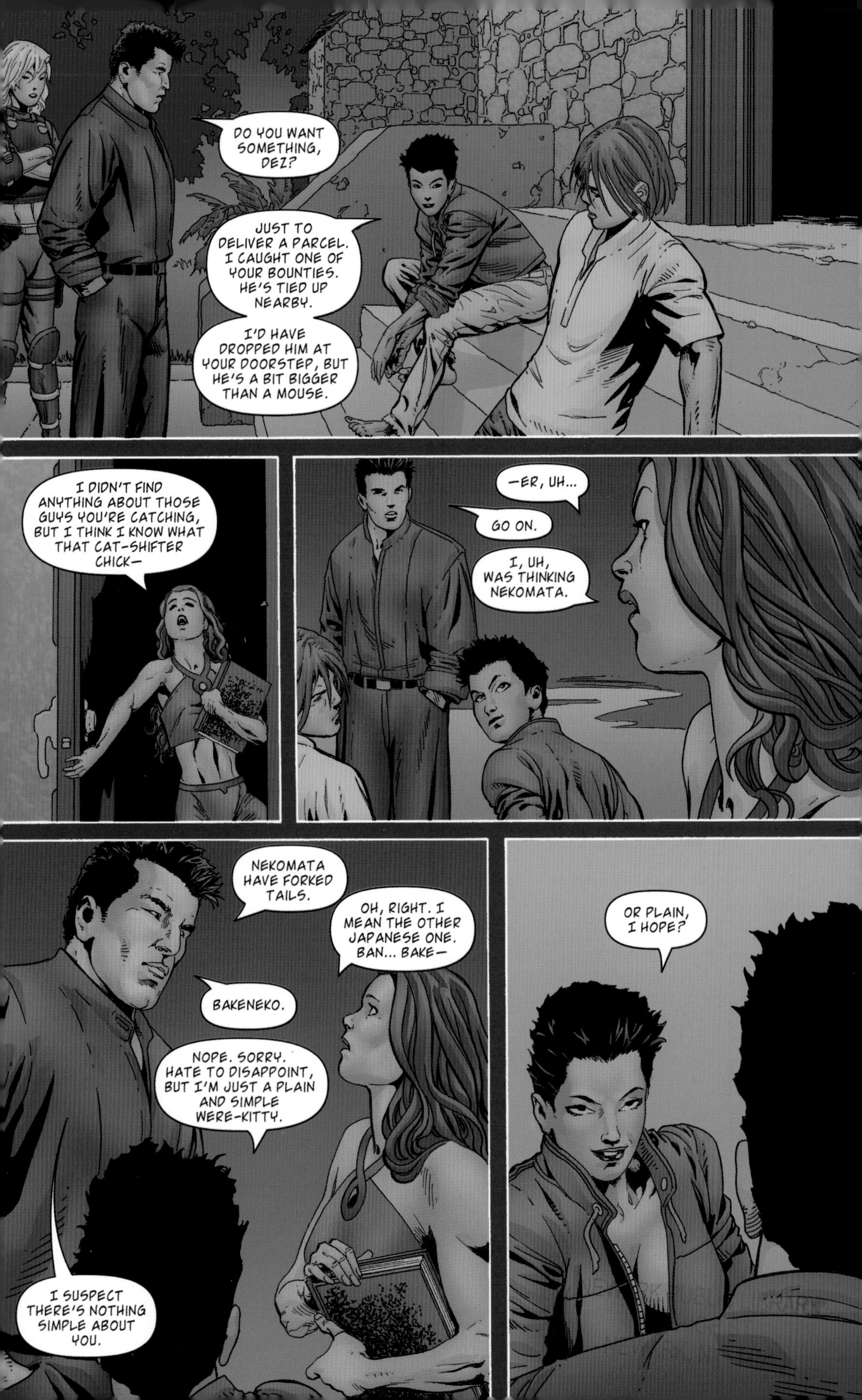
DO YOU WANT SOMETHING, DEZ?
JUST TO DELIVER A PARCEL. I CAUGHT ONE OF YOUR BOUNTIES. HE'S TIED UP NEARBY.
I'D HAVE DROPPED HIM AT YOUR DOORSTEP, BUT HE'S A BIT BIGGER THAN A MOUSE.
I DIDN'T FIND ANYTHING ABOUT THOSE GUYS YOU'RE CATCHING, BUT I THINK I KNOW WHAT THAT CAT-SHIFTER CHICK—
—ER, UH...
GO ON.
I, UH, WAS THINKING NEKOMATA.
NEKOMATA HAVE FORKED TAILS.
OH, RIGHT. I MEAN THE OTHER JAPANESE ONE. BAN... BAKE—
BAKENEKO.
NOPE. SORRY. HATE TO DISAPPOINT, BUT I'M JUST A PLAIN AND SIMPLE WERE-KITTY.
I SUSPECT THERE'S NOTHING SIMPLE ABOUT YOU.
OR PLAIN, I HOPE?

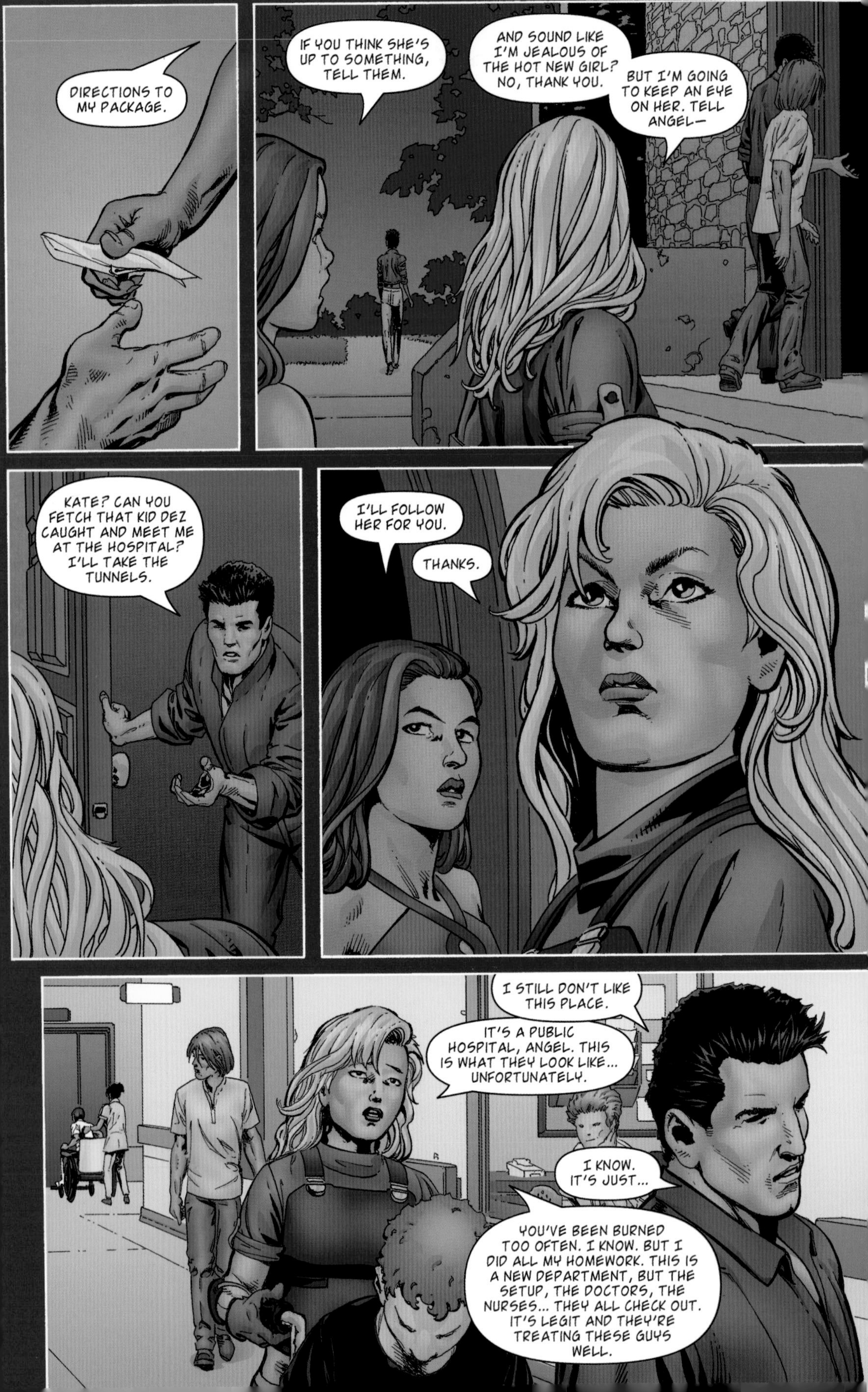
DIRECTIONS TO MY PACKAGE.
IF YOU THINK SHE'S UP TO SOMETHING, TELL THEM.
AND SOUND LIKE I'M JEALOUS OF THE HOT NEW GIRL? NO, THANK YOU.
BUT I'M GOING TO KEEP AN EYE ON HER. TELL ANGEL—
KATE? CAN YOU FETCH THAT KID DEZ CAUGHT AND MEET ME AT THE HOSPITAL? I'LL TAKE THE TUNNELS.
I'LL FOLLOW HER FOR YOU.
THANKS.
I STILL DON'T LIKE THIS PLACE.
IT'S A PUBLIC HOSPITAL, ANGEL. THIS IS WHAT THEY LOOK LIKE... UNFORTUNATELY.
I KNOW. IT'S JUST...
YOU'VE BEEN BURNED TOO OFTEN. I KNOW. BUT I DID ALL MY HOMEWORK. THIS IS A NEW DEPARTMENT, BUT THE SETUP, THE DOCTORS, THE NURSES... THEY ALL CHECK OUT. IT'S LEGIT AND THEY'RE TREATING THESE GUYS WELL.

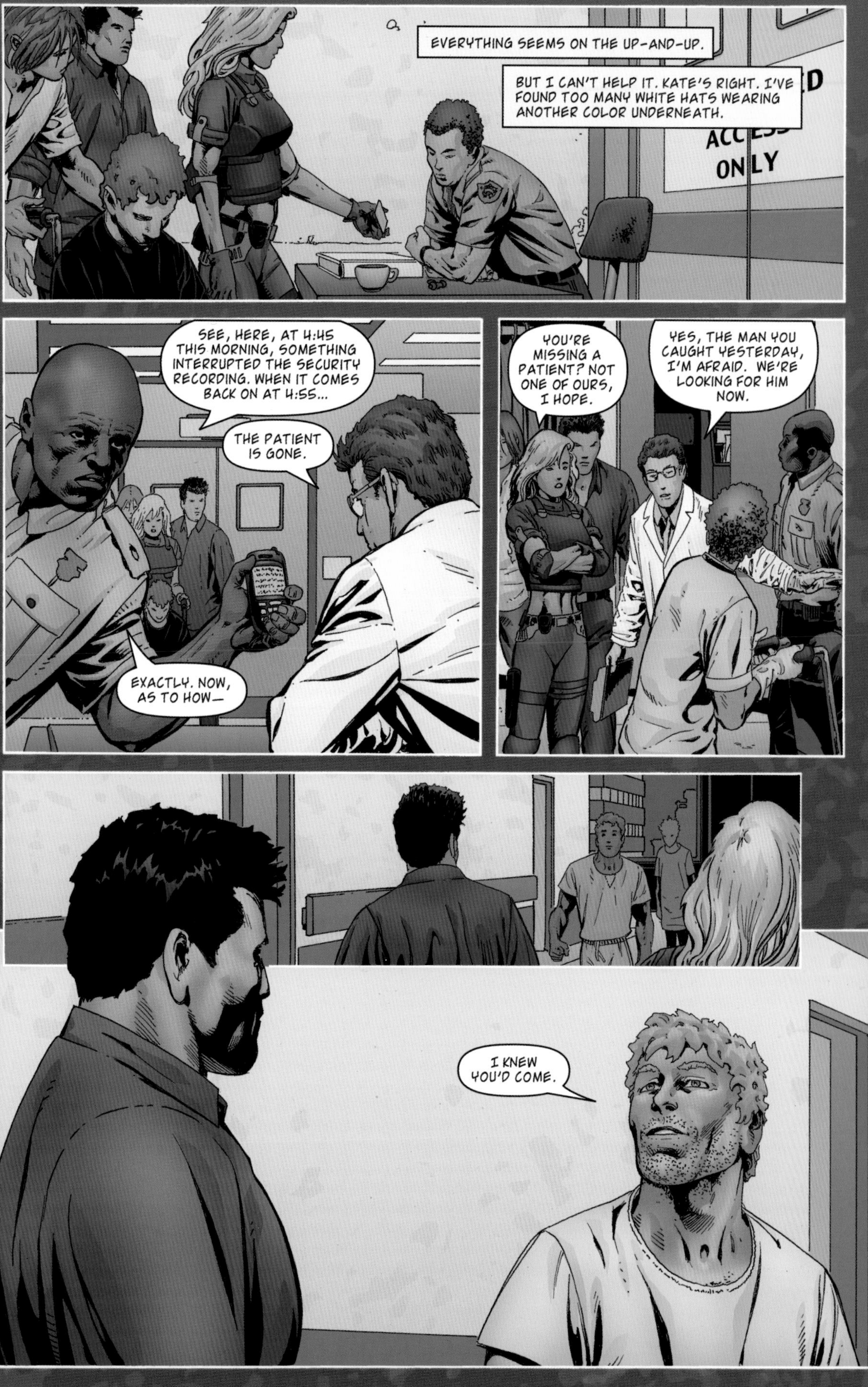
EVERYTHING SEEMS ON THE UP-AND-UP.
BUT I CAN'T HELP IT. KATE'S RIGHT. I'VE FOUND TOO MANY WHITE HATS WEARING ANOTHER COLOR UNDERNEATH.
ACCESS ONLY
SEE, HERE, AT 4:45 THIS MORNING, SOMETHING INTERRUPTED THE SECURITY RECORDING. WHEN IT COMES BACK ON AT 4:55...
THE PATIENT IS GONE.
EXACTLY. NOW, AS TO HOW—
YOU'RE MISSING A PATIENT? NOT ONE OF OURS, I HOPE.
YES, THE MAN YOU CAUGHT YESTERDAY, I'M AFRAID. WE'RE LOOKING FOR HIM NOW.
I KNEW YOU'D COME.

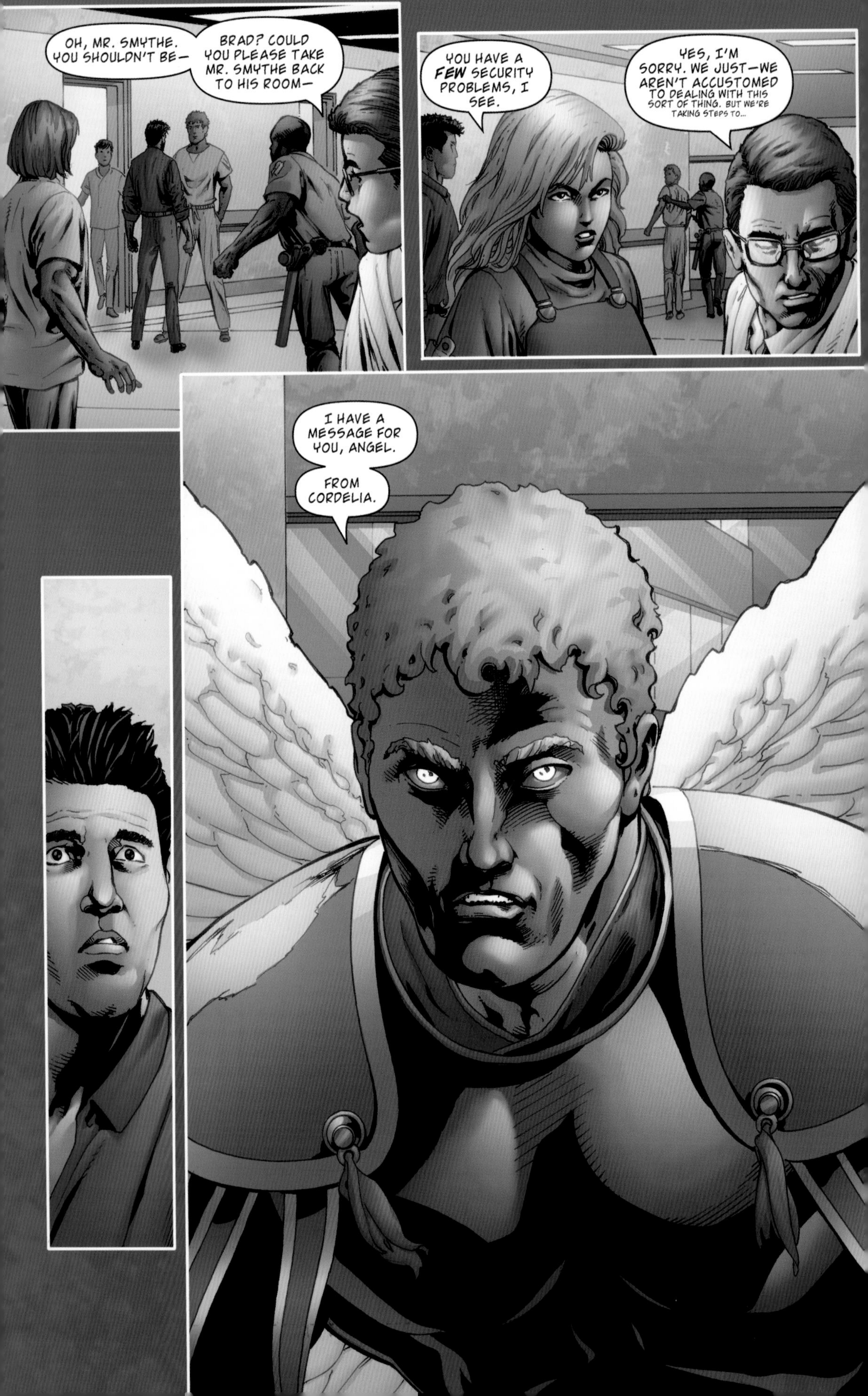
OH, MR. SMYTHE. YOU SHOULDN'T BE—
BRAD? COULD YOU PLEASE TAKE MR. SMYTHE BACK TO HIS ROOM—
YOU HAVE A FEW SECURITY PROBLEMS, I SEE.
YES, I'M SORRY. WE JUST—WE AREN'T ACCUSTOMED TO DEALING WITH THIS SORT OF THING. BUT WE'RE TAKING STEPS TO...
I HAVE A MESSAGE FOR YOU, ANGEL.
FROM CORDELIA.

chapter
three

WAIT!

I'M SURE THEY'LL LET YOU SEE HIM IF YOU REALLY WANT TO, WHEN THE SEDATIVE WEARS OFF.

IS HE SOMEONE YOU KNOW?

YOU DIDN'T SEE ANYTHING? HEAR ANYTHING?

JUST A PATIENT TRYING TO TALK TO YOU.

HE MUST HAVE RECOGNIZED YOU FROM THE NEWS.

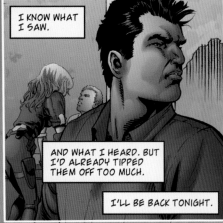

I KNOW WHAT I SAW.

AND WHAT I HEARD. BUT I'D ALREADY TIPPED THEM OFF TOO MUCH.

I'LL BE BACK TONIGHT.

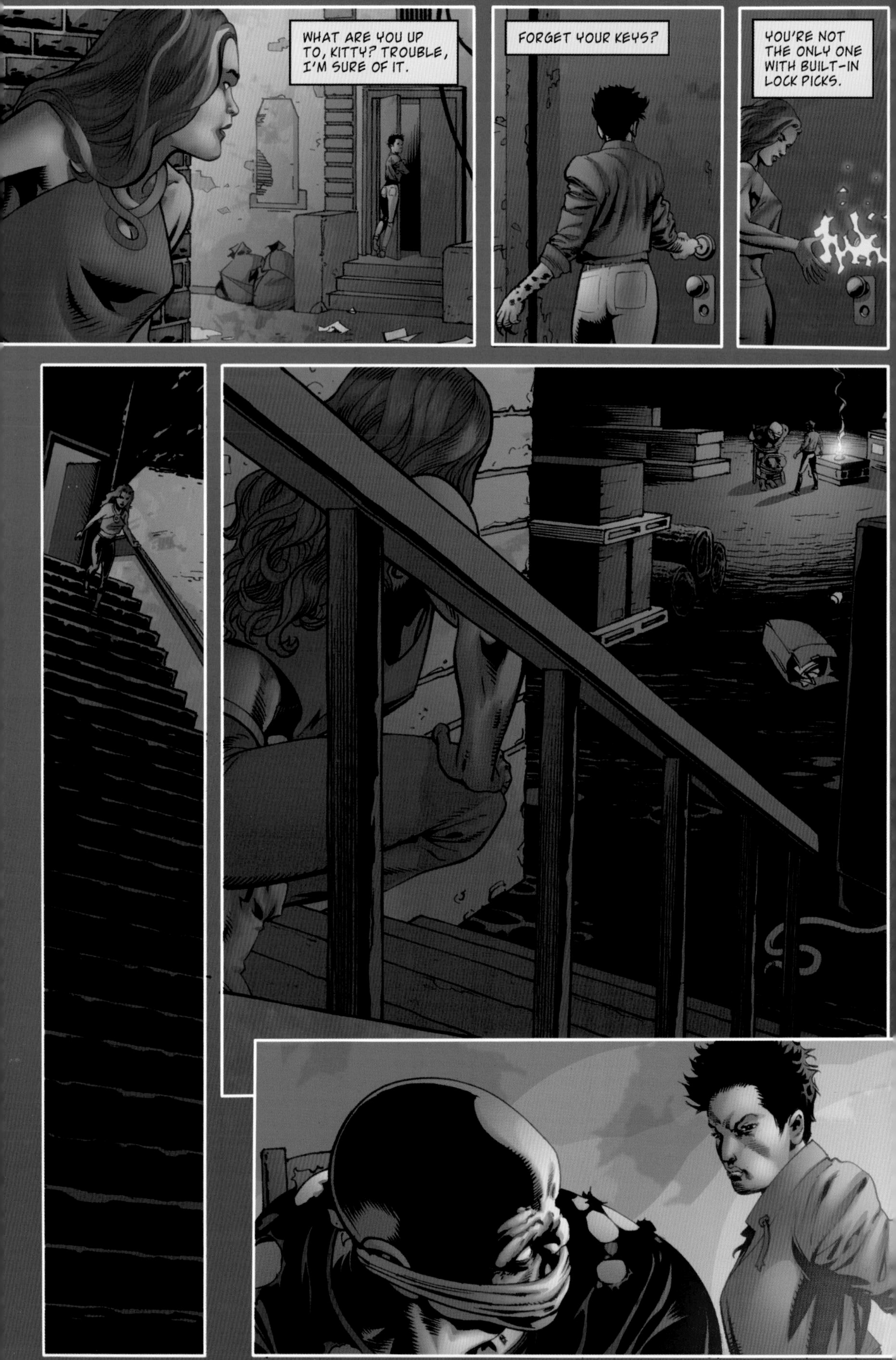
WHAT ARE YOU UP TO, KITTY? TROUBLE, I'M SURE OF IT.
FORGET YOUR KEYS?
YOU'RE NOT THE ONLY ONE WITH BUILT-IN LOCK PICKS.

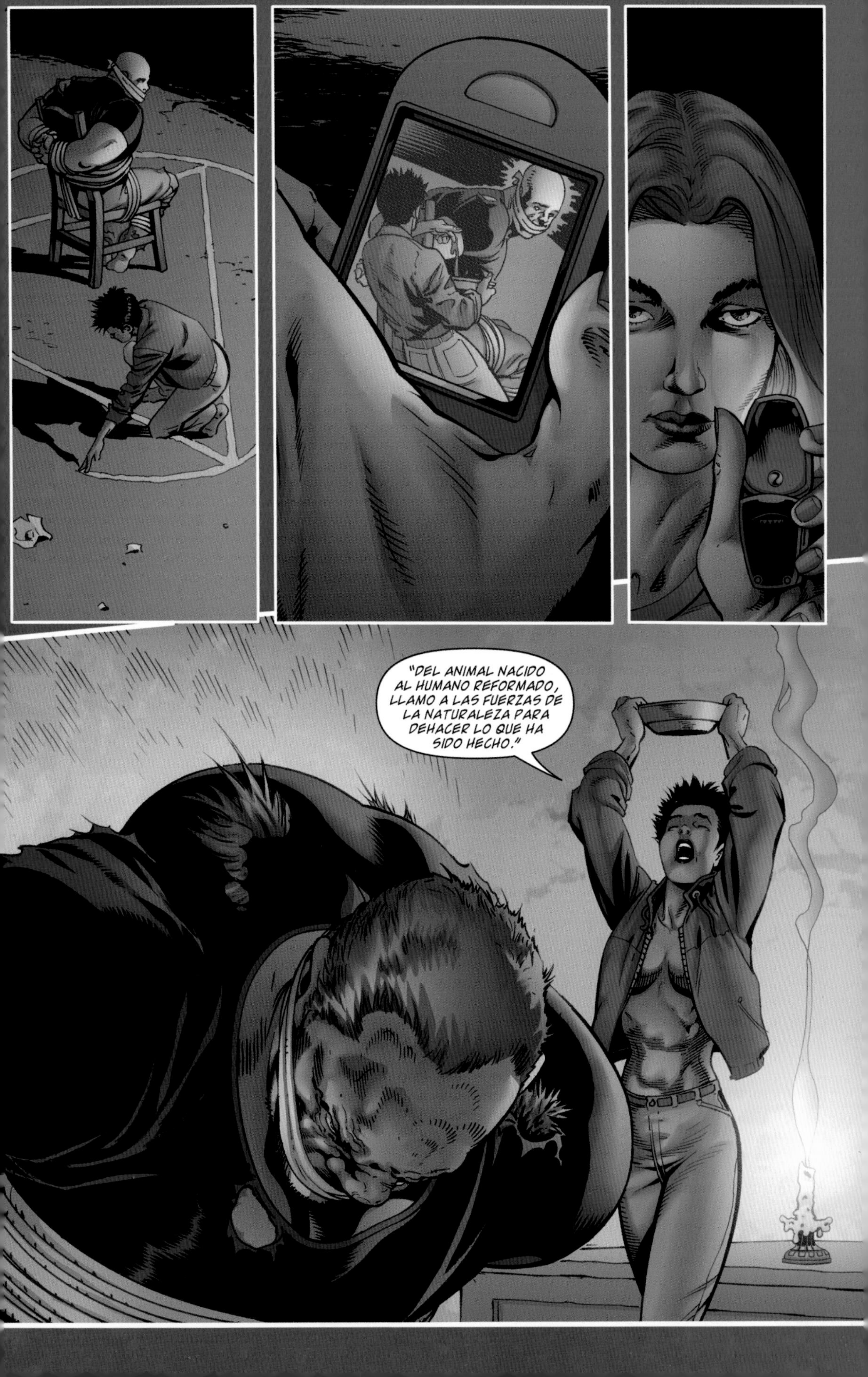
"DEL ANIMAL NACIDO AL HUMANO REFORMADO, LLAMO A LAS FUERZAS DE LA NATURALEZA PARA DEHACER LO QUE HA SIDO HECHO."

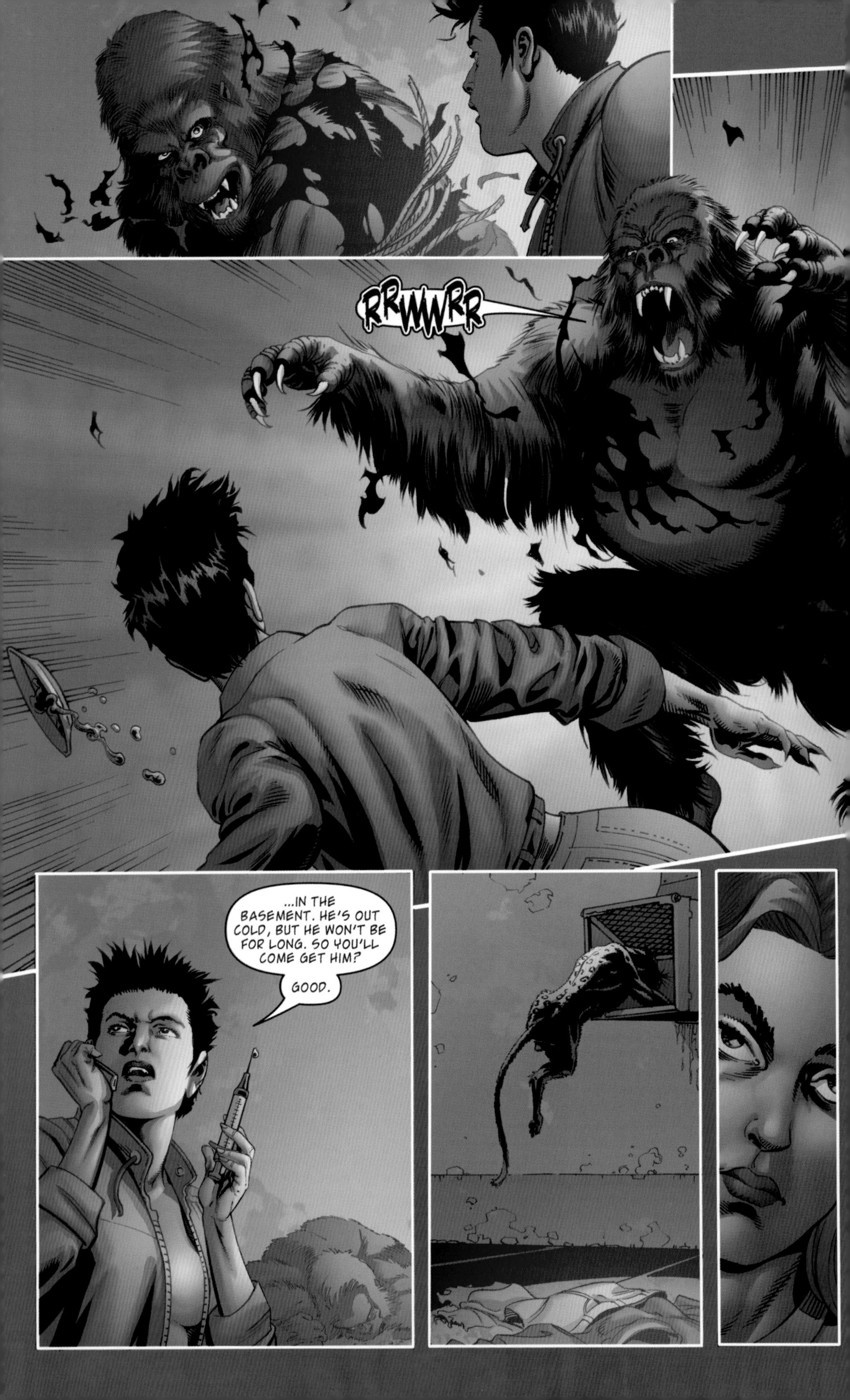
RRWWRR
...IN THE BASEMENT. HE'S OUT COLD, BUT HE WON'T BE FOR LONG. SO YOU'LL COME GET HIM?
GOOD.

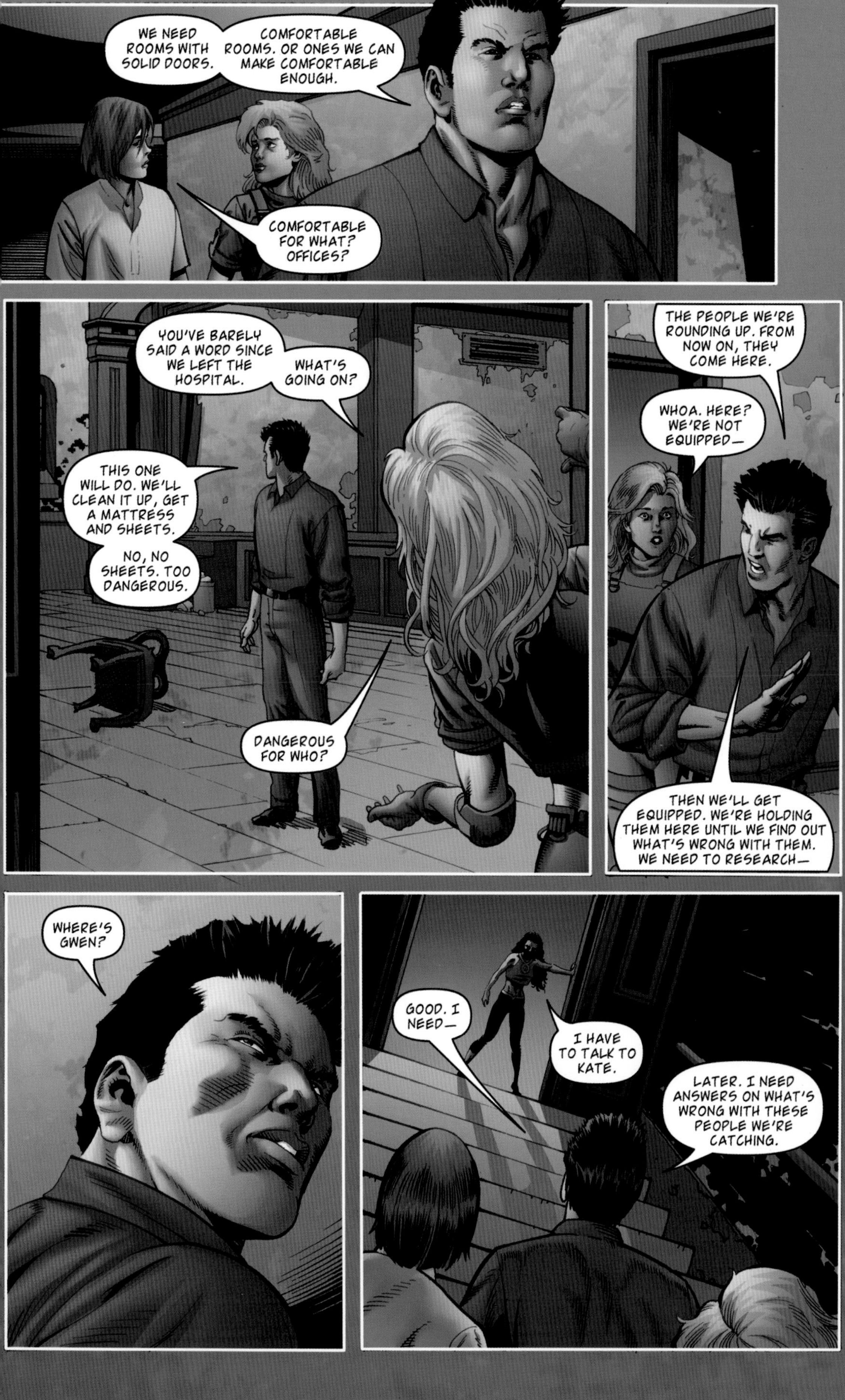
WE NEED ROOMS WITH SOLID DOORS.
COMFORTABLE ROOMS. OR ONES WE CAN MAKE COMFORTABLE ENOUGH.
COMFORTABLE FOR WHAT? OFFICES?
YOU'VE BARELY SAID A WORD SINCE WE LEFT THE HOSPITAL.
WHAT'S GOING ON?
THIS ONE WILL DO. WE'LL CLEAN IT UP, GET A MATTRESS AND SHEETS.
NO, NO SHEETS. TOO DANGEROUS.
DANGEROUS FOR WHO?
THE PEOPLE WE'RE ROUNDING UP. FROM NOW ON, THEY COME HERE.
WHOA. HERE? WE'RE NOT EQUIPPED—
THEN WE'LL GET EQUIPPED. WE'RE HOLDING THEM HERE UNTIL WE FIND OUT WHAT'S WRONG WITH THEM. WE NEED TO RESEARCH—
WHERE'S GWEN?
GOOD. I NEED—
I HAVE TO TALK TO KATE.
LATER. I NEED ANSWERS ON WHAT'S WRONG WITH THESE PEOPLE WE'RE CATCHING.

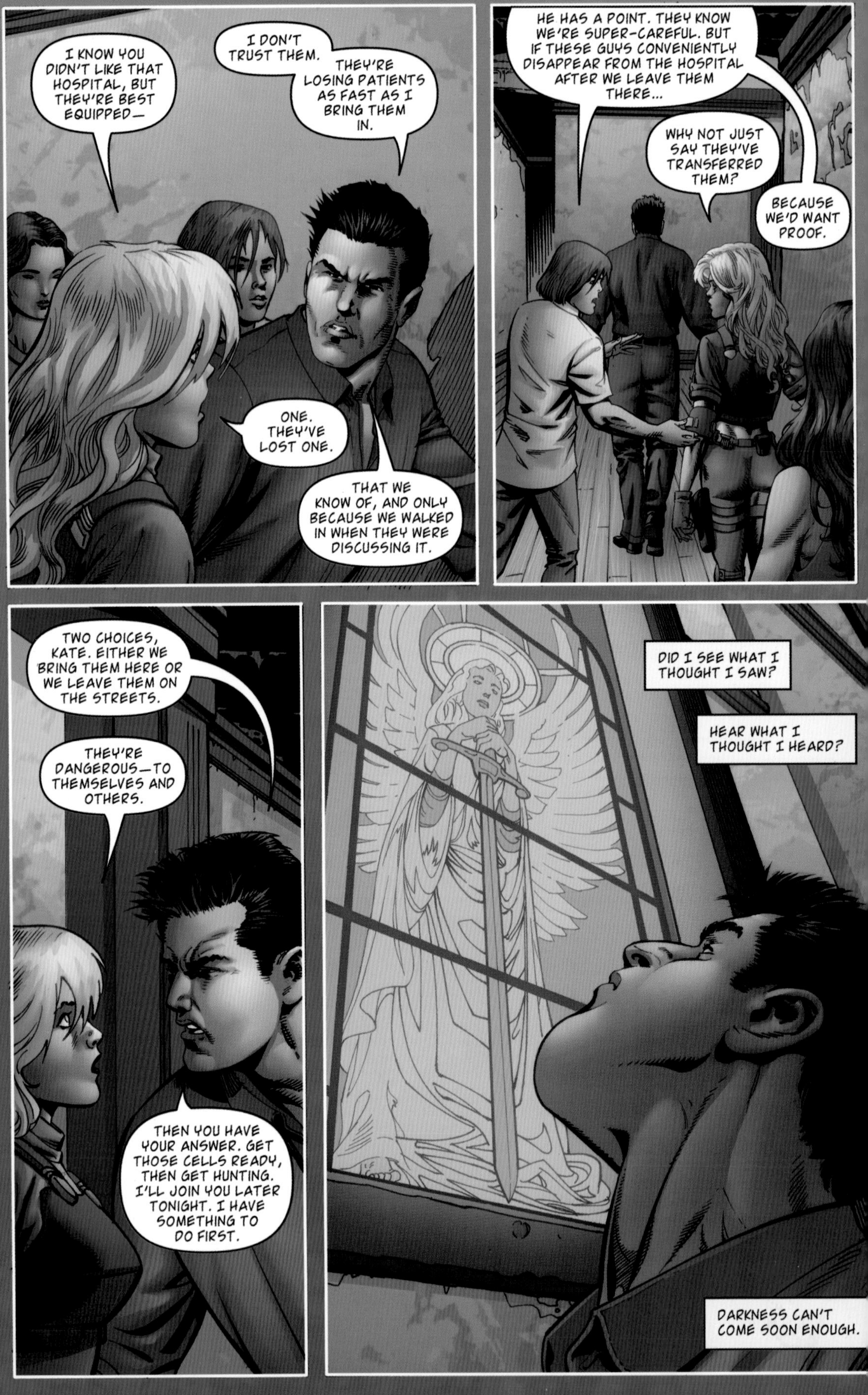
I KNOW YOU DIDN'T LIKE THAT HOSPITAL, BUT THEY'RE BEST EQUIPPED—
I DON'T TRUST THEM.
THEY'RE LOSING PATIENTS AS FAST AS I BRING THEM IN.
ONE. THEY'VE LOST ONE.
THAT WE KNOW OF, AND ONLY BECAUSE WE WALKED IN WHEN THEY WERE DISCUSSING IT.
HE HAS A POINT. THEY KNOW WE'RE SUPER-CAREFUL. BUT IF THESE GUYS CONVENIENTLY DISAPPEAR FROM THE HOSPITAL AFTER WE LEAVE THEM THERE...
WHY NOT JUST SAY THEY'VE TRANSFERRED THEM?
BECAUSE WE'D WANT PROOF.
TWO CHOICES, KATE. EITHER WE BRING THEM HERE OR WE LEAVE THEM ON THE STREETS.
THEY'RE DANGEROUS—TO THEMSELVES AND OTHERS.
THEN YOU HAVE YOUR ANSWER. GET THOSE CELLS READY, THEN GET HUNTING. I'LL JOIN YOU LATER TONIGHT. I HAVE SOMETHING TO DO FIRST.
DID I SEE WHAT I THOUGHT I SAW?
HEAR WHAT I THOUGHT I HEARD?
DARKNESS CAN'T COME SOON ENOUGH.

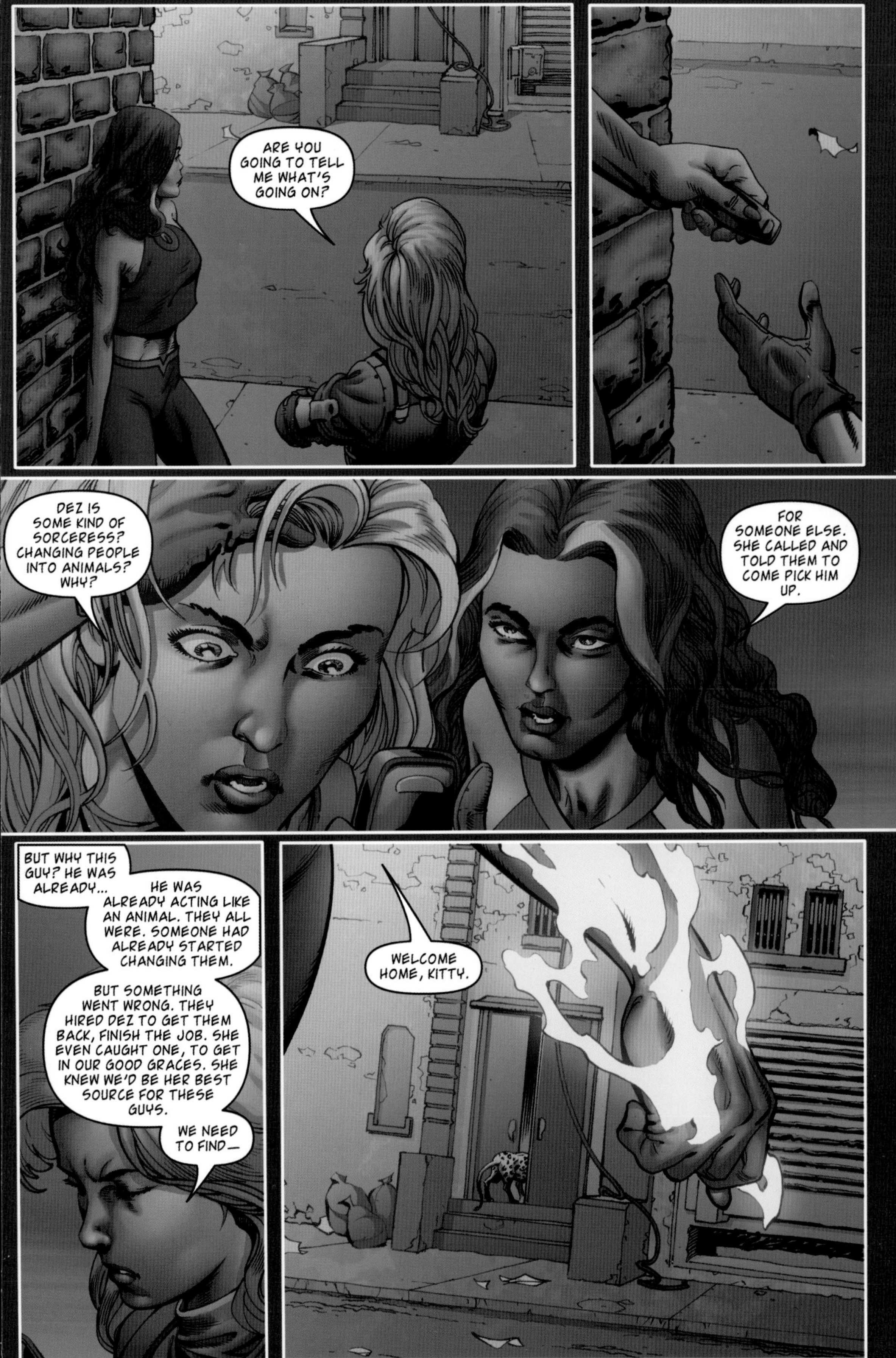
ARE YOU GOING TO TELL ME WHAT'S GOING ON?
DEZ IS SOME KIND OF SORCERESS? CHANGING PEOPLE INTO ANIMALS? WHY?
FOR SOMEONE ELSE. SHE CALLED AND TOLD THEM TO COME PICK HIM UP.
BUT WHY THIS GUY? HE WAS ALREADY...
HE WAS ALREADY ACTING LIKE AN ANIMAL. THEY ALL WERE. SOMEONE HAD ALREADY STARTED CHANGING THEM.
BUT SOMETHING WENT WRONG. THEY HIRED DEZ TO GET THEM BACK, FINISH THE JOB. SHE EVEN CAUGHT ONE, TO GET IN OUR GOOD GRACES. SHE KNEW WE'D BE HER BEST SOURCE FOR THESE GUYS.
WE NEED TO FIND—
WELCOME HOME, KITTY.

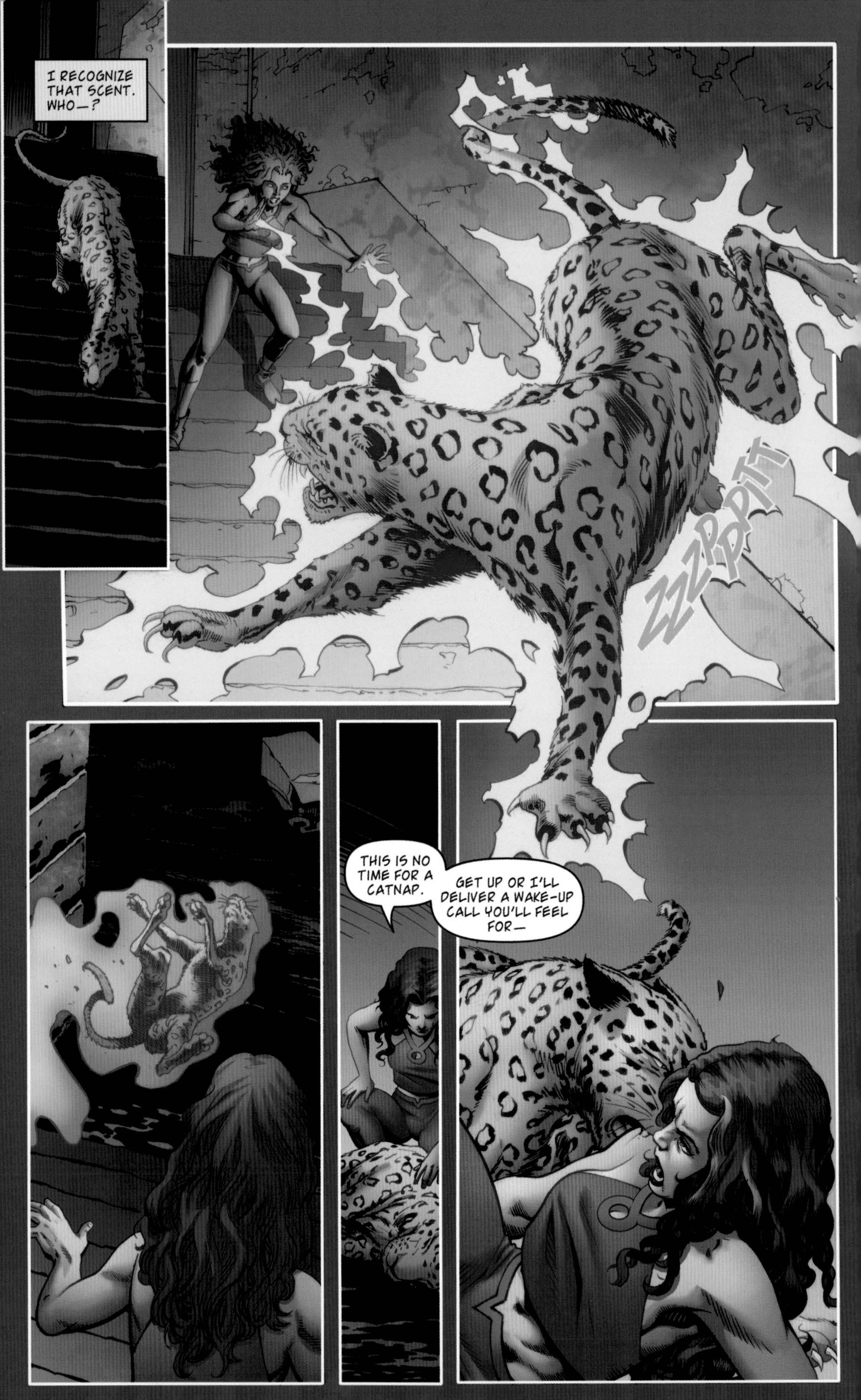
I RECOGNIZE THAT SCENT. WHO—?
ZZZPPPITT
THIS IS NO TIME FOR A CATNAP.
GET UP OR I'LL DELIVER A WAKE-UP CALL YOU'LL FEEL FOR—

LET HER GO.

JUST STEP OFF HER, AND SHE WON'T—

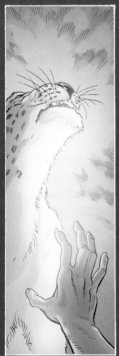

STAY DOWN, KITTY.

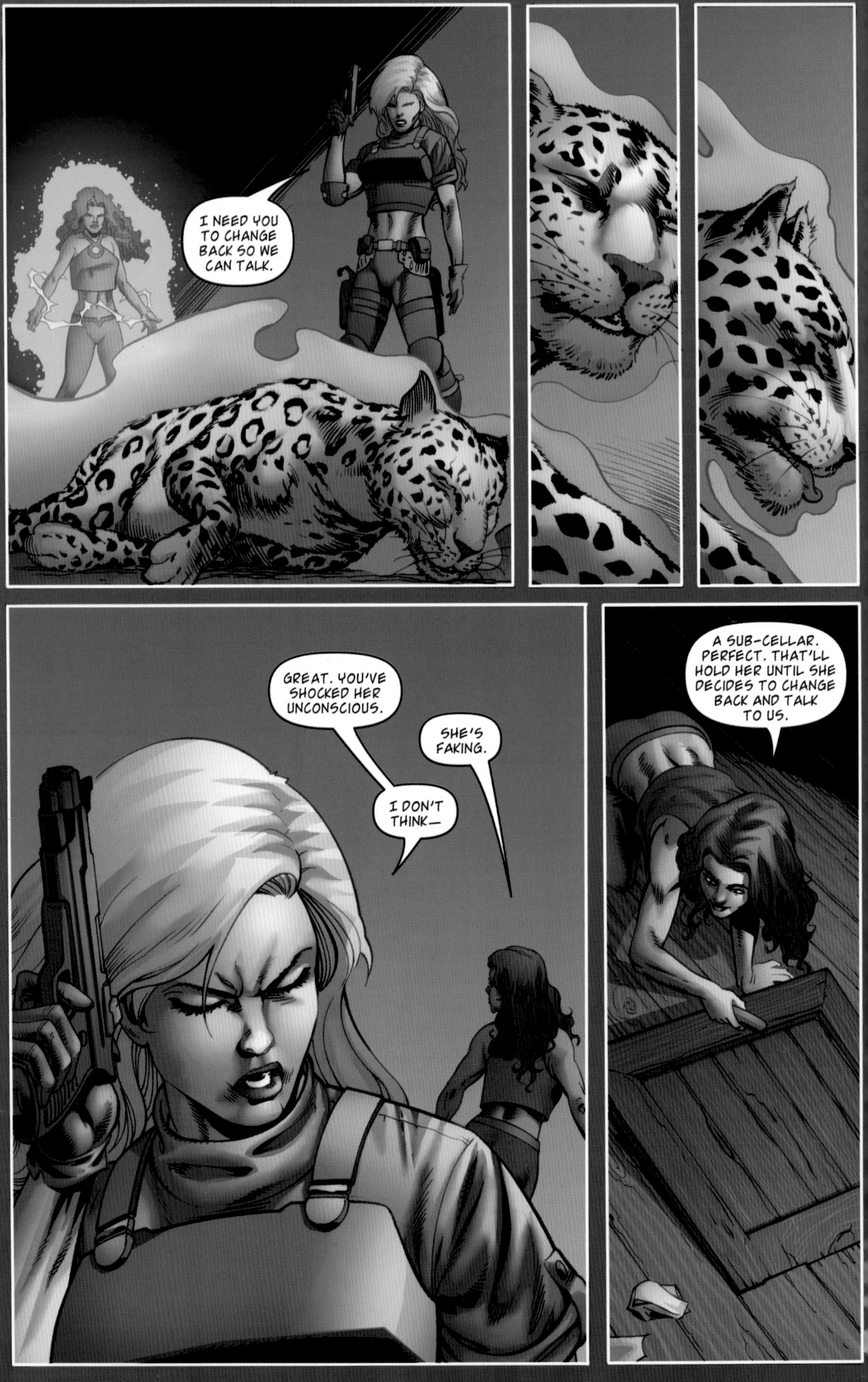
I NEED YOU TO CHANGE BACK SO WE CAN TALK.
GREAT. YOU'VE SHOCKED HER UNCONSCIOUS.
SHE'S FAKING.
I DON'T THINK—
A SUB-CELLAR. PERFECT. THAT'LL HOLD HER UNTIL SHE DECIDES TO CHANGE BACK AND TALK TO US.

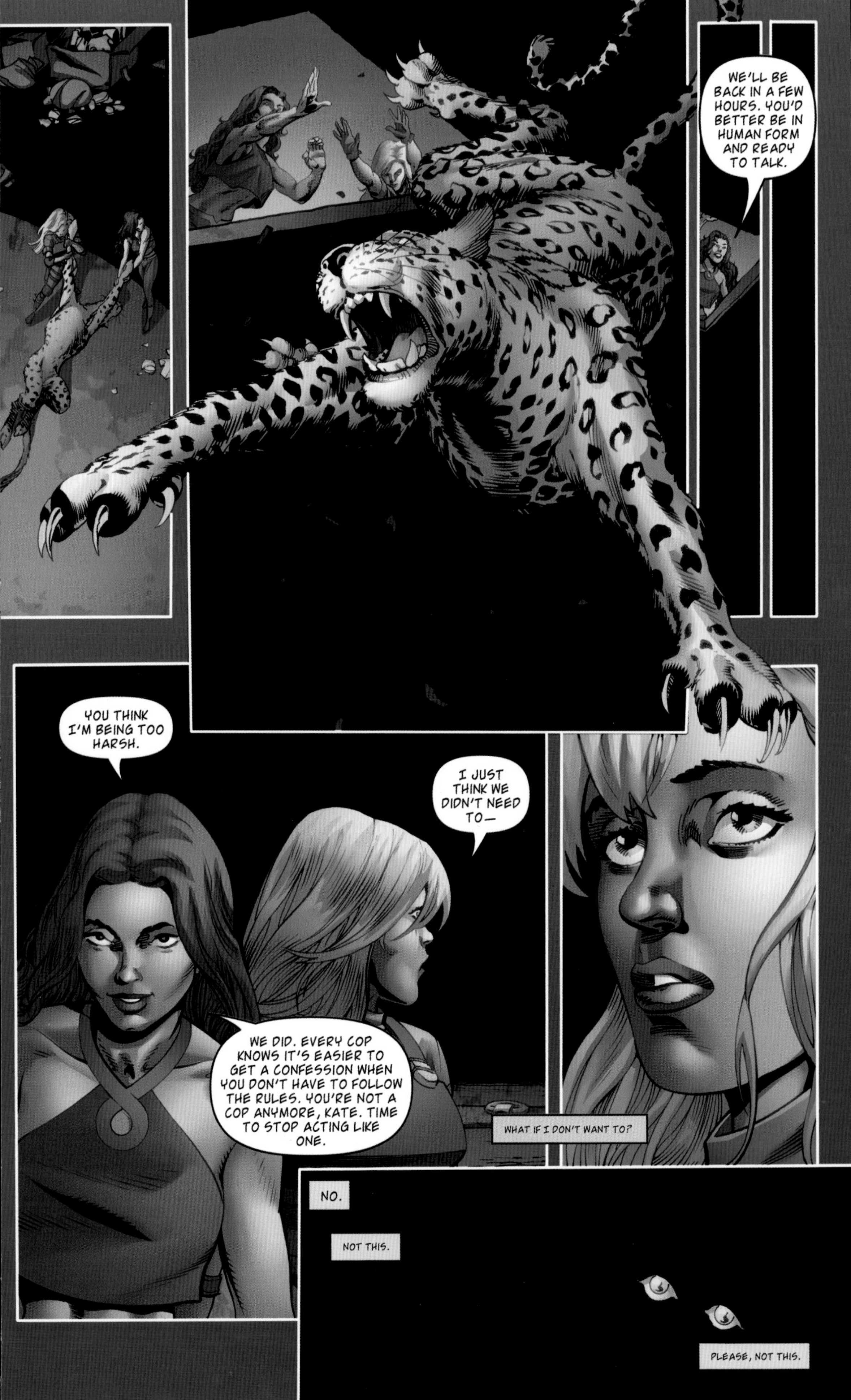
WE'LL BE BACK IN A FEW HOURS. YOU'D BETTER BE IN HUMAN FORM AND READY TO TALK.
YOU THINK I'M BEING TOO HARSH.
I JUST THINK WE DIDN'T NEED TO—
WE DID. EVERY COP KNOWS IT'S EASIER TO GET A CONFESSION WHEN YOU DON'T HAVE TO FOLLOW THE RULES. YOU'RE NOT A COP ANYMORE, KATE. TIME TO STOP ACTING LIKE ONE.
WHAT IF I DON'T WANT TO?
NO.
NOT THIS.
PLEASE, NOT THIS.

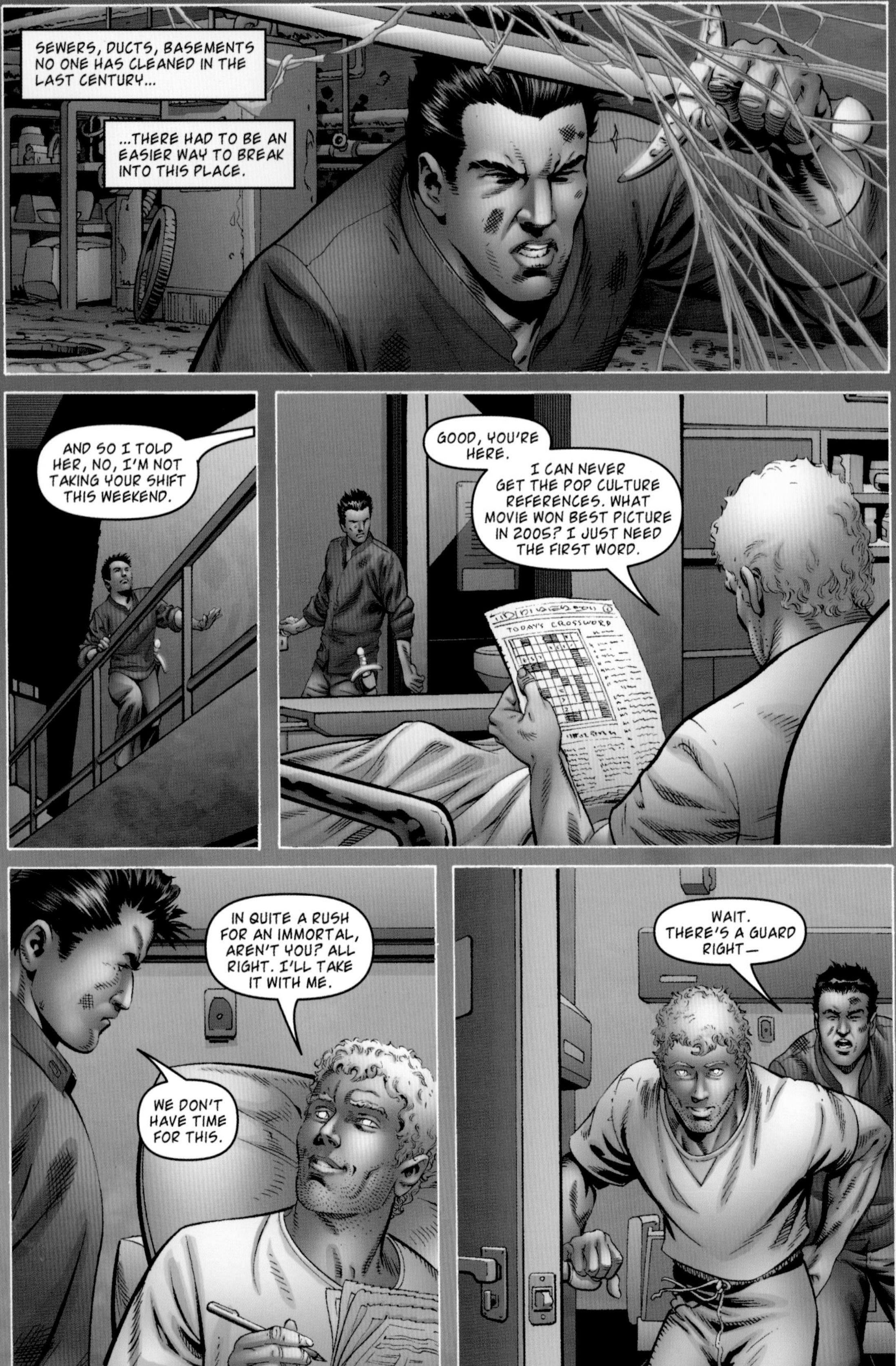
SEWERS, DUCTS, BASEMENTS NO ONE HAS CLEANED IN THE LAST CENTURY...
...THERE HAD TO BE AN EASIER WAY TO BREAK INTO THIS PLACE.
AND SO I TOLD HER, NO, I'M NOT TAKING YOUR SHIFT THIS WEEKEND.
GOOD, YOU'RE HERE.
I CAN NEVER GET THE POP CULTURE REFERENCES. WHAT MOVIE WON BEST PICTURE IN 2005? I JUST NEED THE FIRST WORD.
TODAY'S CROSSWORD
IN QUITE A RUSH FOR AN IMMORTAL, AREN'T YOU? ALL RIGHT. I'LL TAKE IT WITH ME.
WE DON'T HAVE TIME FOR THIS.
WAIT. THERE'S A GUARD RIGHT—

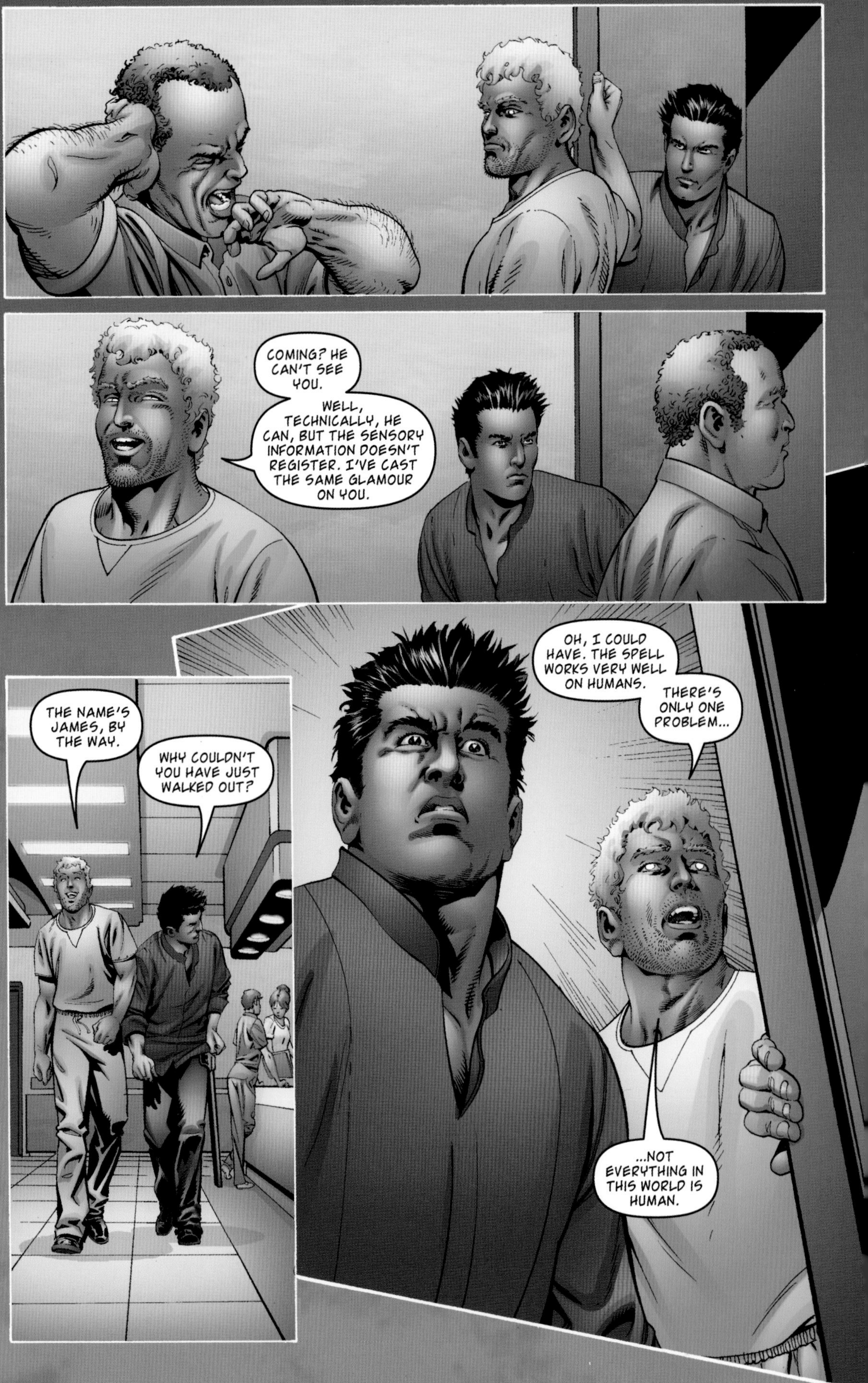
COMING? HE CAN'T SEE YOU.
WELL, TECHNICALLY, HE CAN, BUT THE SENSORY INFORMATION DOESN'T REGISTER. I'VE CAST THE SAME GLAMOUR ON YOU.
THE NAME'S JAMES, BY THE WAY.
WHY COULDN'T YOU HAVE JUST WALKED OUT?
OH, I COULD HAVE. THE SPELL WORKS VERY WELL ON HUMANS.
THERE'S ONLY ONE PROBLEM...
...NOT EVERYTHING IN THIS WORLD IS HUMAN.

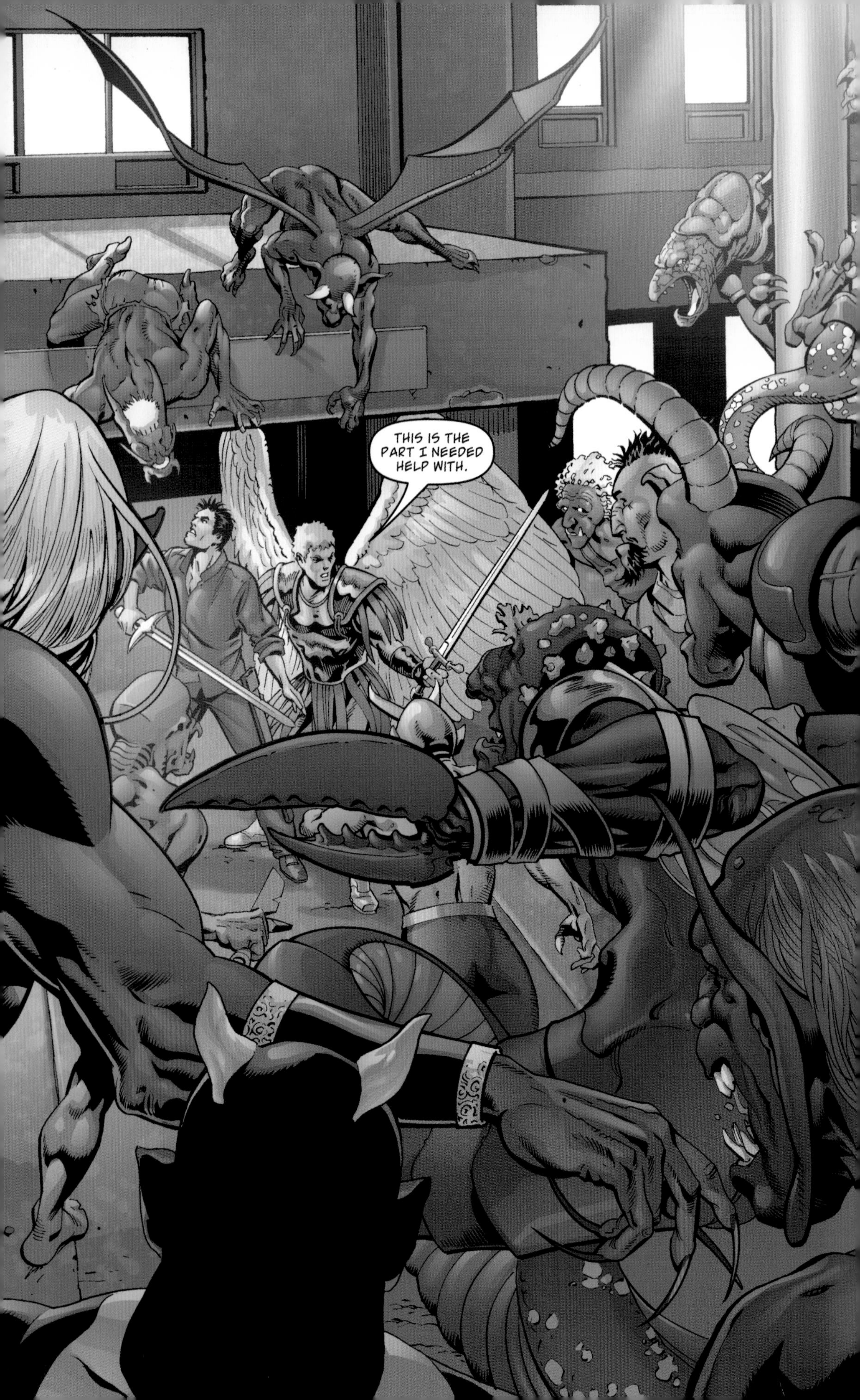
THIS IS THE PART I NEEDED HELP WITH.

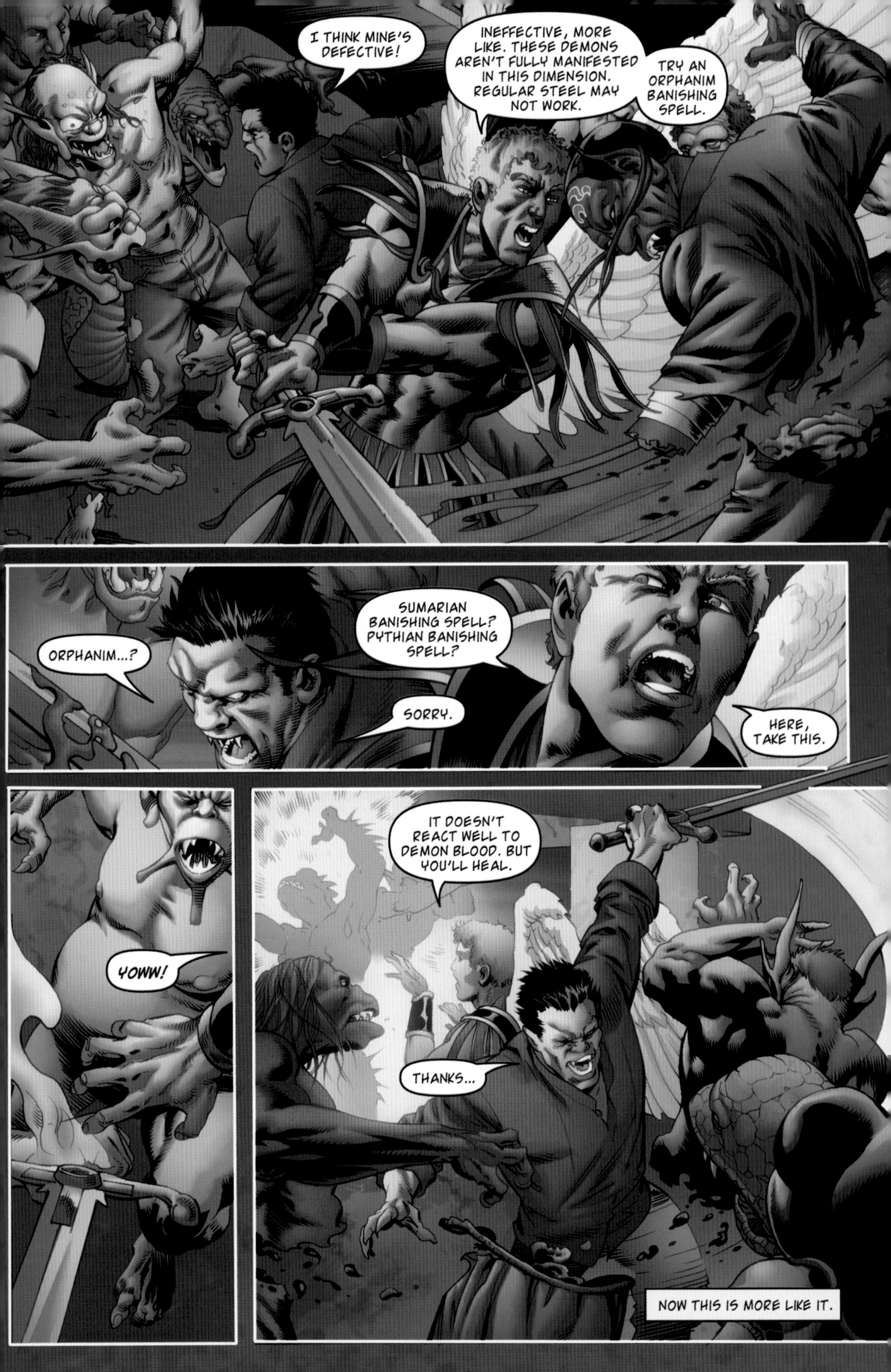
I THINK MINE'S DEFECTIVE!
INEFFECTIVE, MORE LIKE. THESE DEMONS AREN'T FULLY MANIFESTED IN THIS DIMENSION. REGULAR STEEL MAY NOT WORK.
TRY AN ORPHANIM BANISHING SPELL.
ORPHANIM...?
SUMARIAN BANISHING SPELL? PYTHIAN BANISHING SPELL?
SORRY.
HERE, TAKE THIS.
YOWW!
IT DOESN'T REACT WELL TO DEMON BLOOD. BUT YOU'LL HEAL.
THANKS...
NOW THIS IS MORE LIKE IT.

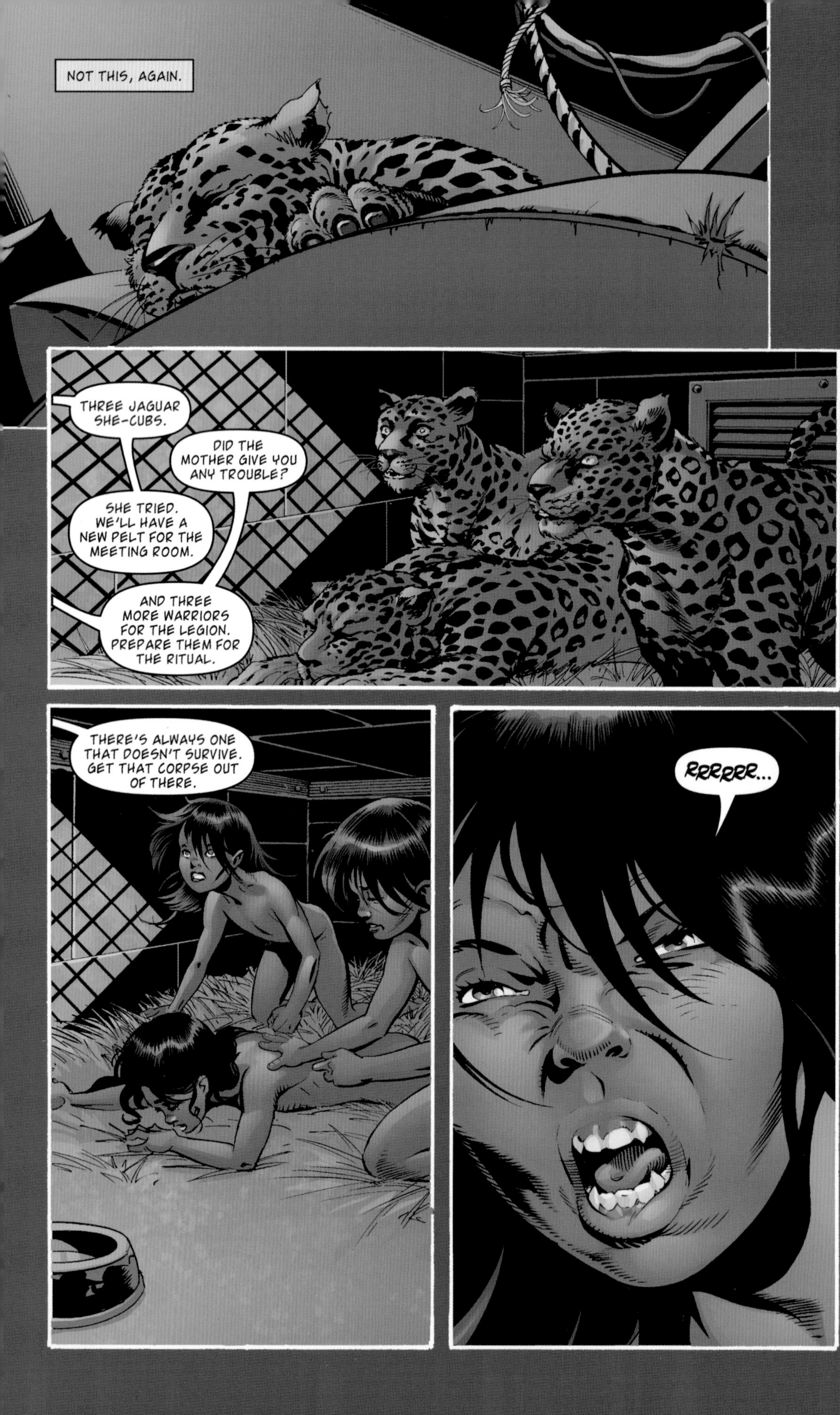
NOT THIS, AGAIN.
THREE JAGUAR SHE-CUBS.
DID THE MOTHER GIVE YOU ANY TROUBLE?
SHE TRIED. WE'LL HAVE A NEW PELT FOR THE MEETING ROOM.
AND THREE MORE WARRIORS FOR THE LEGION. PREPARE THEM FOR THE RITUAL.
THERE'S ALWAYS ONE THAT DOESN'T SURVIVE. GET THAT CORPSE OUT OF THERE.
RRRRRR...

OUR JAGUAR LEGION. THIRTY-SIX WARRIORS STRONG, AS THE PROPHESY REQUIRES. WHEN THE END OF DAYS COMES, THEY WILL BE READY TO FIGHT ALL THOSE THAT OPPOSE US.

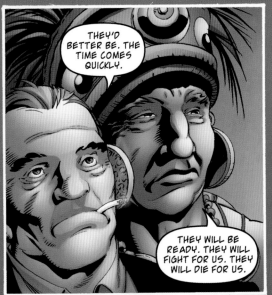

THEY'D BETTER BE. THE TIME COMES QUICKLY.

THEY WILL BE READY. THEY WILL FIGHT FOR US. THEY WILL DIE FOR US.

DIE FOR THEM? RIGHT. BECAUSE THEY'VE GIVEN US SO MUCH REASON.

THE LUXURY ACCOMMODATIONS ALONE ARE INCENTIVE ENOUGH.

SHHH, THEY'LL HEAR YOU.

AND DO WHAT? BEAT ME INTO SUBMISSION? HASN'T WORKED YET.

THEY WANT US TO BE HUMAN, BUT THEY TREAT US LIKE WE'RE STILL ANIMALS. WE OWE THEM NOTHING.

WE OWE THEM OUR HUMANITY. WITHOUT THE MONTHLY RITUALS, WE WOULD BE ANIMALS AGAIN.

SO THEY SAY.

"BUT IT'S A THEORY I'M WILLING TO TEST."

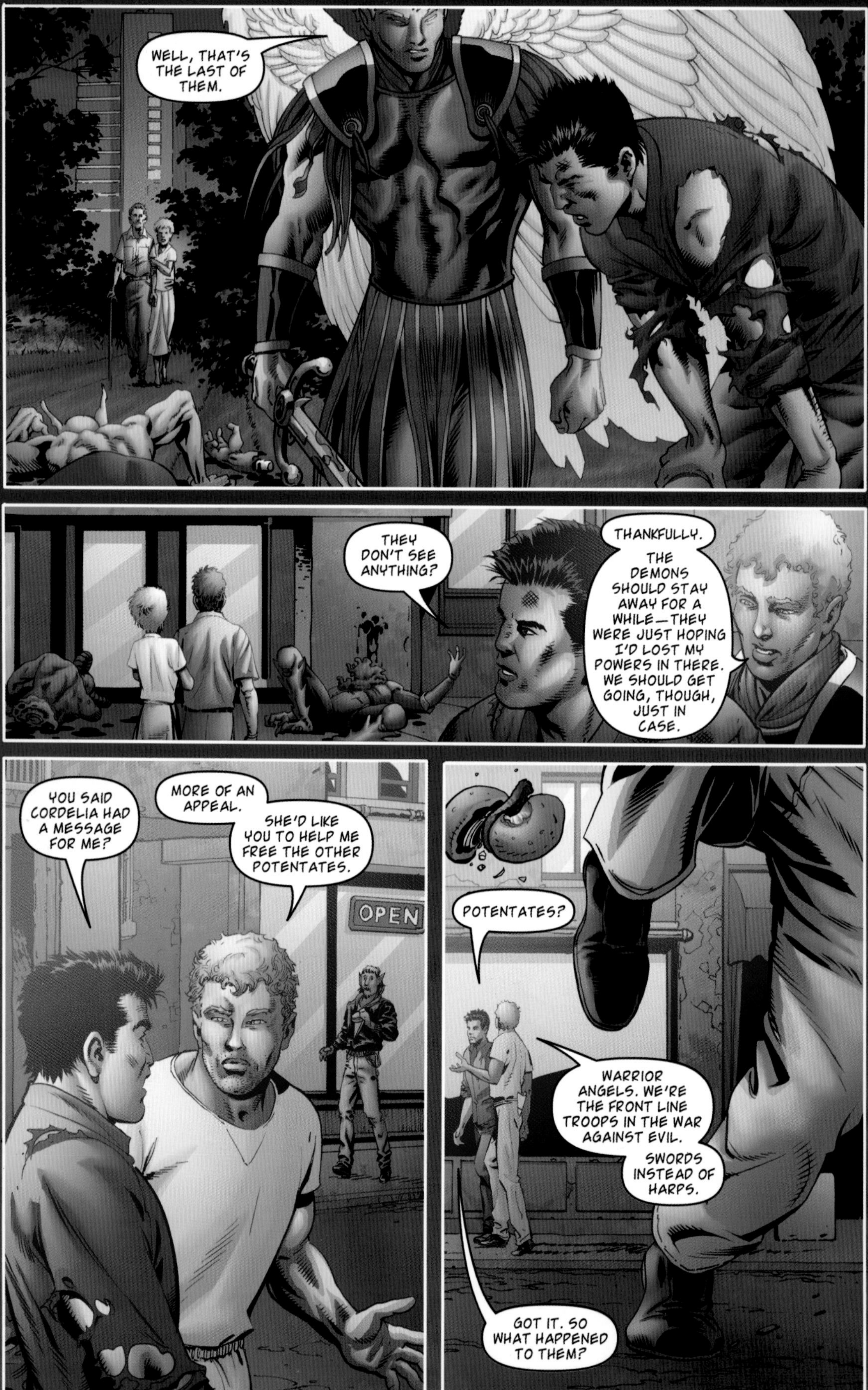
WELL, THAT'S THE LAST OF THEM.
THEY DON'T SEE ANYTHING?
THANKFULLY.
THE DEMONS SHOULD STAY AWAY FOR A WHILE—THEY WERE JUST HOPING I'D LOST MY POWERS IN THERE. WE SHOULD GET GOING, THOUGH, JUST IN CASE.
YOU SAID CORDELIA HAD A MESSAGE FOR ME?
MORE OF AN APPEAL.
SHE'D LIKE YOU TO HELP ME FREE THE OTHER POTENTATES.
OPEN
POTENTATES?
WARRIOR ANGELS. WE'RE THE FRONT LINE TROOPS IN THE WAR AGAINST EVIL.
SWORDS INSTEAD OF HARPS.
GOT IT. SO WHAT HAPPENED TO THEM?

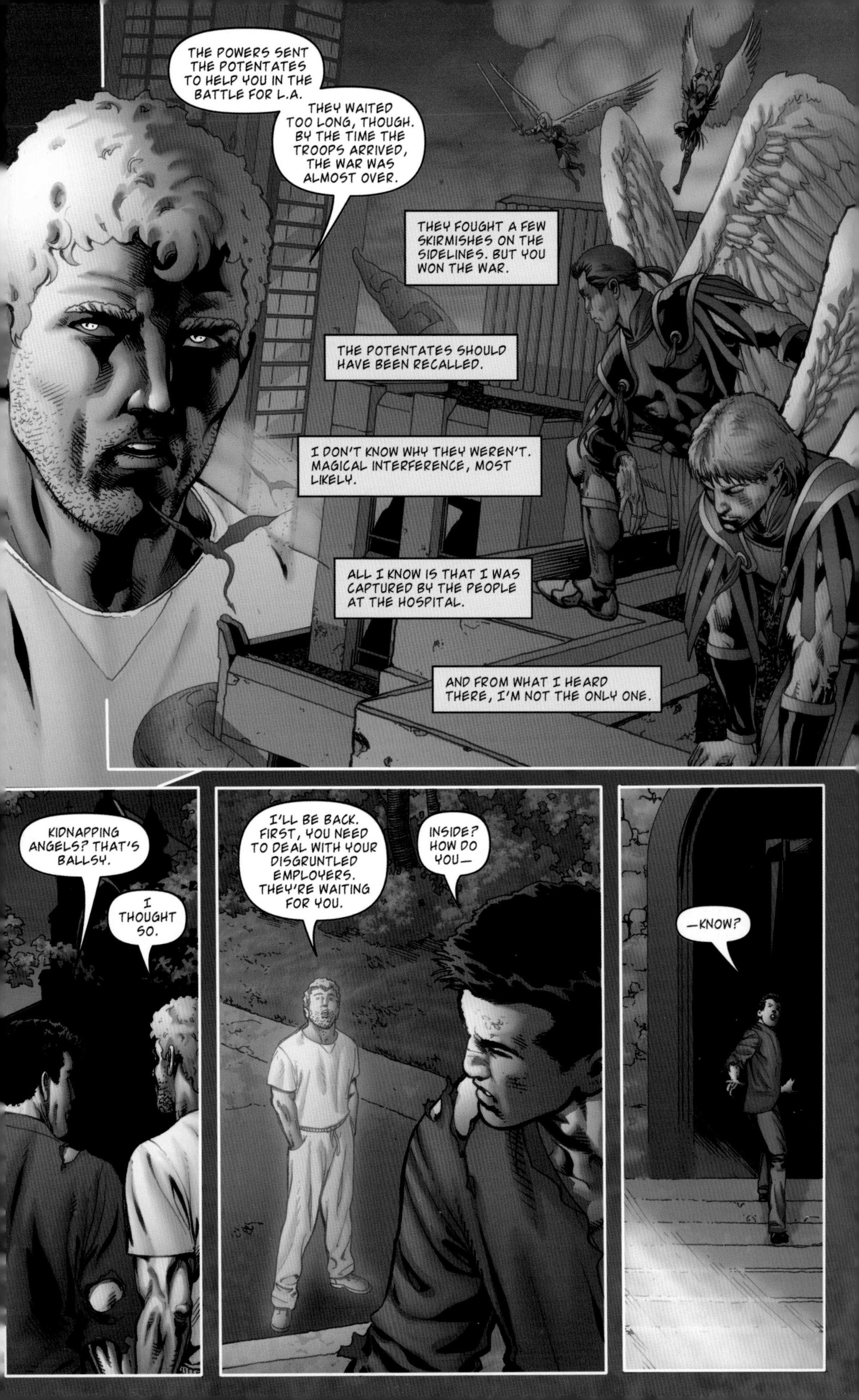
THE POWERS SENT THE POTENTATES TO HELP YOU IN THE BATTLE FOR L.A.
THEY WAITED TOO LONG, THOUGH. BY THE TIME THE TROOPS ARRIVED, THE WAR WAS ALMOST OVER.
THEY FOUGHT A FEW SKIRMISHES ON THE SIDELINES. BUT YOU WON THE WAR.
THE POTENTATES SHOULD HAVE BEEN RECALLED.
I DON'T KNOW WHY THEY WEREN'T. MAGICAL INTERFERENCE, MOST LIKELY.
ALL I KNOW IS THAT I WAS CAPTURED BY THE PEOPLE AT THE HOSPITAL.
AND FROM WHAT I HEARD THERE, I'M NOT THE ONLY ONE.
KIDNAPPING ANGELS? THAT'S BALLSY.
I THOUGHT SO.
I'LL BE BACK. FIRST, YOU NEED TO DEAL WITH YOUR DISGRUNTLED EMPLOYERS. THEY'RE WAITING FOR YOU.
INSIDE? HOW DO YOU—
—KNOW?

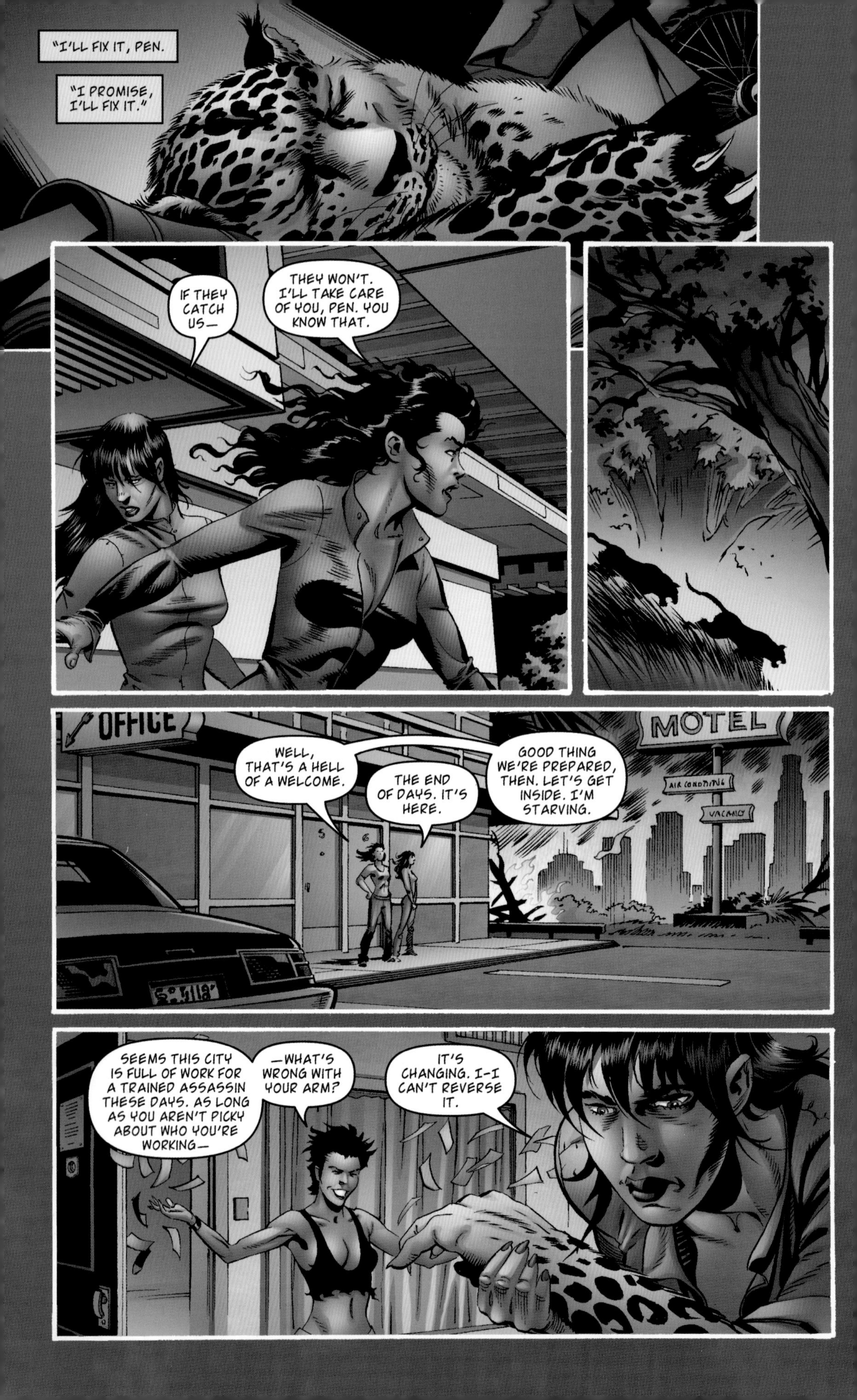
"I'LL FIX IT, PEN.
"I PROMISE, I'LL FIX IT."
IF THEY CATCH US—
THEY WON'T. I'LL TAKE CARE OF YOU, PEN. YOU KNOW THAT.
OFFICE
MOTEL
AIR CONDITIONING
VACANCY
WELL, THAT'S A HELL OF A WELCOME.
THE END OF DAYS. IT'S HERE.
GOOD THING WE'RE PREPARED, THEN. LET'S GET INSIDE. I'M STARVING.
SEEMS THIS CITY IS FULL OF WORK FOR A TRAINED ASSASSIN THESE DAYS. AS LONG AS YOU AREN'T PICKY ABOUT WHO YOU'RE WORKING—
—WHAT'S WRONG WITH YOUR ARM?
IT'S CHANGING. I-I CAN'T REVERSE IT.

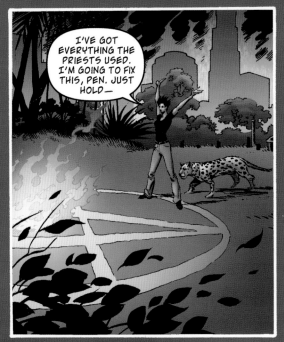

I'VE GOT EVERYTHING THE PRIESTS USED. I'M GOING TO FIX THIS, PEN. JUST HOLD—

WHA-WHAT HAPPENED?

PEN?

PENELOPE!

STILL NOT AWAKE? THE BEST CHANCE I HAVE OF PROVING MYSELF TO CONNOR IS TO GET ANSWERS FROM YOU. PROVE MY WORTH. MY LOYALTY.

AND I'M GOING TO GET THEM. ONE WAY OR ANOTHER.

THOSE SUITS ARE HERE. IN YOUR OFFICE.

GOT IT.

DO YOU WANT US TO—

GOT IT.

AH, IT SEEMS WE WERE CORRECT.

OUR NEW EMPLOYEE WISHES TO TERMINATE HIS CONTRACT.

IF THAT'S SOME FORGED CONTRACT, I NEVER SIGNED ANYTHING—

WE KNOW. WE MEANT **CONTRACT** FIGURATIVELY.

THIS IS A CHECK FOR SERVICES RENDERED.

WE'RE A GOVERNMENT AGENCY. WE PAY OUR EMPLOYEES PROMPTLY AND FULLY.

UNIONS. PERSONALLY, I'D RATHER DEAL WITH FALANJOID DEMONS.

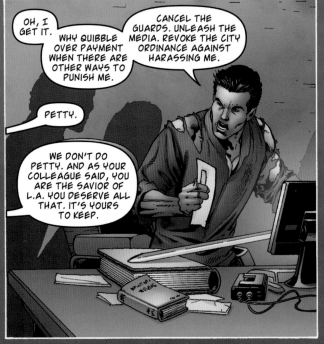

OH, I GET IT.

WHY QUIBBLE OVER PAYMENT WHEN THERE ARE OTHER WAYS TO PUNISH ME.

CANCEL THE GUARDS. UNLEASH THE MEDIA. REVOKE THE CITY ORDINANCE AGAINST HARASSING ME.

PETTY.

WE DON'T DO PETTY. AND AS YOUR COLLEAGUE SAID, YOU ARE THE SAVIOR OF L.A. YOU DESERVE ALL THAT. IT'S YOURS TO KEEP.

IT WAS A PLEASURE WORKING WITH YOU, ANGEL. IF ONLY BRIEFLY.

WE WISH YOU ALL THE BEST IN YOUR NEW ENDEAVOR.

NEW ENDEAVOR?

WORKING WITH JAMAERAH.

JAMES. HE CALLS HIMSELF JAMES HERE.

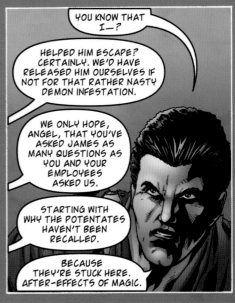

YOU KNOW THAT I—?

HELPED HIM ESCAPE? CERTAINLY. WE'D HAVE RELEASED HIM OURSELVES IF NOT FOR THAT RATHER NASTY DEMON INFESTATION.

WE ONLY HOPE, ANGEL, THAT YOU'VE ASKED JAMES AS MANY QUESTIONS AS YOU AND YOUR EMPLOYEES ASKED US.

STARTING WITH WHY THE POTENTATES HAVEN'T BEEN RECALLED.

BECAUSE THEY'RE STUCK HERE. AFTER-EFFECTS OF MAGIC.

THE POWERS THAT BE CAN'T GET THEIR ANGELS HOME? HARDLY. THEY'RE ON A MISSION.

THEY'RE ALWAYS ON A MISSION. JAMES MAY NOT KNOW IT, THOUGH, GIVEN THE CIRCUMSTANCES.

WHAT CIRCUMSTANCES?

ASK HIM. HE'S AN HONEST IMMORTAL.

WHEN YOU'RE READY TO SPEAK TO US, JUST CALL.

AS ARE WE. BUT WE DON'T EXPECT YOU TO BELIEVE THAT. NOT YET.

YOU HAVE THE NUMBER.

WE'LL BE WAITING.

chapter four

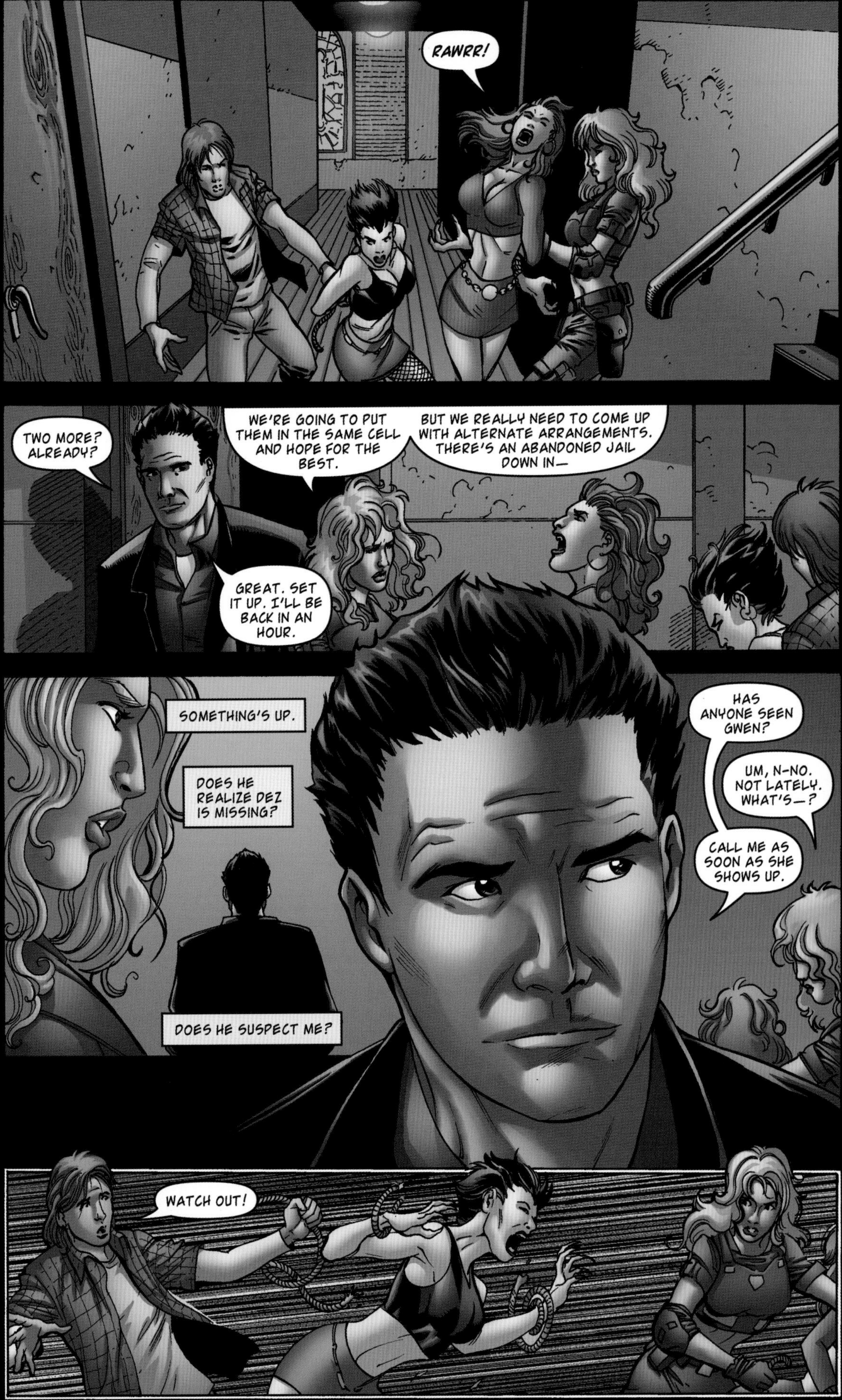
RAWRR!
TWO MORE? ALREADY?
WE'RE GOING TO PUT THEM IN THE SAME CELL AND HOPE FOR THE BEST.
BUT WE REALLY NEED TO COME UP WITH ALTERNATE ARRANGEMENTS. THERE'S AN ABANDONED JAIL DOWN IN—
GREAT. SET IT UP. I'LL BE BACK IN AN HOUR.
SOMETHING'S UP.
DOES HE REALIZE DEZ IS MISSING?
DOES HE SUSPECT ME?
HAS ANYONE SEEN GWEN?
UM, N-NO. NOT LATELY. WHAT'S—?
CALL ME AS SOON AS SHE SHOWS UP.
WATCH OUT!

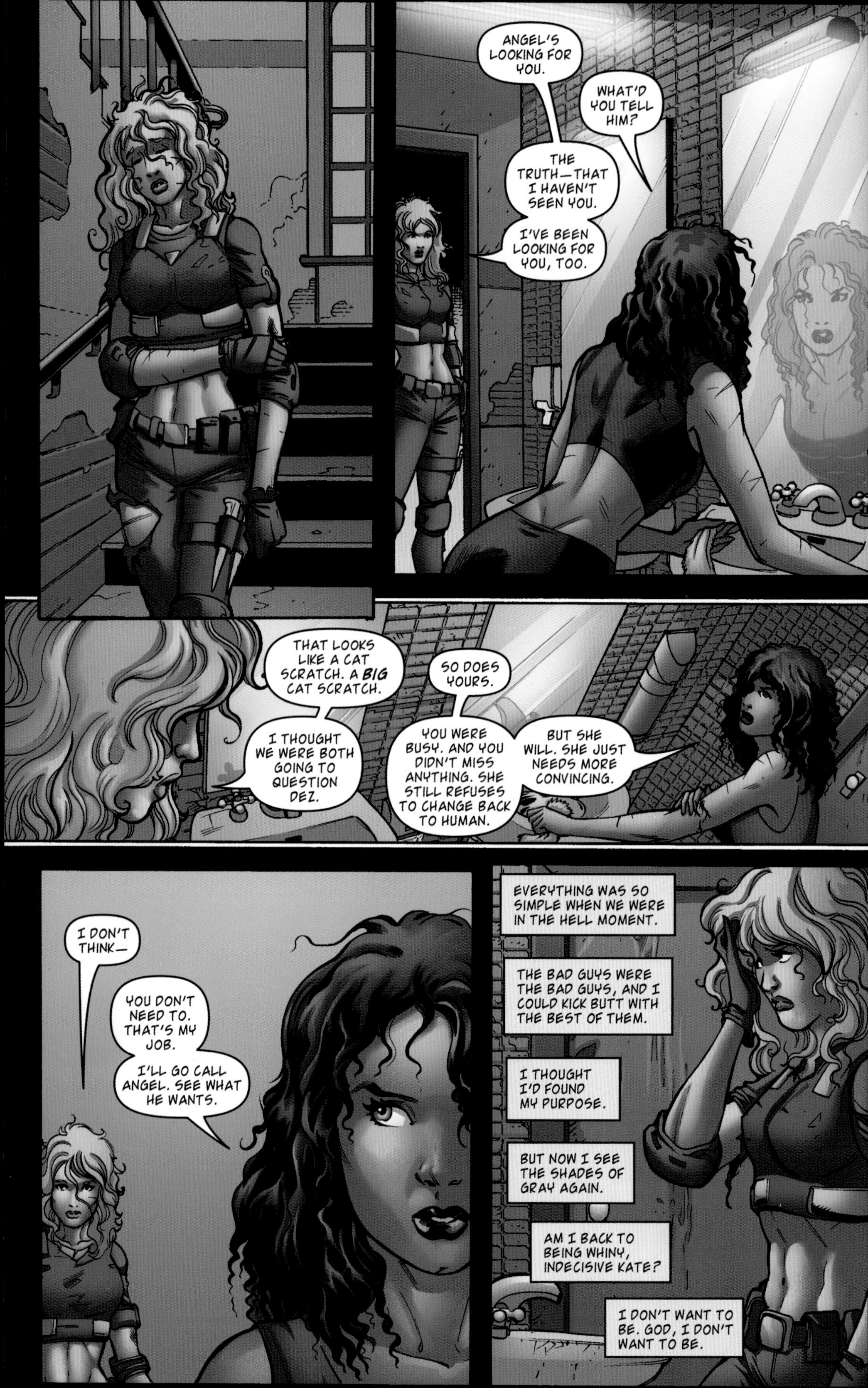
ANGEL'S LOOKING FOR YOU.
WHAT'D YOU TELL HIM?
THE TRUTH—THAT I HAVEN'T SEEN YOU.
I'VE BEEN LOOKING FOR YOU, TOO.
THAT LOOKS LIKE A CAT SCRATCH. A BIG CAT SCRATCH.
SO DOES YOURS.
I THOUGHT WE WERE BOTH GOING TO QUESTION DEZ.
YOU WERE BUSY. AND YOU DIDN'T MISS ANYTHING. SHE STILL REFUSES TO CHANGE BACK TO HUMAN.
BUT SHE WILL. SHE JUST NEEDS MORE CONVINCING.
I DON'T THINK—
YOU DON'T NEED TO. THAT'S MY JOB.
I'LL GO CALL ANGEL. SEE WHAT HE WANTS.
EVERYTHING WAS SO SIMPLE WHEN WE WERE IN THE HELL MOMENT.
THE BAD GUYS WERE THE BAD GUYS, AND I COULD KICK BUTT WITH THE BEST OF THEM.
I THOUGHT I'D FOUND MY PURPOSE.
BUT NOW I SEE THE SHADES OF GRAY AGAIN.
AM I BACK TO BEING WHINY, INDECISIVE KATE?
I DON'T WANT TO BE. GOD, I DON'T WANT TO BE.

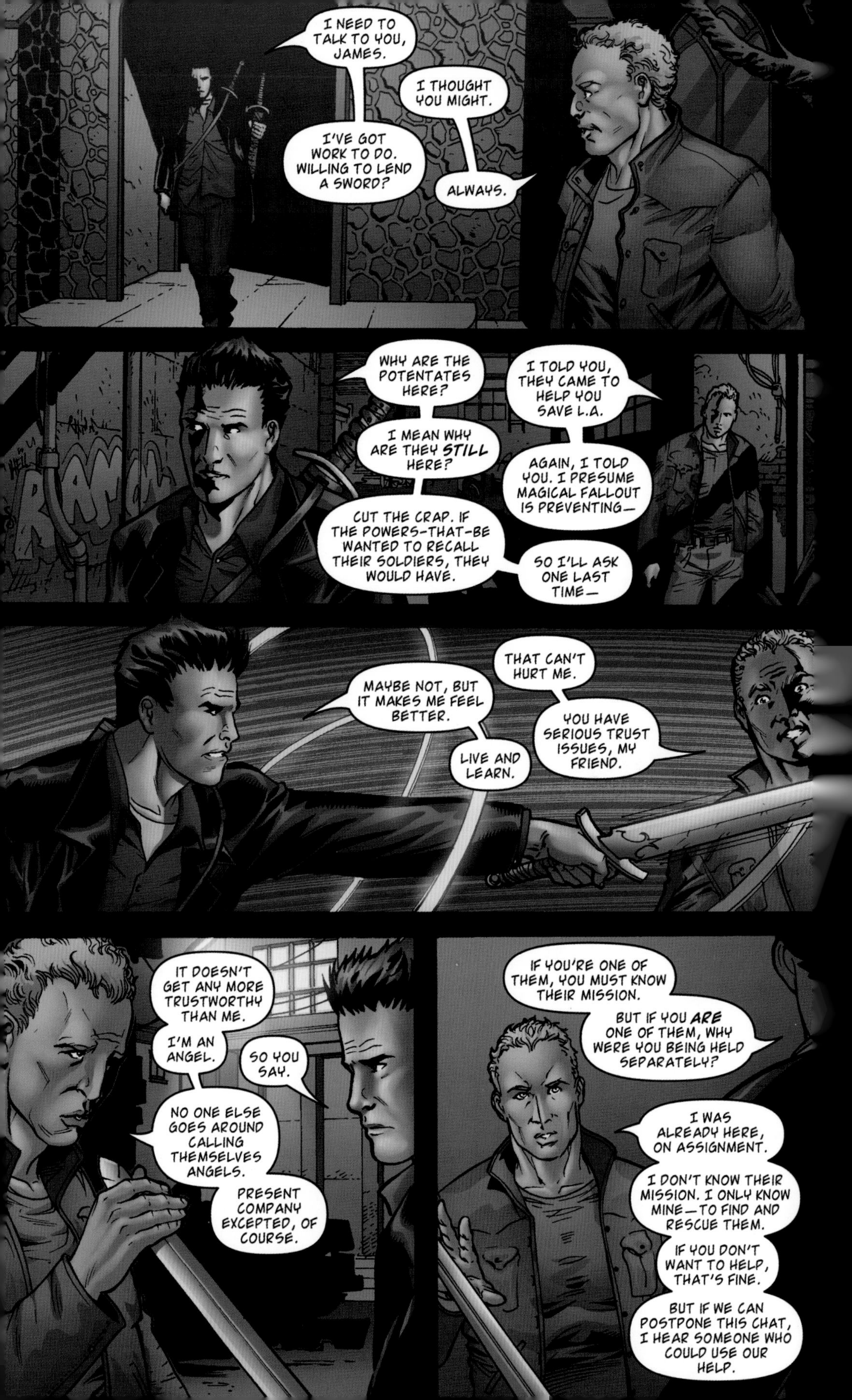

I NEED TO TALK TO YOU, JAMES.
I THOUGHT YOU MIGHT.
I'VE GOT WORK TO DO. WILLING TO LEND A SWORD?
ALWAYS.
WHY ARE THE POTENTATES HERE?
I MEAN WHY ARE THEY *STILL* HERE?
I TOLD YOU, THEY CAME TO HELP YOU SAVE L.A.
AGAIN, I TOLD YOU. I PRESUME MAGICAL FALLOUT IS PREVENTING—
CUT THE CRAP. IF THE POWERS-THAT-BE WANTED TO RECALL THEIR SOLDIERS, THEY WOULD HAVE.
SO I'LL ASK ONE LAST TIME—
THAT CAN'T HURT ME.
MAYBE NOT, BUT IT MAKES ME FEEL BETTER.
YOU HAVE SERIOUS TRUST ISSUES, MY FRIEND.
LIVE AND LEARN.
IT DOESN'T GET ANY MORE TRUSTWORTHY THAN ME.
I'M AN ANGEL.
SO YOU SAY.
NO ONE ELSE GOES AROUND CALLING THEMSELVES ANGELS.
PRESENT COMPANY EXCEPTED, OF COURSE.
IF YOU'RE ONE OF THEM, YOU MUST KNOW THEIR MISSION.
BUT IF YOU *ARE* ONE OF THEM, WHY WERE YOU BEING HELD SEPARATELY?
I WAS ALREADY HERE, ON ASSIGNMENT.
I DON'T KNOW THEIR MISSION. I ONLY KNOW MINE—TO FIND AND RESCUE THEM.
IF YOU DON'T WANT TO HELP, THAT'S FINE.
BUT IF WE CAN POSTPONE THIS CHAT, I HEAR SOMEONE WHO COULD USE OUR HELP.

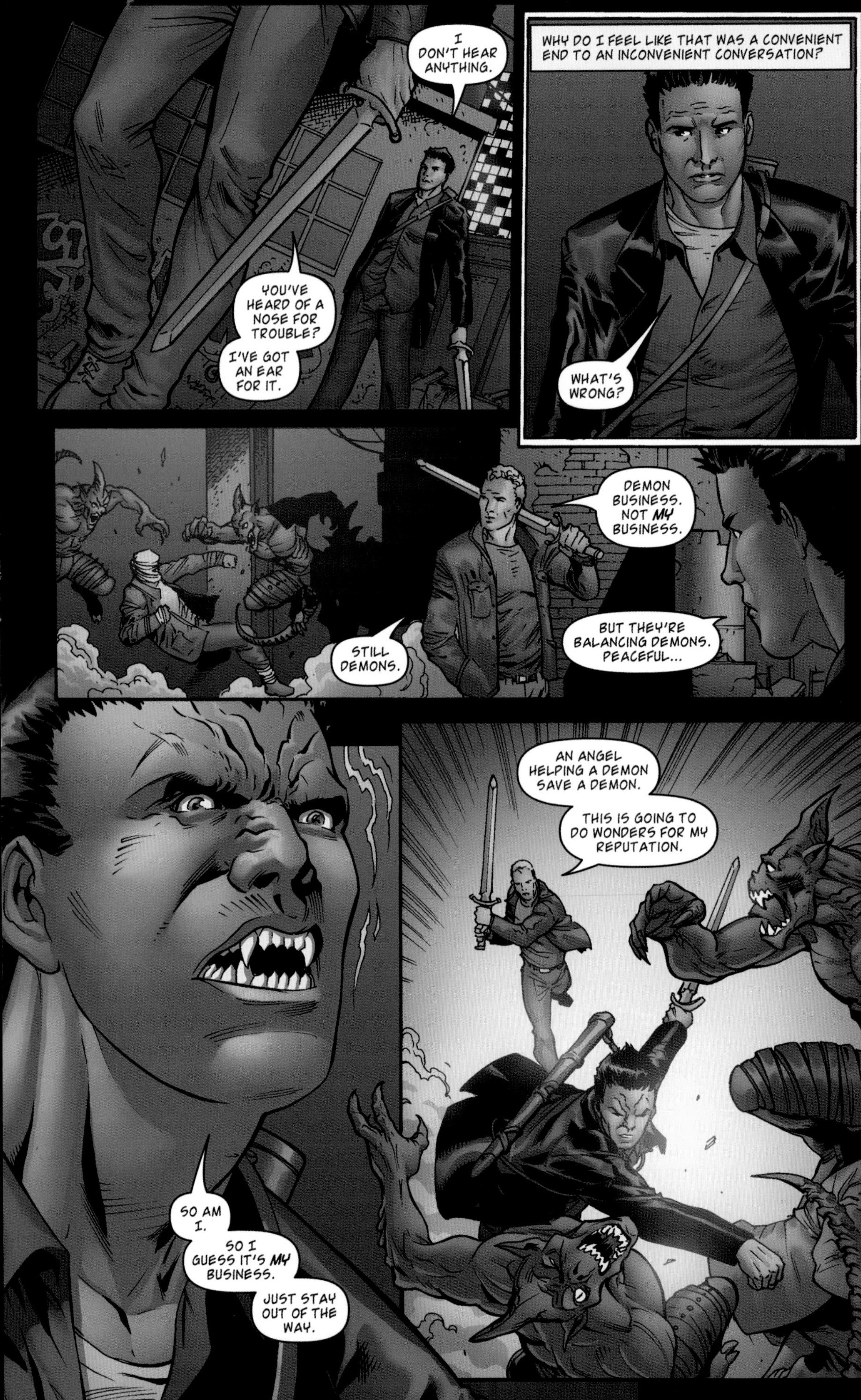
I DON'T HEAR ANYTHING.
YOU'VE HEARD OF A NOSE FOR TROUBLE?
I'VE GOT AN EAR FOR IT.
WHY DO I FEEL LIKE THAT WAS A CONVENIENT END TO AN INCONVENIENT CONVERSATION?
WHAT'S WRONG?
DEMON BUSINESS. NOT MY BUSINESS.
BUT THEY'RE BALANCING DEMONS. PEACEFUL...
STILL DEMONS.
SO AM I.
SO I GUESS IT'S MY BUSINESS.
JUST STAY OUT OF THE WAY.
AN ANGEL HELPING A DEMON SAVE A DEMON.
THIS IS GOING TO DO WONDERS FOR MY REPUTATION.

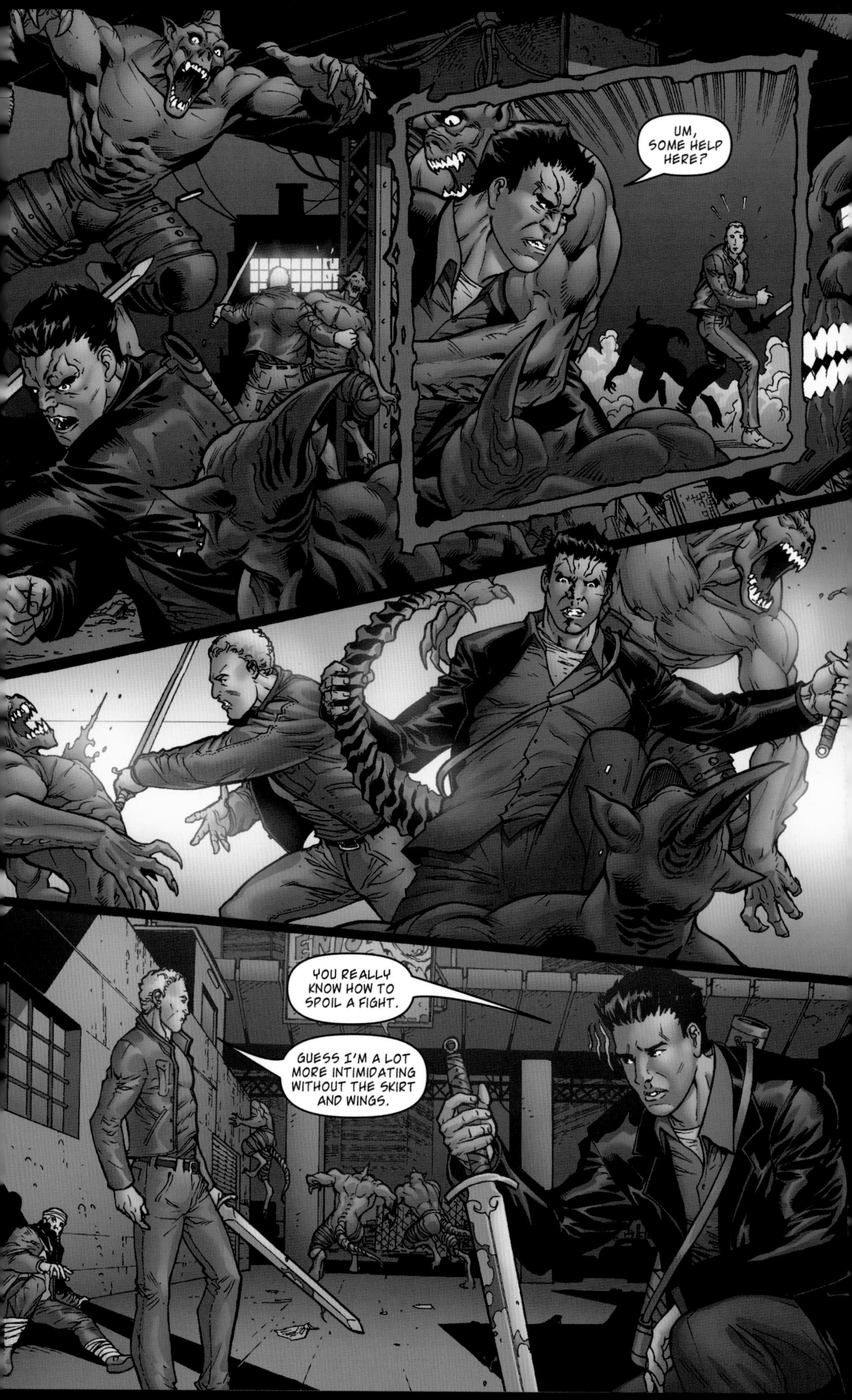
UM, SOME HELP HERE?
YOU REALLY KNOW HOW TO SPOIL A FIGHT.
GUESS I'M A LOT MORE INTIMIDATING WITHOUT THE SKIRT AND WINGS.

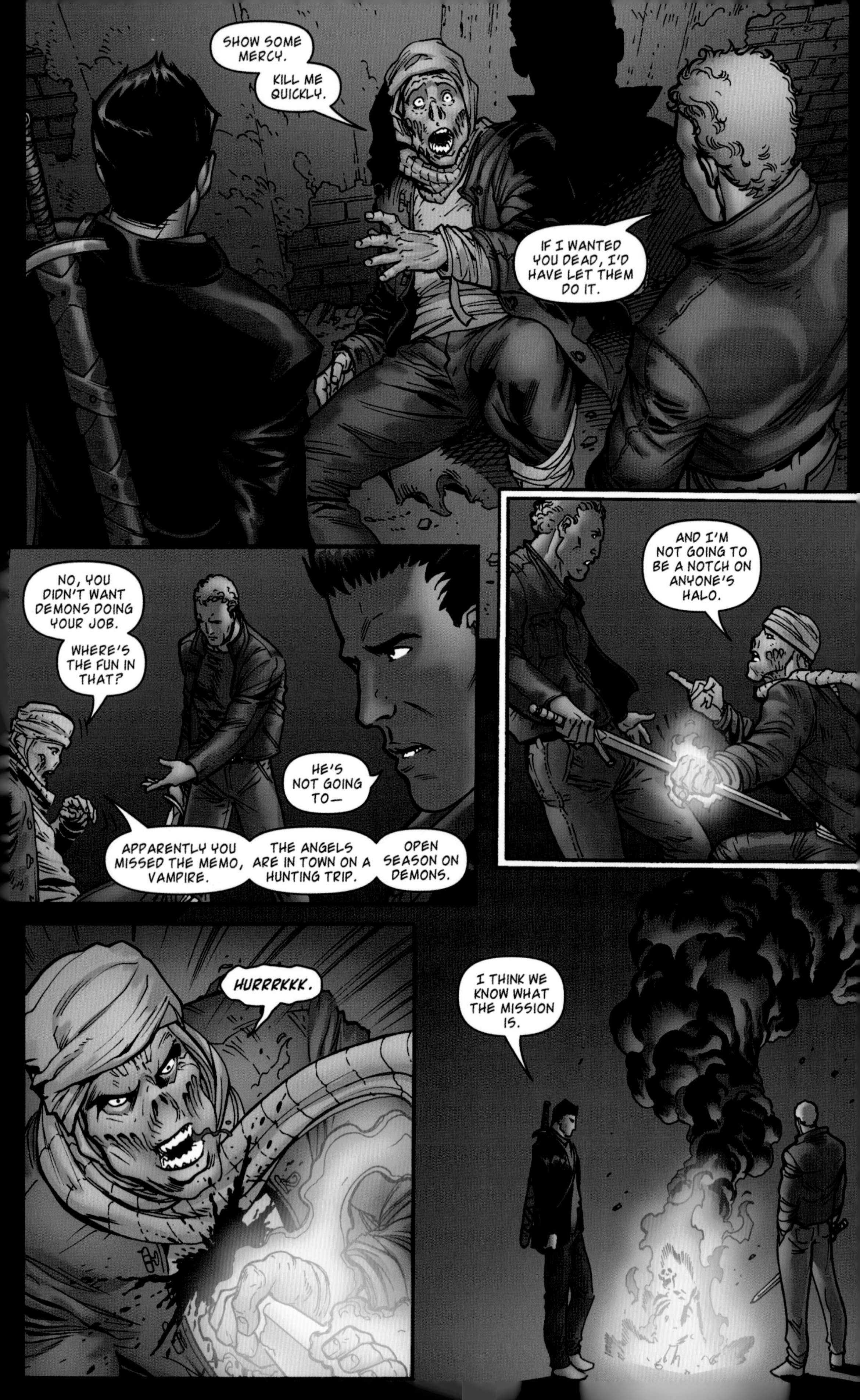
SHOW SOME MERCY.
KILL ME QUICKLY.
IF I WANTED YOU DEAD, I'D HAVE LET THEM DO IT.
NO, YOU DIDN'T WANT DEMONS DOING YOUR JOB.
WHERE'S THE FUN IN THAT?
HE'S NOT GOING TO—
APPARENTLY YOU MISSED THE MEMO, VAMPIRE.
THE ANGELS ARE IN TOWN ON A HUNTING TRIP.
OPEN SEASON ON DEMONS.
AND I'M NOT GOING TO BE A NOTCH ON ANYONE'S HALO.
HURRRKKK.
I THINK WE KNOW WHAT THE MISSION IS.

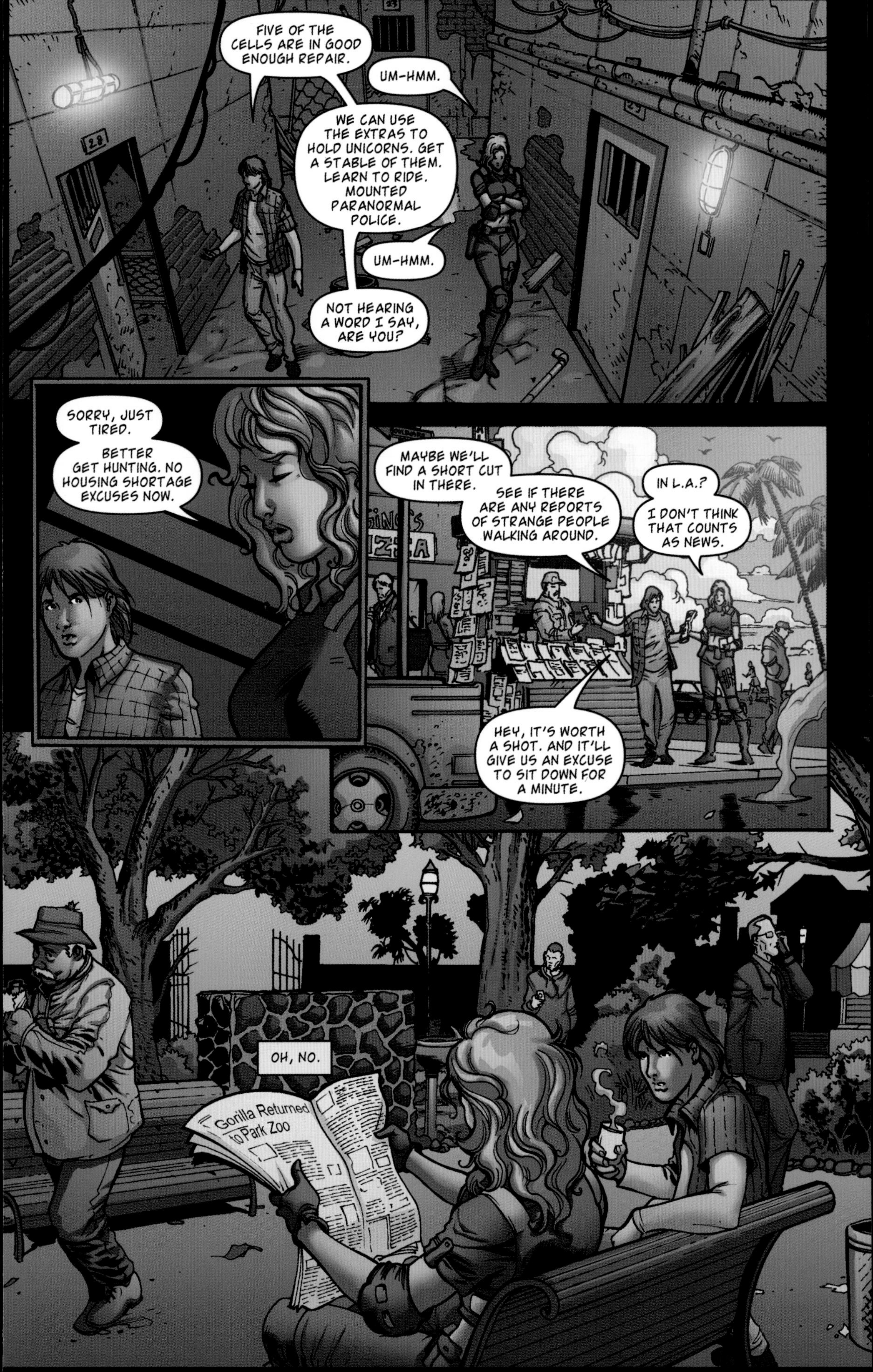
FIVE OF THE CELLS ARE IN GOOD ENOUGH REPAIR.
UM-HMM.
WE CAN USE THE EXTRAS TO HOLD UNICORNS. GET A STABLE OF THEM. LEARN TO RIDE. MOUNTED PARANORMAL POLICE.
UM-HMM.
NOT HEARING A WORD I SAY, ARE YOU?
SORRY, JUST TIRED.
BETTER GET HUNTING. NO HOUSING SHORTAGE EXCUSES NOW.
MAYBE WE'LL FIND A SHORT CUT IN THERE.
SEE IF THERE ARE ANY REPORTS OF STRANGE PEOPLE WALKING AROUND.
IN L.A.?
I DON'T THINK THAT COUNTS AS NEWS.
HEY, IT'S WORTH A SHOT. AND IT'LL GIVE US AN EXCUSE TO SIT DOWN FOR A MINUTE.
OH, NO.
Gorilla Returned to Park Zoo

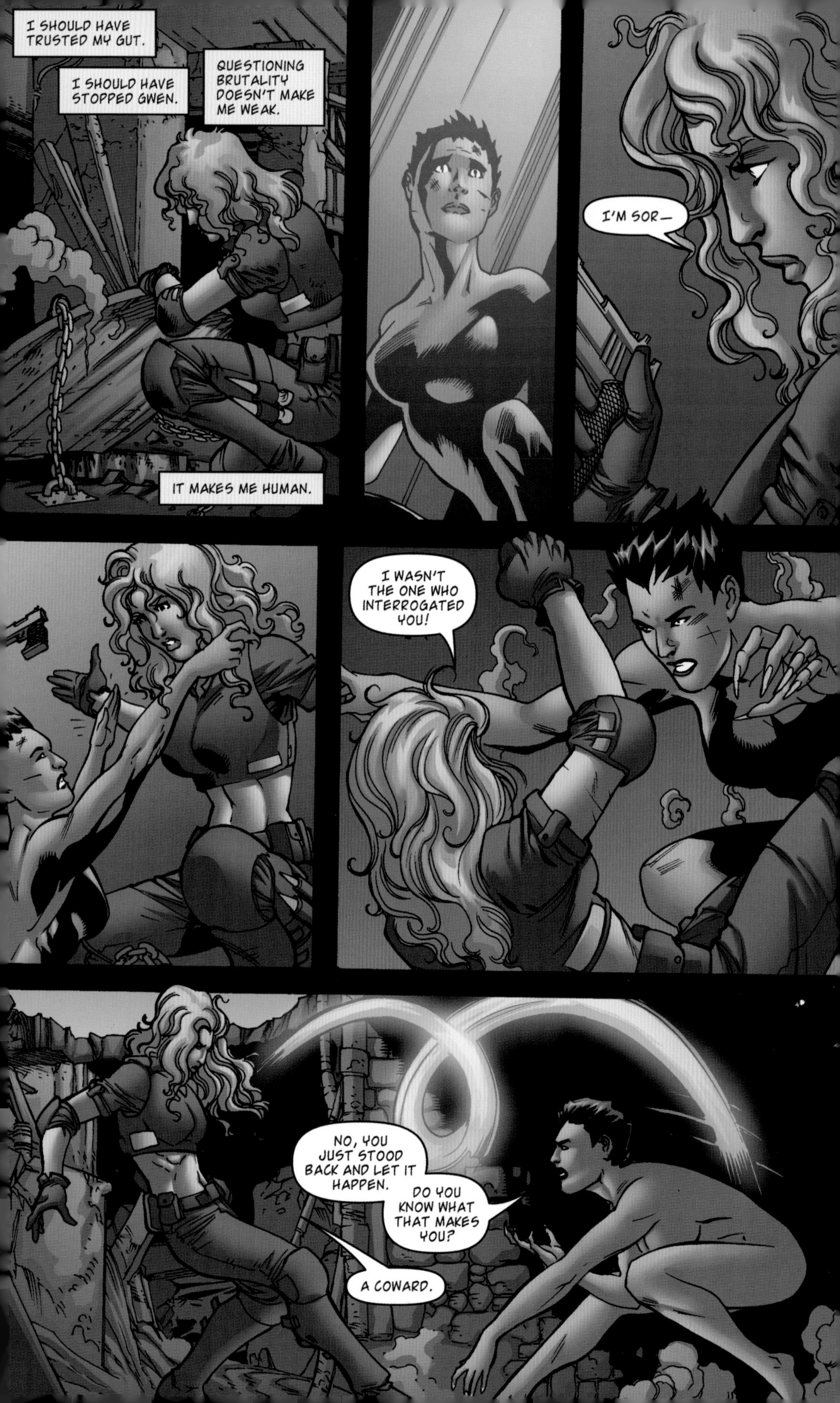
I SHOULD HAVE TRUSTED MY GUT.
I SHOULD HAVE STOPPED GWEN.
QUESTIONING BRUTALITY DOESN'T MAKE ME WEAK.
IT MAKES ME HUMAN.
I'M SOR—
I WASN'T THE ONE WHO INTERROGATED YOU!
NO, YOU JUST STOOD BACK AND LET IT HAPPEN.
DO YOU KNOW WHAT THAT MAKES YOU?
A COWARD.

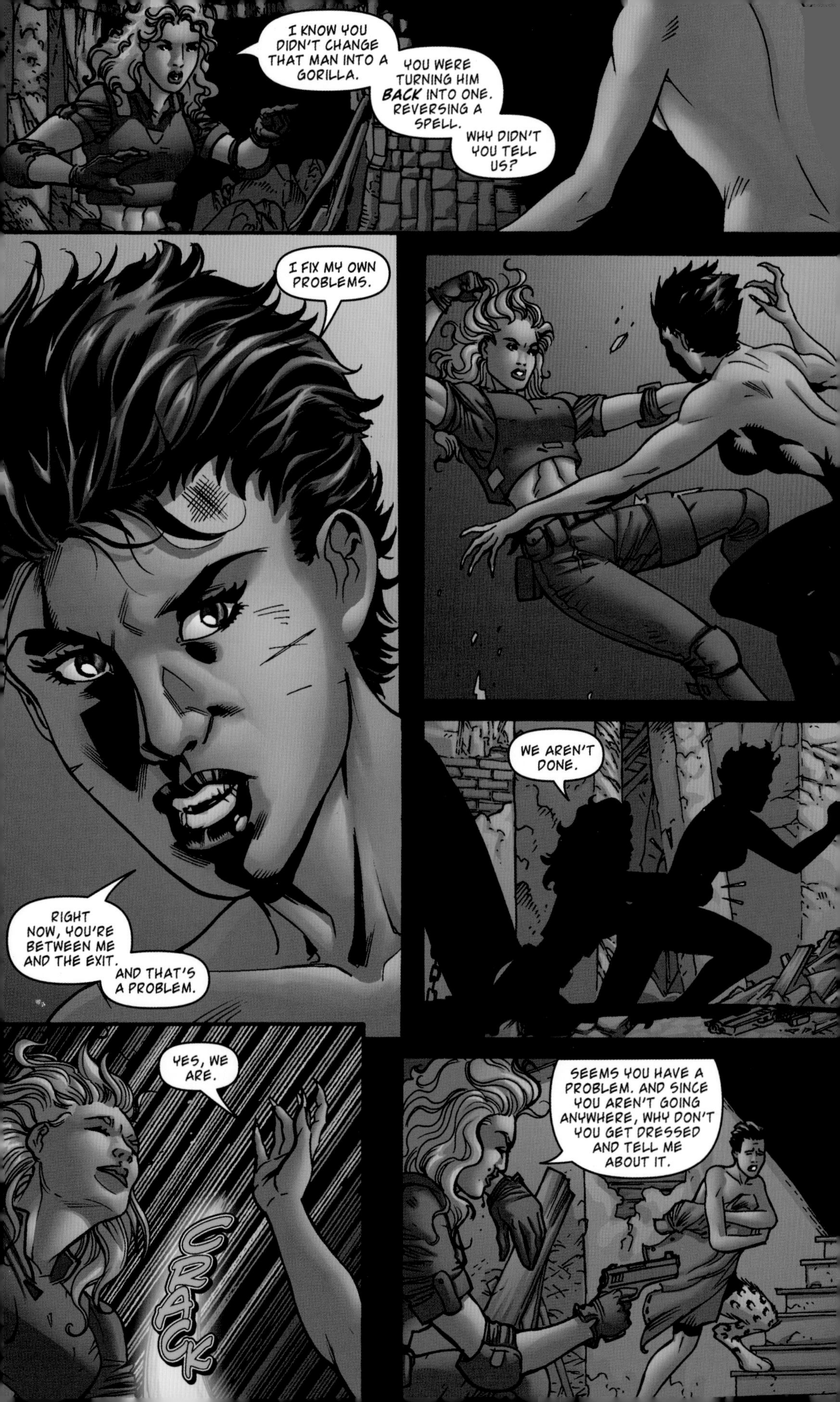
I KNOW YOU DIDN'T CHANGE THAT MAN INTO A GORILLA.
YOU WERE TURNING HIM BACK INTO ONE. REVERSING A SPELL.
WHY DIDN'T YOU TELL US?
I FIX MY OWN PROBLEMS.
RIGHT NOW, YOU'RE BETWEEN ME AND THE EXIT.
AND THAT'S A PROBLEM.
WE AREN'T DONE.
YES, WE ARE.
CRACK
SEEMS YOU HAVE A PROBLEM. AND SINCE YOU AREN'T GOING ANYWHERE, WHY DON'T YOU GET DRESSED AND TELL ME ABOUT IT.

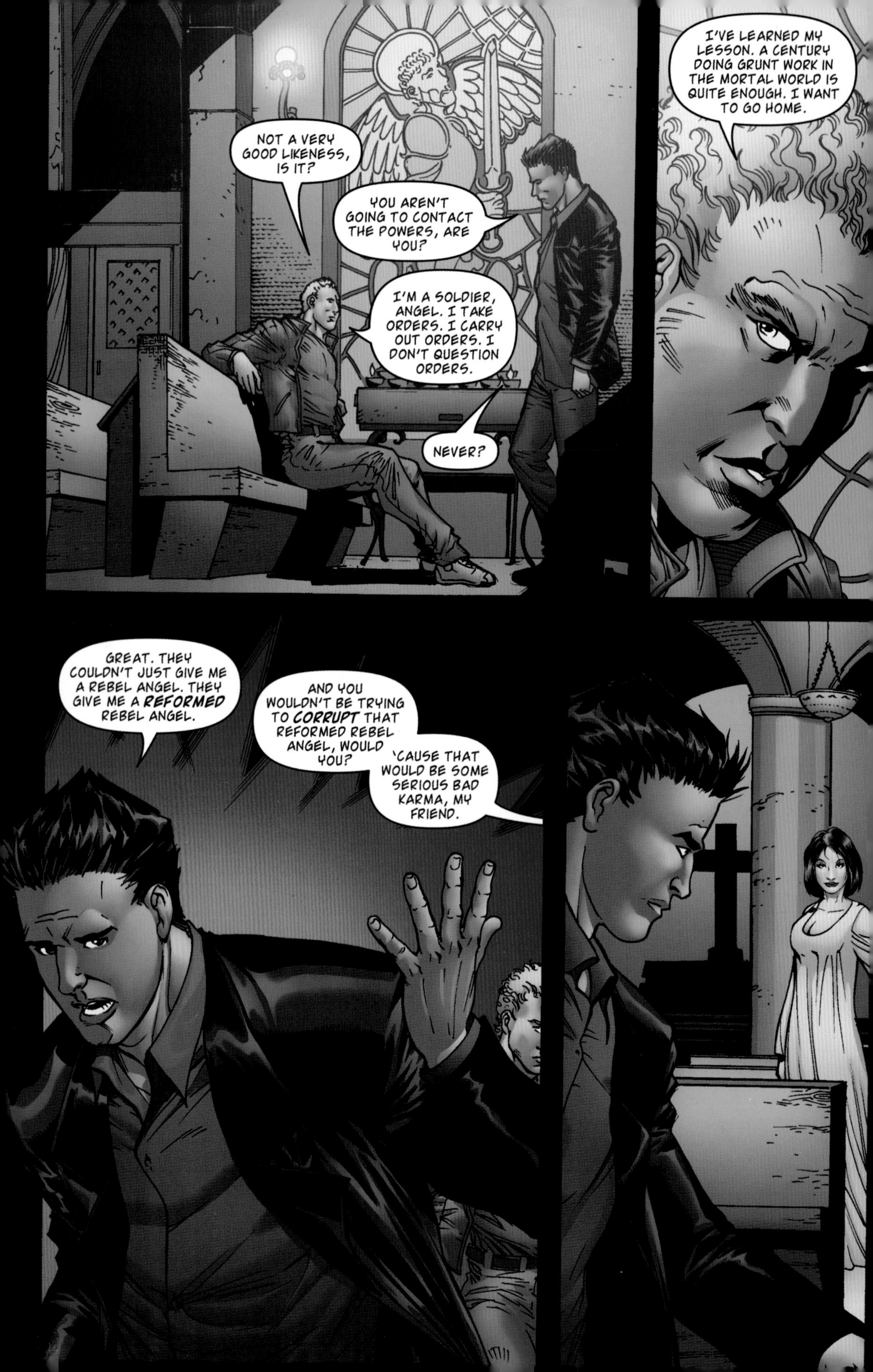
NOT A VERY GOOD LIKENESS, IS IT?
YOU AREN'T GOING TO CONTACT THE POWERS, ARE YOU?
I'M A SOLDIER, ANGEL. I TAKE ORDERS. I CARRY OUT ORDERS. I DON'T QUESTION ORDERS.
NEVER?
I'VE LEARNED MY LESSON. A CENTURY DOING GRUNT WORK IN THE MORTAL WORLD IS QUITE ENOUGH. I WANT TO GO HOME.
GREAT. THEY COULDN'T JUST GIVE ME A REBEL ANGEL. THEY GIVE ME A REFORMED REBEL ANGEL.
AND YOU WOULDN'T BE TRYING TO CORRUPT THAT REFORMED REBEL ANGEL, WOULD YOU?
'CAUSE THAT WOULD BE SOME SERIOUS BAD KARMA, MY FRIEND.

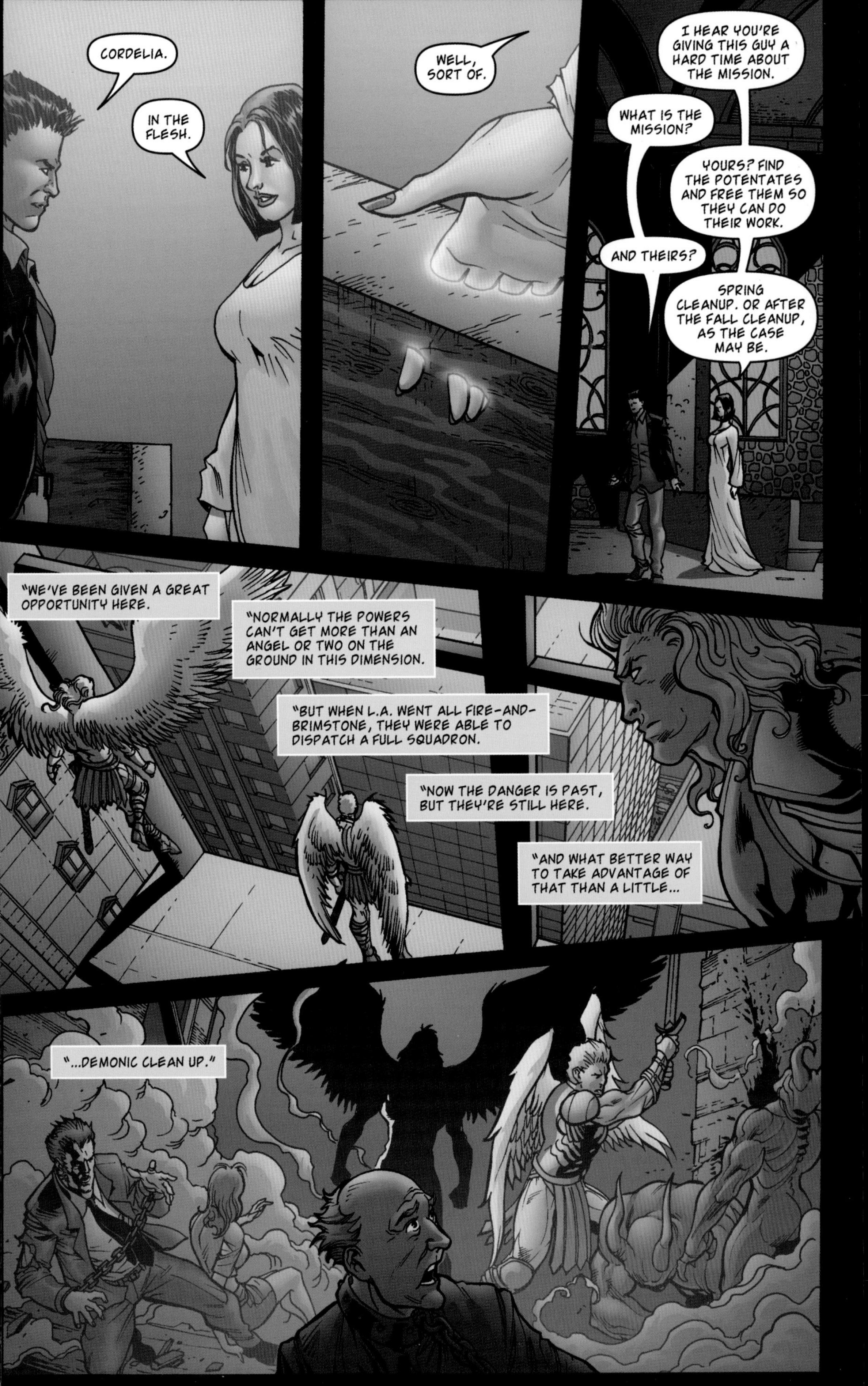
CORDELIA.
IN THE FLESH.
WELL, SORT OF.
I HEAR YOU'RE GIVING THIS GUY A HARD TIME ABOUT THE MISSION.
WHAT IS THE MISSION?
YOURS? FIND THE POTENTATES AND FREE THEM SO THEY CAN DO THEIR WORK.
AND THEIRS?
SPRING CLEANUP. OR AFTER THE FALL CLEANUP, AS THE CASE MAY BE.
"WE'VE BEEN GIVEN A GREAT OPPORTUNITY HERE.
"NORMALLY THE POWERS CAN'T GET MORE THAN AN ANGEL OR TWO ON THE GROUND IN THIS DIMENSION.
"BUT WHEN L.A. WENT ALL FIRE-AND-BRIMSTONE, THEY WERE ABLE TO DISPATCH A FULL SQUADRON.
"NOW THE DANGER IS PAST, BUT THEY'RE STILL HERE.
"AND WHAT BETTER WAY TO TAKE ADVANTAGE OF THAT THAN A LITTLE...
"...DEMONIC CLEAN UP."

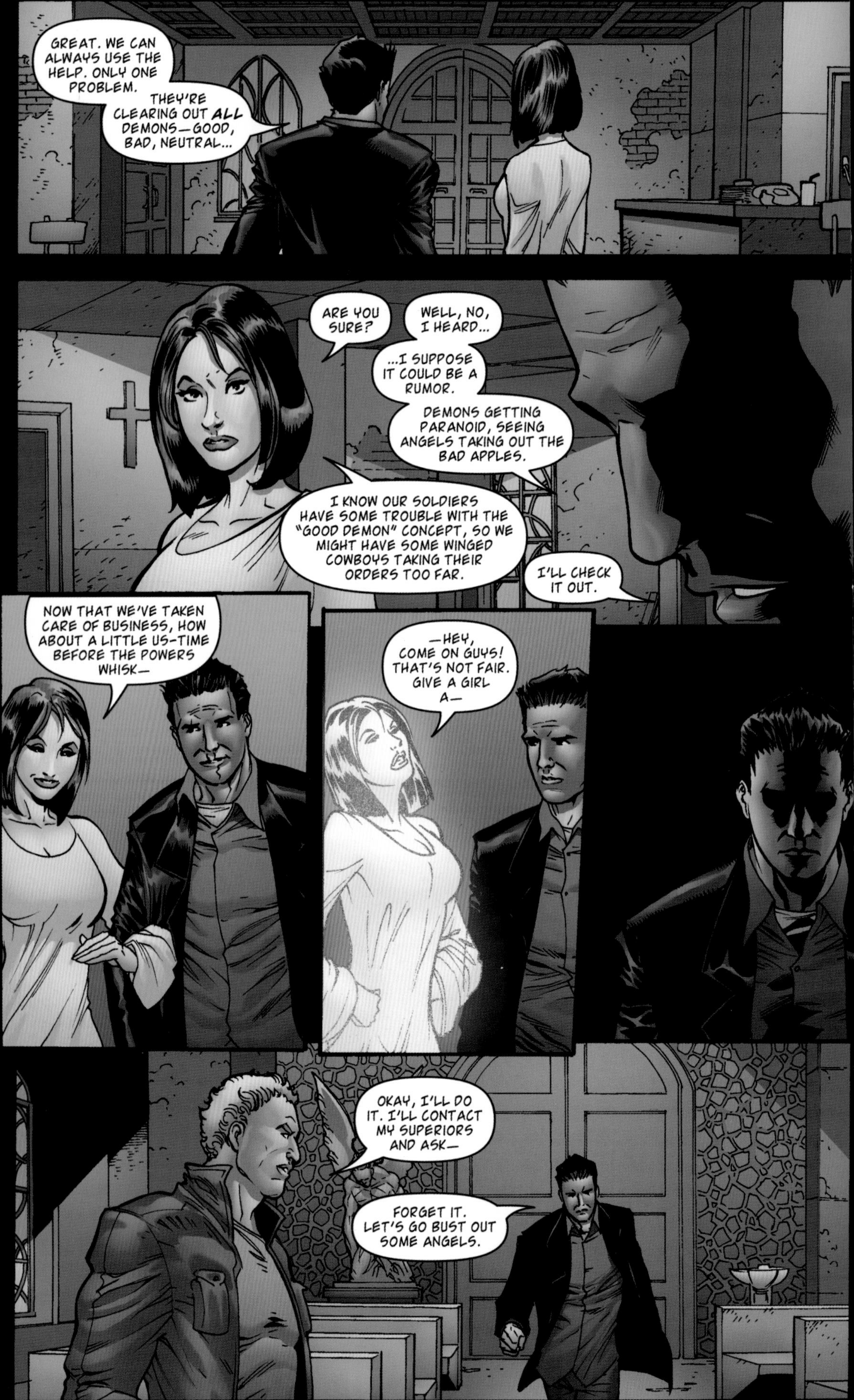
GREAT. WE CAN ALWAYS USE THE HELP. ONLY ONE PROBLEM.
THEY'RE CLEARING OUT ALL DEMONS—GOOD, BAD, NEUTRAL...
ARE YOU SURE?
WELL, NO, I HEARD...
...I SUPPOSE IT COULD BE A RUMOR.
DEMONS GETTING PARANOID, SEEING ANGELS TAKING OUT THE BAD APPLES.
I KNOW OUR SOLDIERS HAVE SOME TROUBLE WITH THE "GOOD DEMON" CONCEPT, SO WE MIGHT HAVE SOME WINGED COWBOYS TAKING THEIR ORDERS TOO FAR.
I'LL CHECK IT OUT.
NOW THAT WE'VE TAKEN CARE OF BUSINESS, HOW ABOUT A LITTLE US-TIME BEFORE THE POWERS WHISK—
—HEY, COME ON GUYS! THAT'S NOT FAIR. GIVE A GIRL A—
OKAY, I'LL DO IT. I'LL CONTACT MY SUPERIORS AND ASK—
FORGET IT. LET'S GO BUST OUT SOME ANGELS.

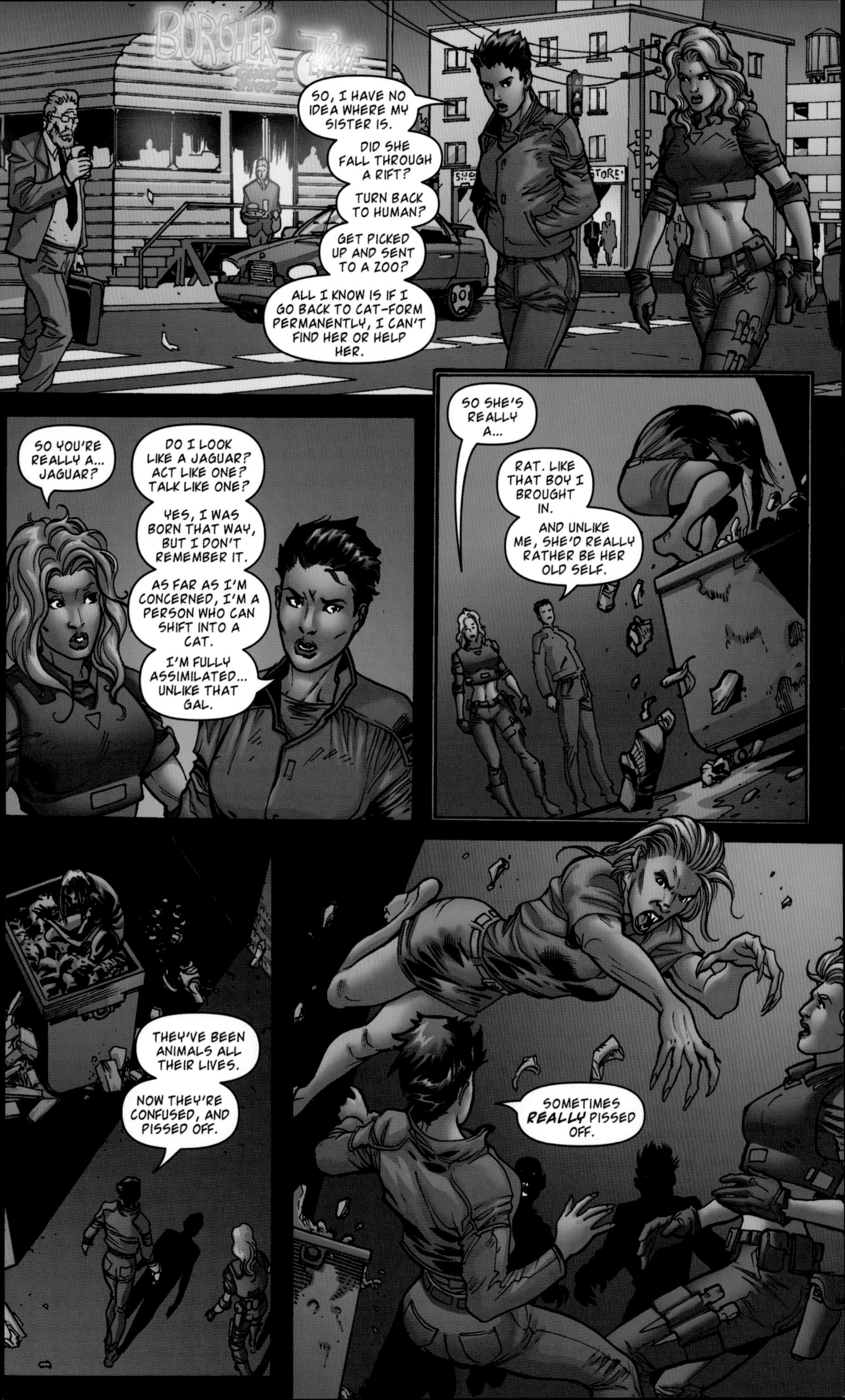
BURGHER Quick Stop
SO, I HAVE NO IDEA WHERE MY SISTER IS.
DID SHE FALL THROUGH A RIFT?
TURN BACK TO HUMAN?
GET PICKED UP AND SENT TO A ZOO?
ALL I KNOW IS IF I GO BACK TO CAT-FORM PERMANENTLY, I CAN'T FIND HER OR HELP HER.
SO YOU'RE REALLY A... JAGUAR?
DO I LOOK LIKE A JAGUAR? ACT LIKE ONE? TALK LIKE ONE?
YES, I WAS BORN THAT WAY, BUT I DON'T REMEMBER IT.
AS FAR AS I'M CONCERNED, I'M A PERSON WHO CAN SHIFT INTO A CAT.
I'M FULLY ASSIMILATED... UNLIKE THAT GAL.
SO SHE'S REALLY A...
RAT. LIKE THAT BOY I BROUGHT IN.
AND UNLIKE ME, SHE'D REALLY RATHER BE HER OLD SELF.
THEY'VE BEEN ANIMALS ALL THEIR LIVES.
NOW THEY'RE CONFUSED, AND PISSED OFF.
SOMETIMES ***REALLY*** PISSED OFF.

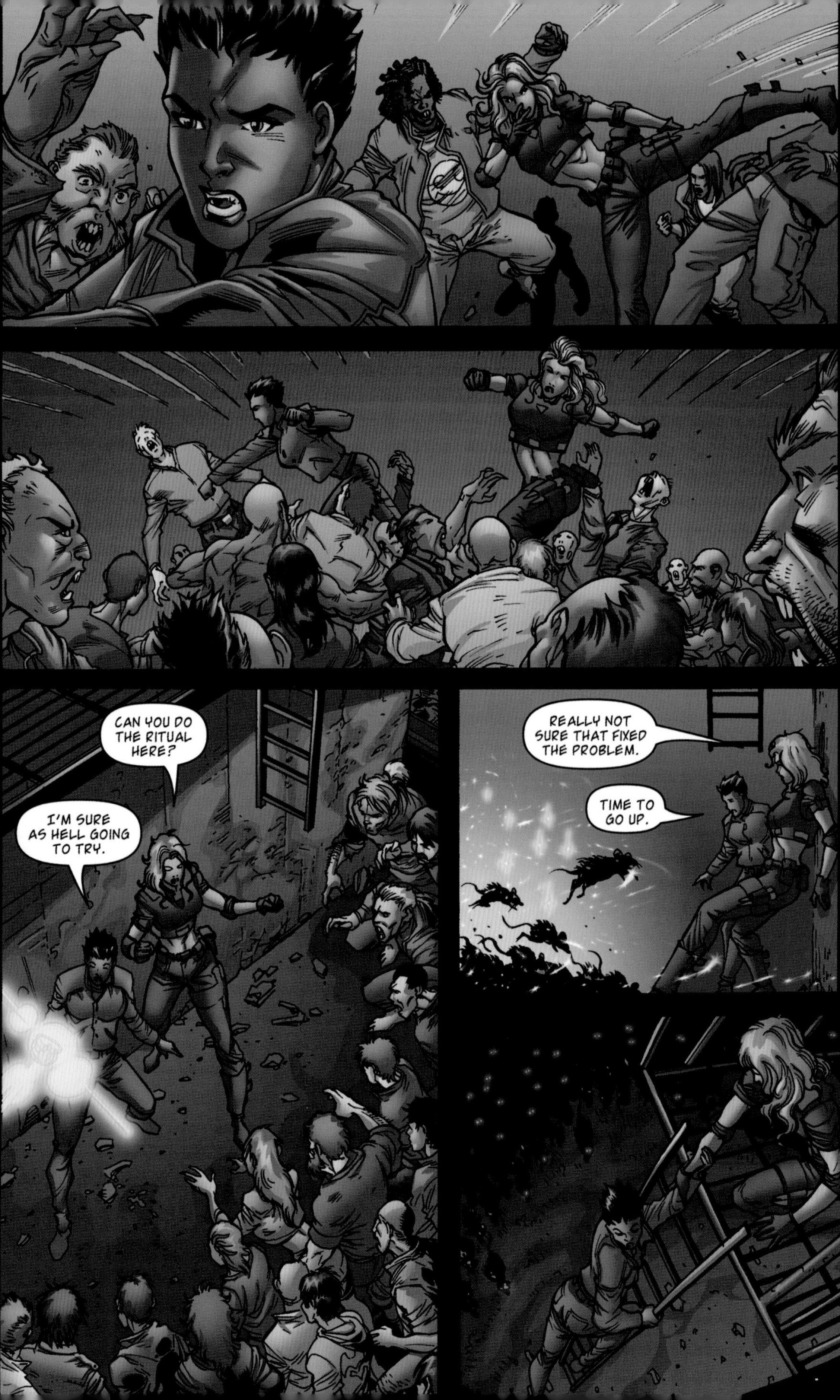
CAN YOU DO THE RITUAL HERE?
I'M SURE AS HELL GOING TO TRY.
REALLY NOT SURE THAT FIXED THE PROBLEM.
TIME TO GO UP.

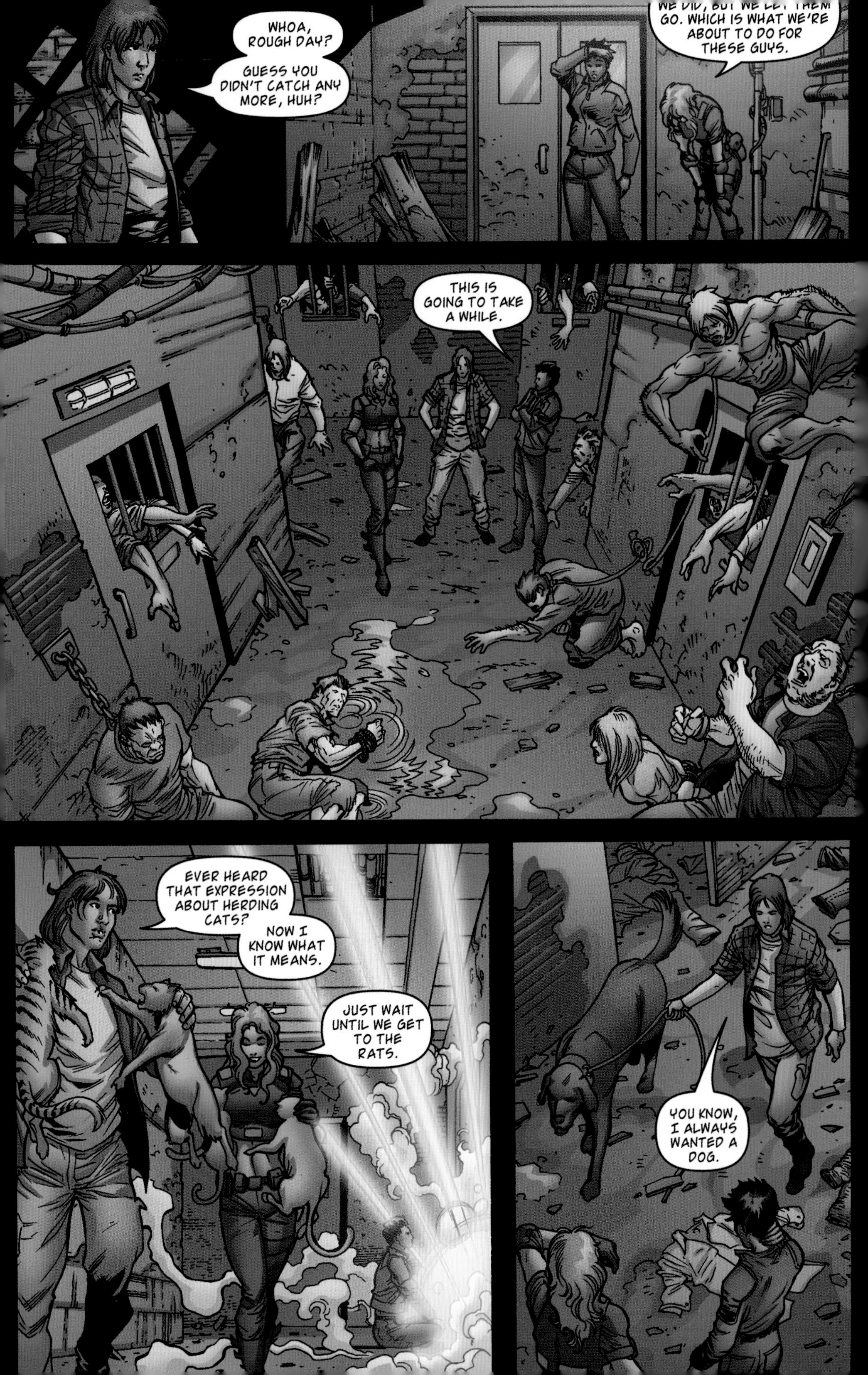

WHOA, ROUGH DAY?
GUESS YOU DIDN'T CATCH ANY MORE, HUH?
WE DID, BUT WE LET THEM GO. WHICH IS WHAT WE'RE ABOUT TO DO FOR THESE GUYS.
THIS IS GOING TO TAKE A WHILE.
EVER HEARD THAT EXPRESSION ABOUT HERDING CATS?
NOW I KNOW WHAT IT MEANS.
JUST WAIT UNTIL WE GET TO THE RATS.
YOU KNOW, I ALWAYS WANTED A DOG.

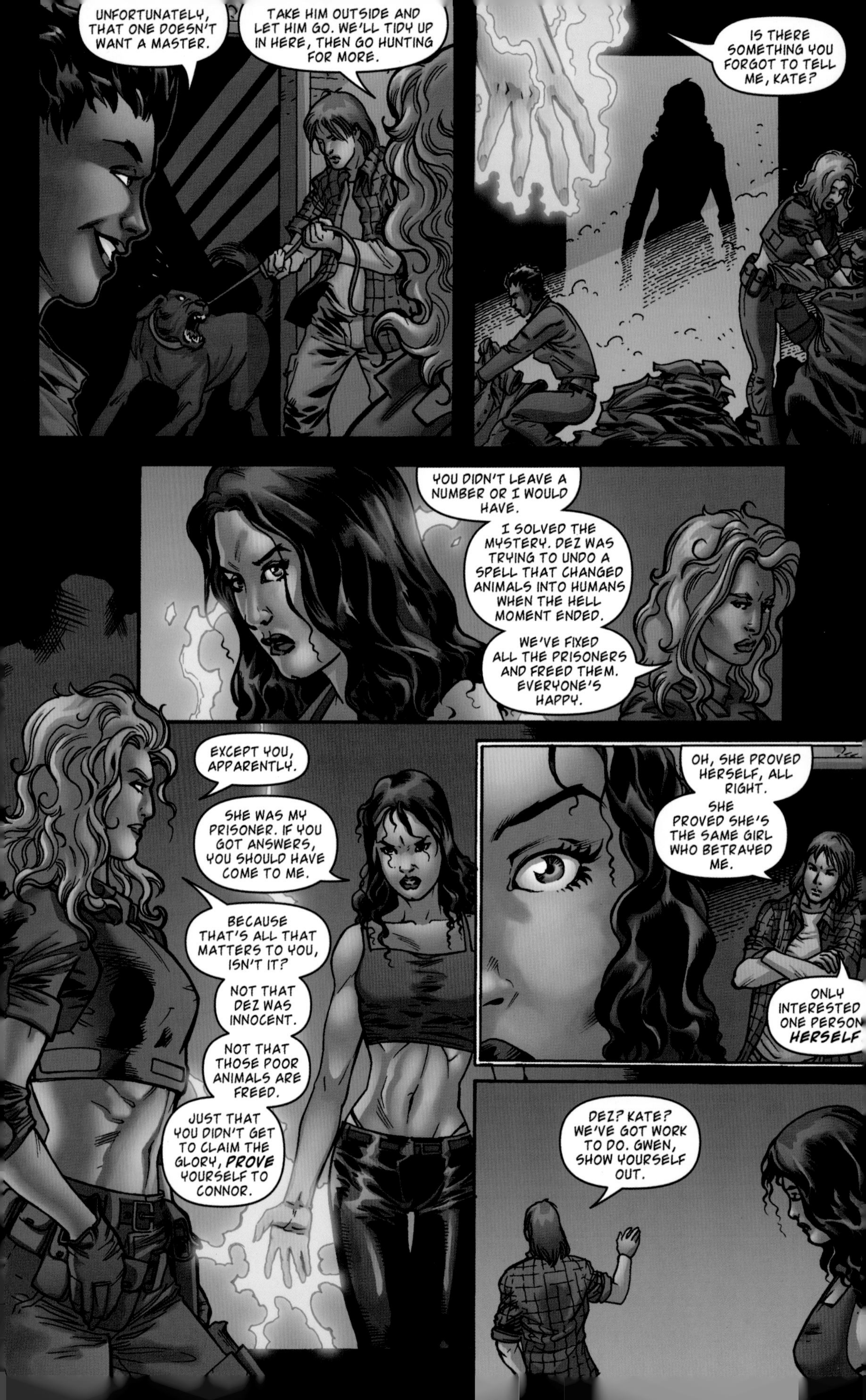
UNFORTUNATELY, THAT ONE DOESN'T WANT A MASTER.
TAKE HIM OUTSIDE AND LET HIM GO. WE'LL TIDY UP IN HERE, THEN GO HUNTING FOR MORE.
IS THERE SOMETHING YOU FORGOT TO TELL ME, KATE?
YOU DIDN'T LEAVE A NUMBER OR I WOULD HAVE.
I SOLVED THE MYSTERY. DEZ WAS TRYING TO UNDO A SPELL THAT CHANGED ANIMALS INTO HUMANS WHEN THE HELL MOMENT ENDED.
WE'VE FIXED ALL THE PRISONERS AND FREED THEM. EVERYONE'S HAPPY.
EXCEPT YOU, APPARENTLY.
SHE WAS MY PRISONER. IF YOU GOT ANSWERS, YOU SHOULD HAVE COME TO ME.
BECAUSE THAT'S ALL THAT MATTERS TO YOU, ISN'T IT?
NOT THAT DEZ WAS INNOCENT.
NOT THAT THOSE POOR ANIMALS ARE FREED.
JUST THAT YOU DIDN'T GET TO CLAIM THE GLORY, PROVE YOURSELF TO CONNOR.
OH, SHE PROVED HERSELF, ALL RIGHT.
SHE PROVED SHE'S THE SAME GIRL WHO BETRAYED ME.
ONLY INTERESTED ONE PERSON HERSELF
DEZ? KATE? WE'VE GOT WORK TO DO. GWEN, SHOW YOURSELF OUT.

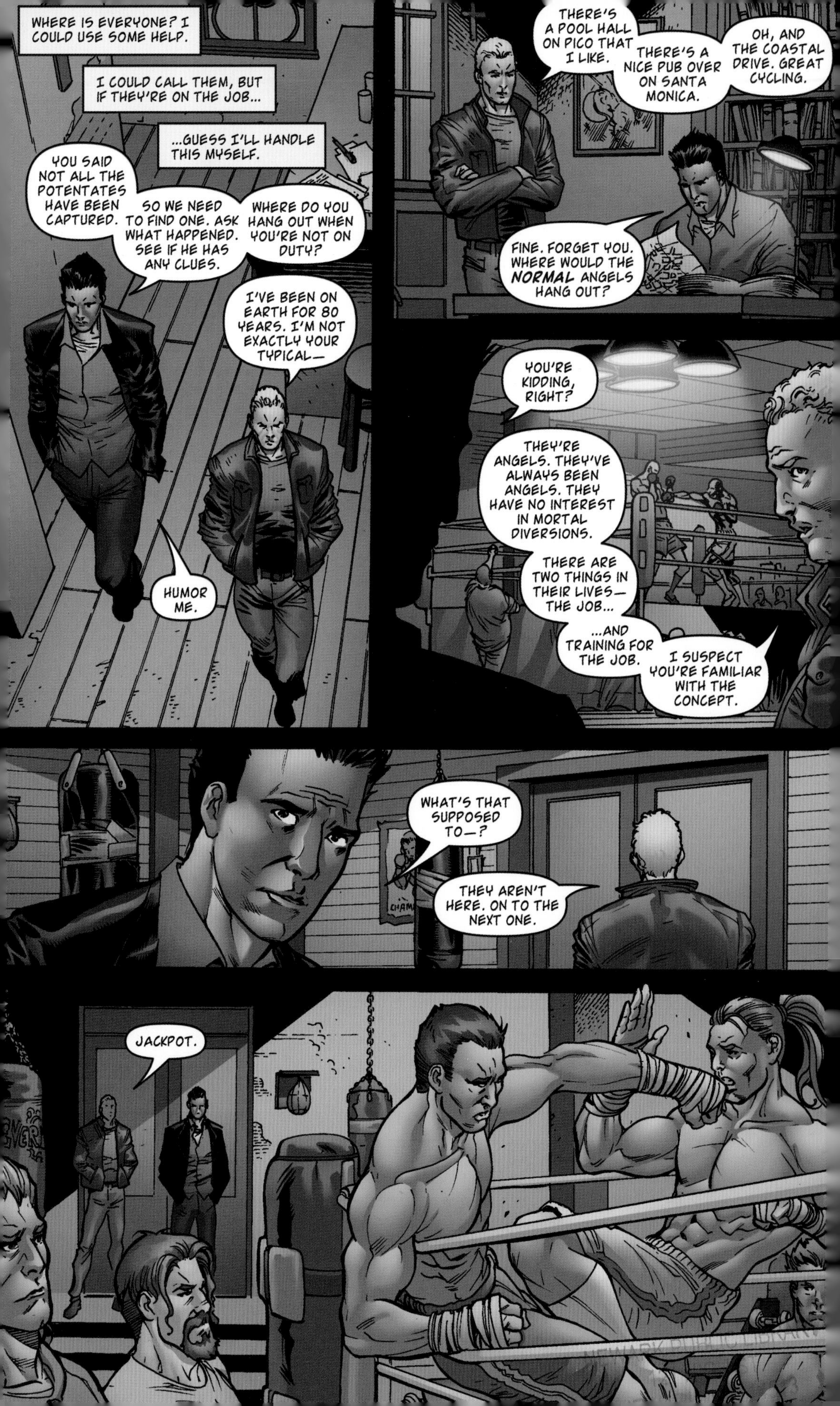
WHERE IS EVERYONE? I COULD USE SOME HELP.
I COULD CALL THEM, BUT IF THEY'RE ON THE JOB...
...GUESS I'LL HANDLE THIS MYSELF.
YOU SAID NOT ALL THE POTENTATES HAVE BEEN CAPTURED.
SO WE NEED TO FIND ONE. ASK WHAT HAPPENED. SEE IF HE HAS ANY CLUES.
WHERE DO YOU HANG OUT WHEN YOU'RE NOT ON DUTY?
I'VE BEEN ON EARTH FOR 80 YEARS. I'M NOT EXACTLY YOUR TYPICAL—
HUMOR ME.
THERE'S A POOL HALL ON PICO THAT I LIKE.
THERE'S A NICE PUB OVER ON SANTA MONICA.
OH, AND THE COASTAL DRIVE. GREAT CYCLING.
FINE. FORGET YOU. WHERE WOULD THE NORMAL ANGELS HANG OUT?
YOU'RE KIDDING, RIGHT?
THEY'RE ANGELS. THEY'VE ALWAYS BEEN ANGELS. THEY HAVE NO INTEREST IN MORTAL DIVERSIONS.
THERE ARE TWO THINGS IN THEIR LIVES— THE JOB...
...AND TRAINING FOR THE JOB.
I SUSPECT YOU'RE FAMILIAR WITH THE CONCEPT.
WHAT'S THAT SUPPOSED TO—?
THEY AREN'T HERE. ON TO THE NEXT ONE.
JACKPOT.

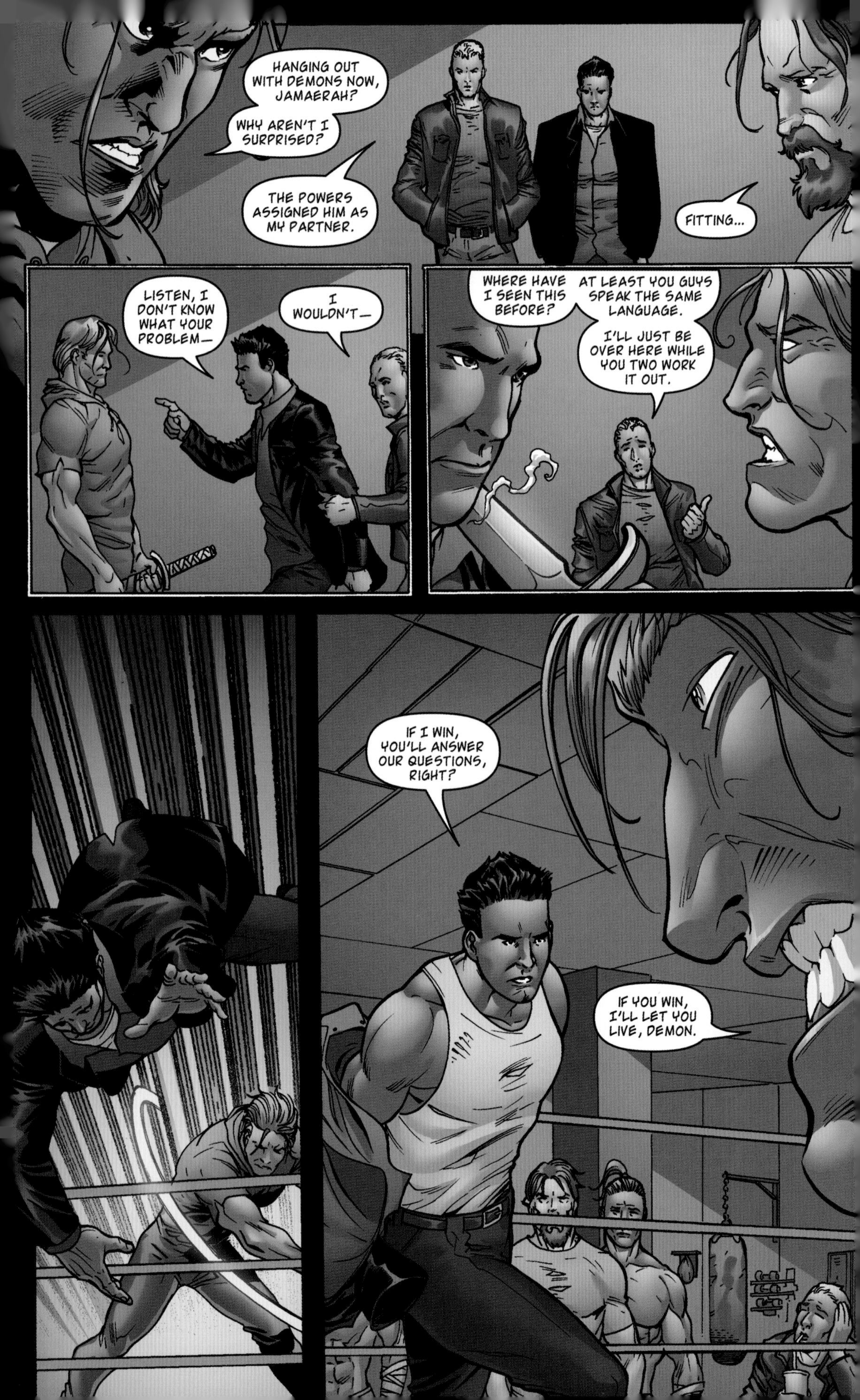
HANGING OUT WITH DEMONS NOW, JAMAERAH?
WHY AREN'T I SURPRISED?
THE POWERS ASSIGNED HIM AS MY PARTNER.
FITTING...
LISTEN, I DON'T KNOW WHAT YOUR PROBLEM—
I WOULDN'T—
WHERE HAVE I SEEN THIS BEFORE?
AT LEAST YOU GUYS SPEAK THE SAME LANGUAGE.
I'LL JUST BE OVER HERE WHILE YOU TWO WORK IT OUT.
IF I WIN, YOU'LL ANSWER OUR QUESTIONS, RIGHT?
IF YOU WIN, I'LL LET YOU LIVE, DEMON.

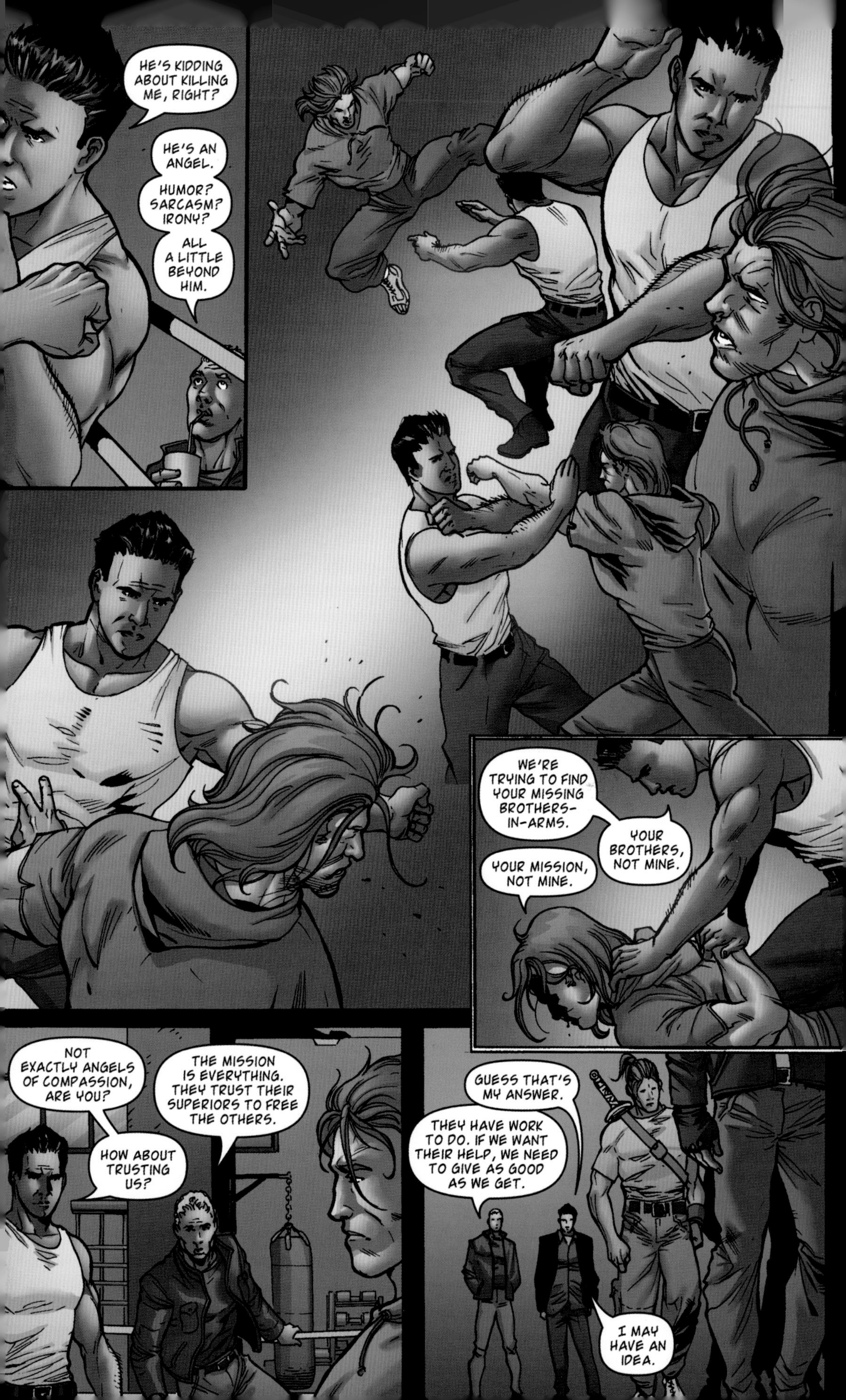
HE'S KIDDING ABOUT KILLING ME, RIGHT?
HE'S AN ANGEL.
HUMOR? SARCASM? IRONY?
ALL A LITTLE BEYOND HIM.
WE'RE TRYING TO FIND YOUR MISSING BROTHERS-IN-ARMS.
YOUR BROTHERS, NOT MINE.
YOUR MISSION, NOT MINE.
NOT EXACTLY ANGELS OF COMPASSION, ARE YOU?
THE MISSION IS EVERYTHING. THEY TRUST THEIR SUPERIORS TO FREE THE OTHERS.
HOW ABOUT TRUSTING US?
GUESS THAT'S MY ANSWER.
THEY HAVE WORK TO DO. IF WE WANT THEIR HELP, WE NEED TO GIVE AS GOOD AS WE GET.
I MAY HAVE AN IDEA.

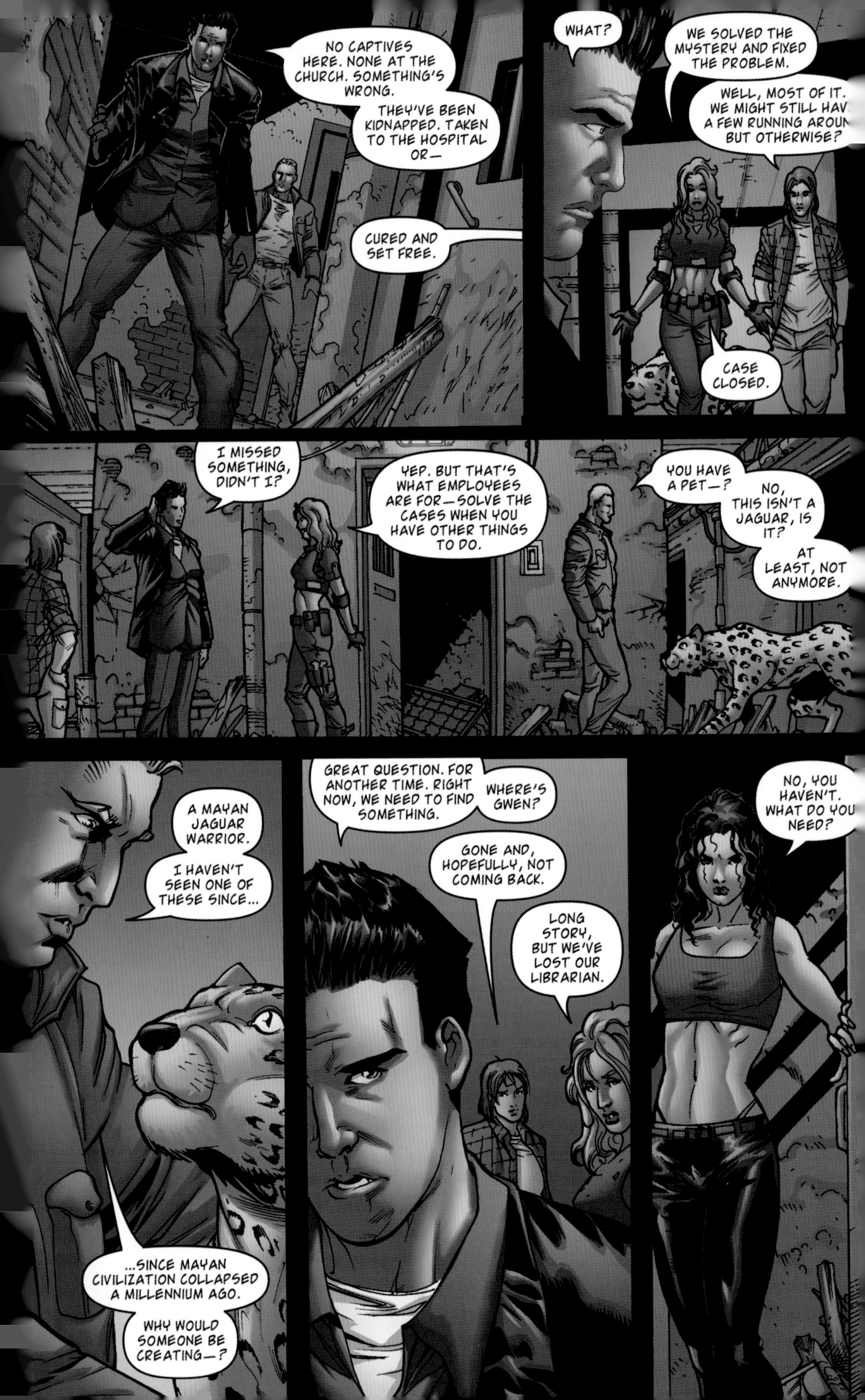
NO CAPTIVES HERE. NONE AT THE CHURCH. SOMETHING'S WRONG.
THEY'VE BEEN KIDNAPPED. TAKEN TO THE HOSPITAL OR—
CURED AND SET FREE.
WHAT?
WE SOLVED THE MYSTERY AND FIXED THE PROBLEM.
WELL, MOST OF IT. WE MIGHT STILL HAV A FEW RUNNING AROUN BUT OTHERWISE?
CASE CLOSED.
I MISSED SOMETHING, DIDN'T I?
YEP. BUT THAT'S WHAT EMPLOYEES ARE FOR—SOLVE THE CASES WHEN YOU HAVE OTHER THINGS TO DO.
YOU HAVE A PET—?
NO, THIS ISN'T A JAGUAR, IS IT?
AT LEAST, NOT ANYMORE.
A MAYAN JAGUAR WARRIOR.
I HAVEN'T SEEN ONE OF THESE SINCE...
...SINCE MAYAN CIVILIZATION COLLAPSED A MILLENNIUM AGO.
WHY WOULD SOMEONE BE CREATING—?
GREAT QUESTION. FOR ANOTHER TIME. RIGHT NOW, WE NEED TO FIND SOMETHING.
WHERE'S GWEN?
GONE AND, HOPEFULLY, NOT COMING BACK.
LONG STORY, BUT WE'VE LOST OUR LIBRARIAN.
NO, YOU HAVEN'T. WHAT DO YOU NEED?

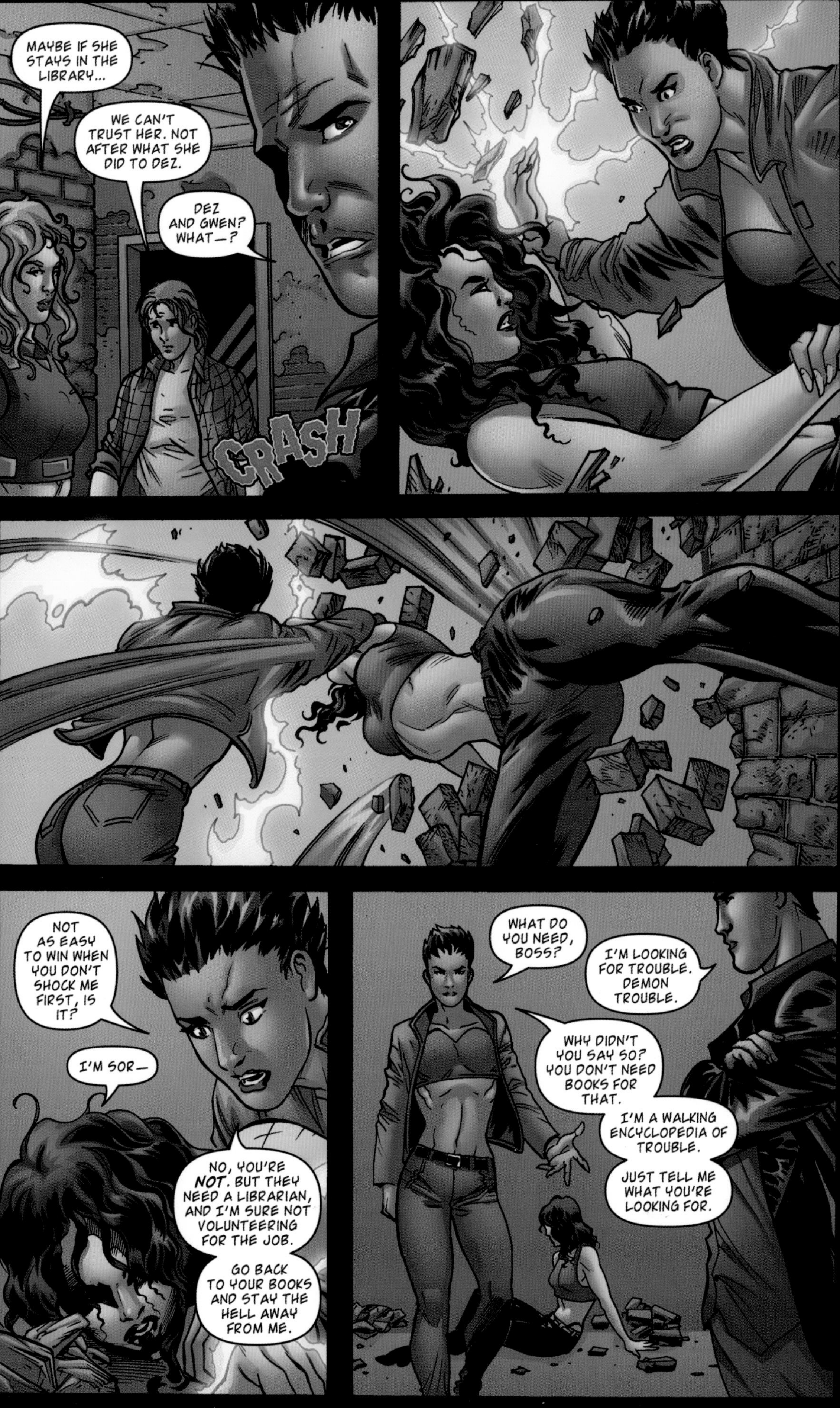
MAYBE IF SHE STAYS IN THE LIBRARY...
WE CAN'T TRUST HER. NOT AFTER WHAT SHE DID TO DEZ.
DEZ AND GWEN? WHAT—?
CRASH
NOT AS EASY TO WIN WHEN YOU DON'T SHOCK ME FIRST, IS IT?
I'M SOR—
NO, YOU'RE NOT. BUT THEY NEED A LIBRARIAN, AND I'M SURE NOT VOLUNTEERING FOR THE JOB.
GO BACK TO YOUR BOOKS AND STAY THE HELL AWAY FROM ME.
WHAT DO YOU NEED, BOSS?
I'M LOOKING FOR TROUBLE. DEMON TROUBLE.
WHY DIDN'T YOU SAY SO? YOU DON'T NEED BOOKS FOR THAT.
I'M A WALKING ENCYCLOPEDIA OF TROUBLE.
JUST TELL ME WHAT YOU'RE LOOKING FOR.

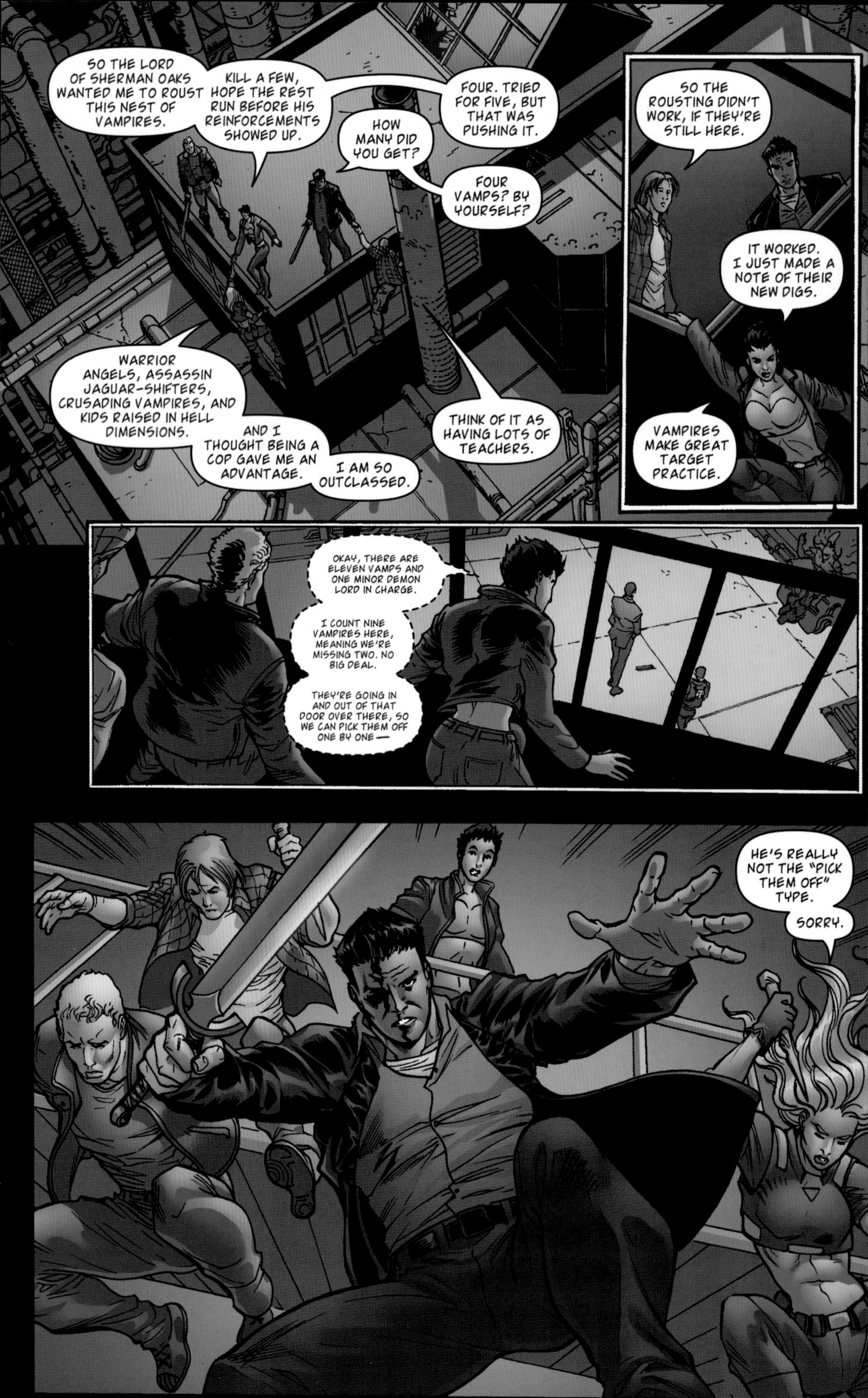
SO THE LORD OF SHERMAN OAKS WANTED ME TO ROUST THIS NEST OF VAMPIRES.
KILL A FEW, HOPE THE REST RUN BEFORE HIS REINFORCEMENTS SHOWED UP.
HOW MANY DID YOU GET?
FOUR. TRIED FOR FIVE, BUT THAT WAS PUSHING IT.
FOUR VAMPS? BY YOURSELF?
WARRIOR ANGELS, ASSASSIN JAGUAR-SHIFTERS, CRUSADING VAMPIRES, AND KIDS RAISED IN HELL DIMENSIONS.
AND I THOUGHT BEING A COP GAVE ME AN ADVANTAGE.
I AM SO OUTCLASSED.
THINK OF IT AS HAVING LOTS OF TEACHERS.
SO THE ROUSTING DIDN'T WORK, IF THEY'RE STILL HERE.
IT WORKED. I JUST MADE A NOTE OF THEIR NEW DIGS.
VAMPIRES MAKE GREAT TARGET PRACTICE.
OKAY, THERE ARE ELEVEN VAMPS AND ONE MINOR DEMON LORD IN CHARGE.
I COUNT NINE VAMPIRES HERE, MEANING WE'RE MISSING TWO. NO BIG DEAL.
THEY'RE GOING IN AND OUT OF THAT DOOR OVER THERE, SO WE CAN PICK THEM OFF ONE BY ONE —
HE'S REALLY NOT THE "PICK THEM OFF" TYPE.
SORRY.

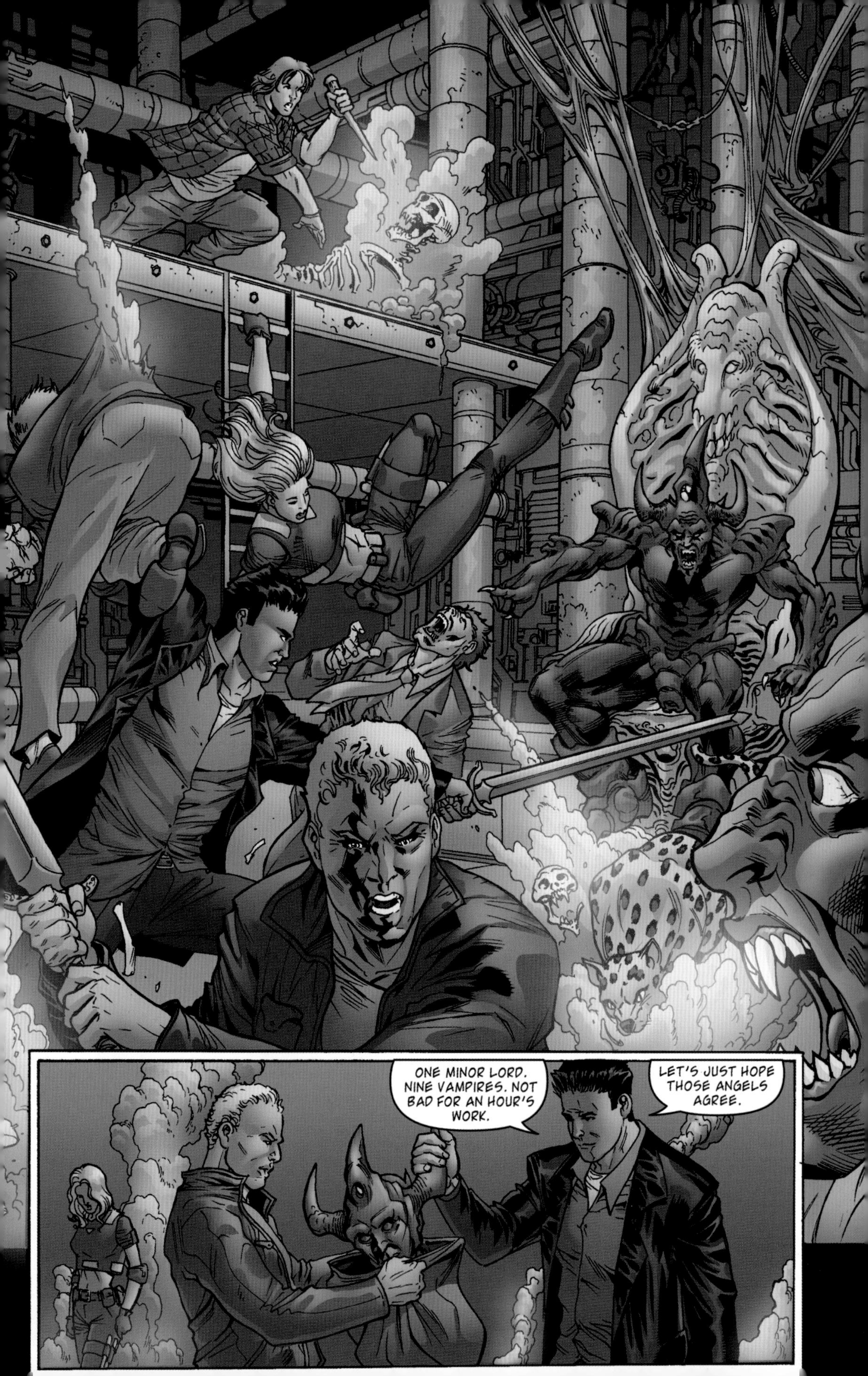
ONE MINOR LORD. NINE VAMPIRES. NOT BAD FOR AN HOUR'S WORK.
LET'S JUST HOPE THOSE ANGELS AGREE.

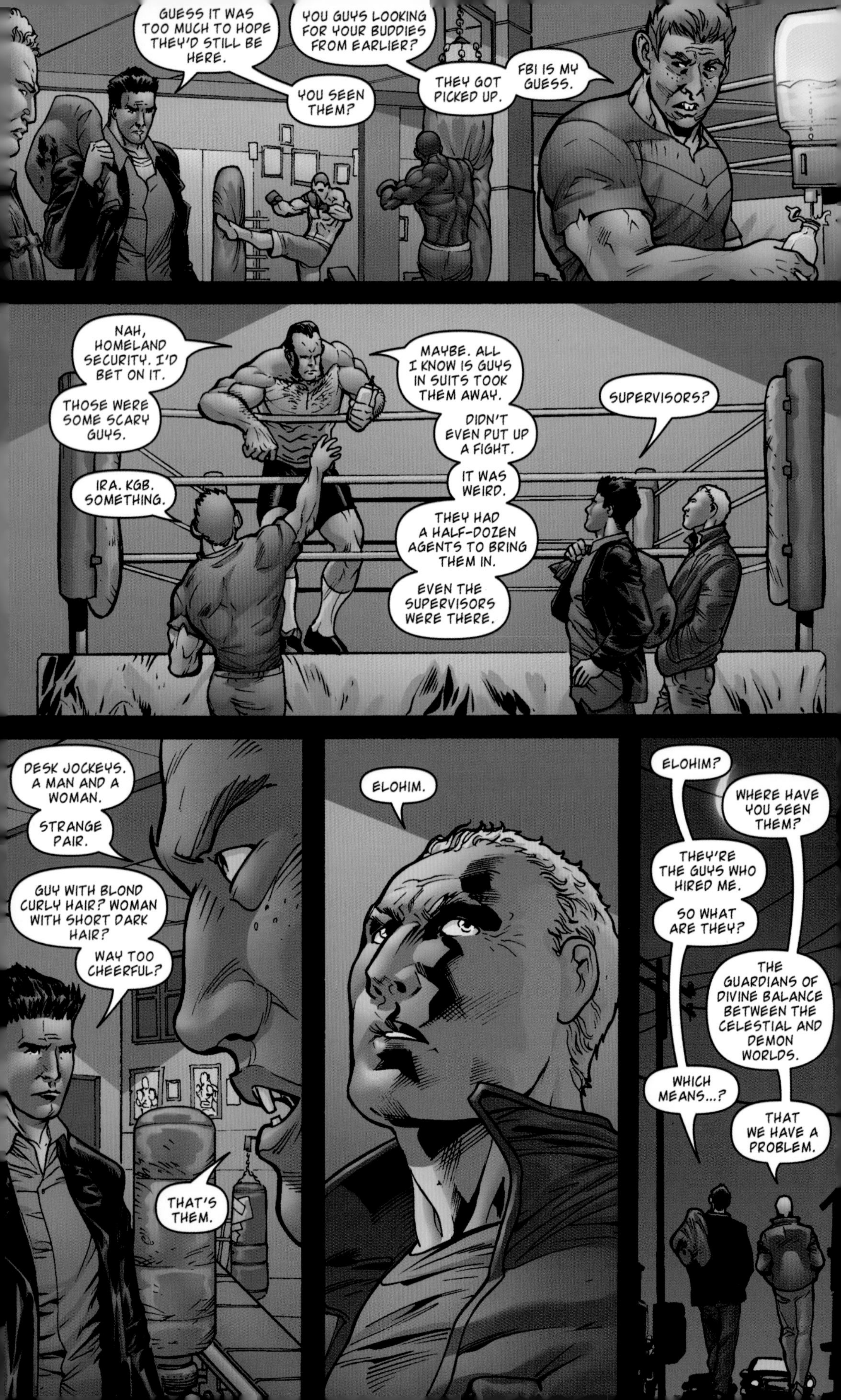
GUESS IT WAS TOO MUCH TO HOPE THEY'D STILL BE HERE.
YOU GUYS LOOKING FOR YOUR BUDDIES FROM EARLIER?
YOU SEEN THEM?
THEY GOT PICKED UP.
FBI IS MY GUESS.
NAH, HOMELAND SECURITY. I'D BET ON IT.
THOSE WERE SOME SCARY GUYS.
IRA. KGB. SOMETHING.
MAYBE. ALL I KNOW IS GUYS IN SUITS TOOK THEM AWAY.
DIDN'T EVEN PUT UP A FIGHT.
IT WAS WEIRD.
THEY HAD A HALF-DOZEN AGENTS TO BRING THEM IN.
EVEN THE SUPERVISORS WERE THERE.
SUPERVISORS?
DESK JOCKEYS. A MAN AND A WOMAN.
STRANGE PAIR.
GUY WITH BLOND CURLY HAIR? WOMAN WITH SHORT DARK HAIR?
WAY TOO CHEERFUL?
THAT'S THEM.
ELOHIM.
ELOHIM?
WHERE HAVE YOU SEEN THEM?
THEY'RE THE GUYS WHO HIRED ME.
SO WHAT ARE THEY?
THE GUARDIANS OF DIVINE BALANCE BETWEEN THE CELESTIAL AND DEMON WORLDS.
WHICH MEANS...?
THAT WE HAVE A PROBLEM.

chapter five

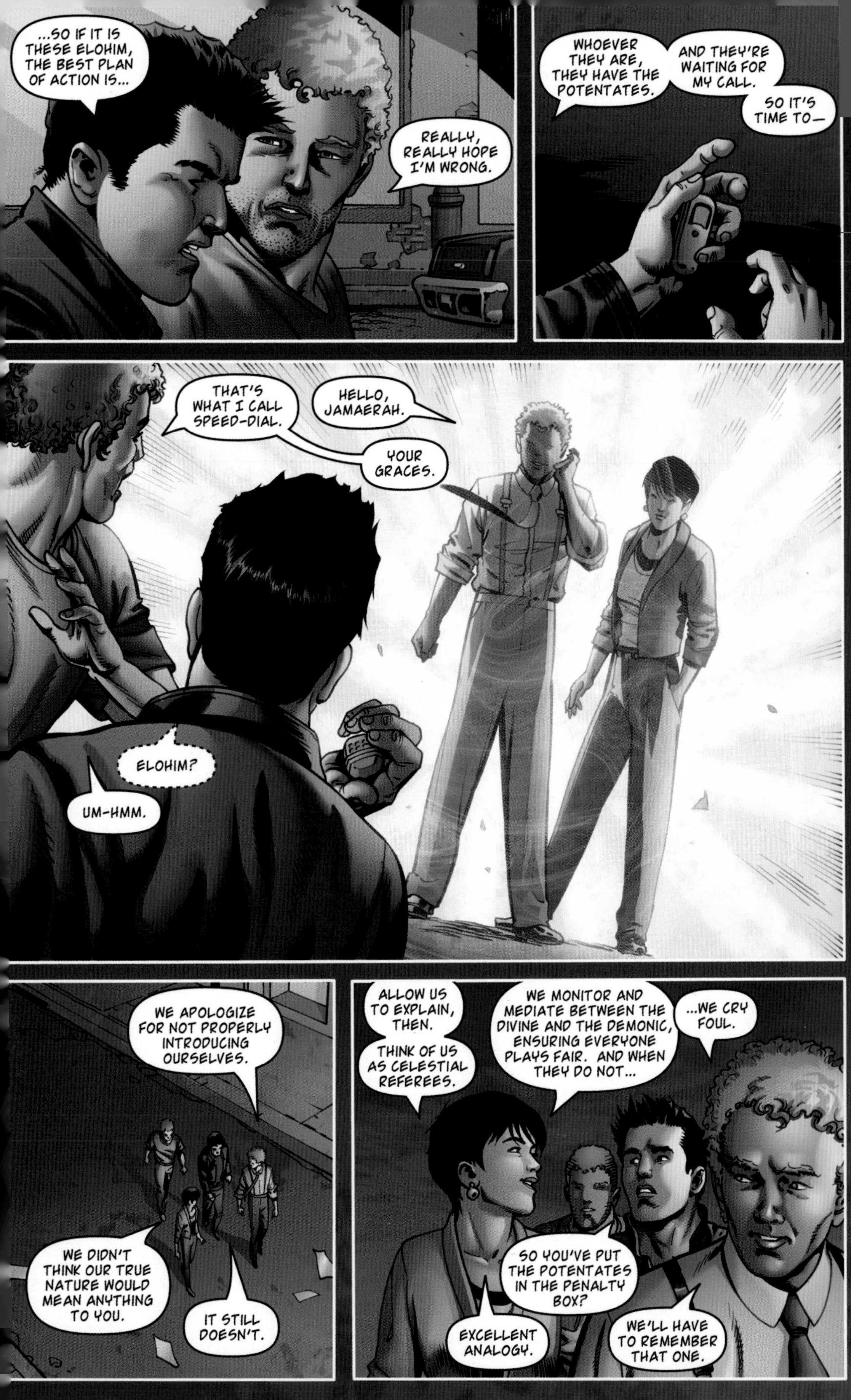
...SO IF IT IS THESE ELOHIM, THE BEST PLAN OF ACTION IS...
REALLY, REALLY HOPE I'M WRONG.
WHOEVER THEY ARE, THEY HAVE THE POTENTATES.
AND THEY'RE WAITING FOR MY CALL.
SO IT'S TIME TO—
THAT'S WHAT I CALL SPEED-DIAL.
HELLO, JAMAERAH.
YOUR GRACES.
ELOHIM?
UM-HMM.
WE APOLOGIZE FOR NOT PROPERLY INTRODUCING OURSELVES.
WE DIDN'T THINK OUR TRUE NATURE WOULD MEAN ANYTHING TO YOU.
IT STILL DOESN'T.
ALLOW US TO EXPLAIN, THEN.
THINK OF US AS CELESTIAL REFEREES.
WE MONITOR AND MEDIATE BETWEEN THE DIVINE AND THE DEMONIC, ENSURING EVERYONE PLAYS FAIR. AND WHEN THEY DO NOT...
...WE CRY FOUL.
SO YOU'VE PUT THE POTENTATES IN THE PENALTY BOX?
EXCELLENT ANALOGY.
WE'LL HAVE TO REMEMBER THAT ONE.

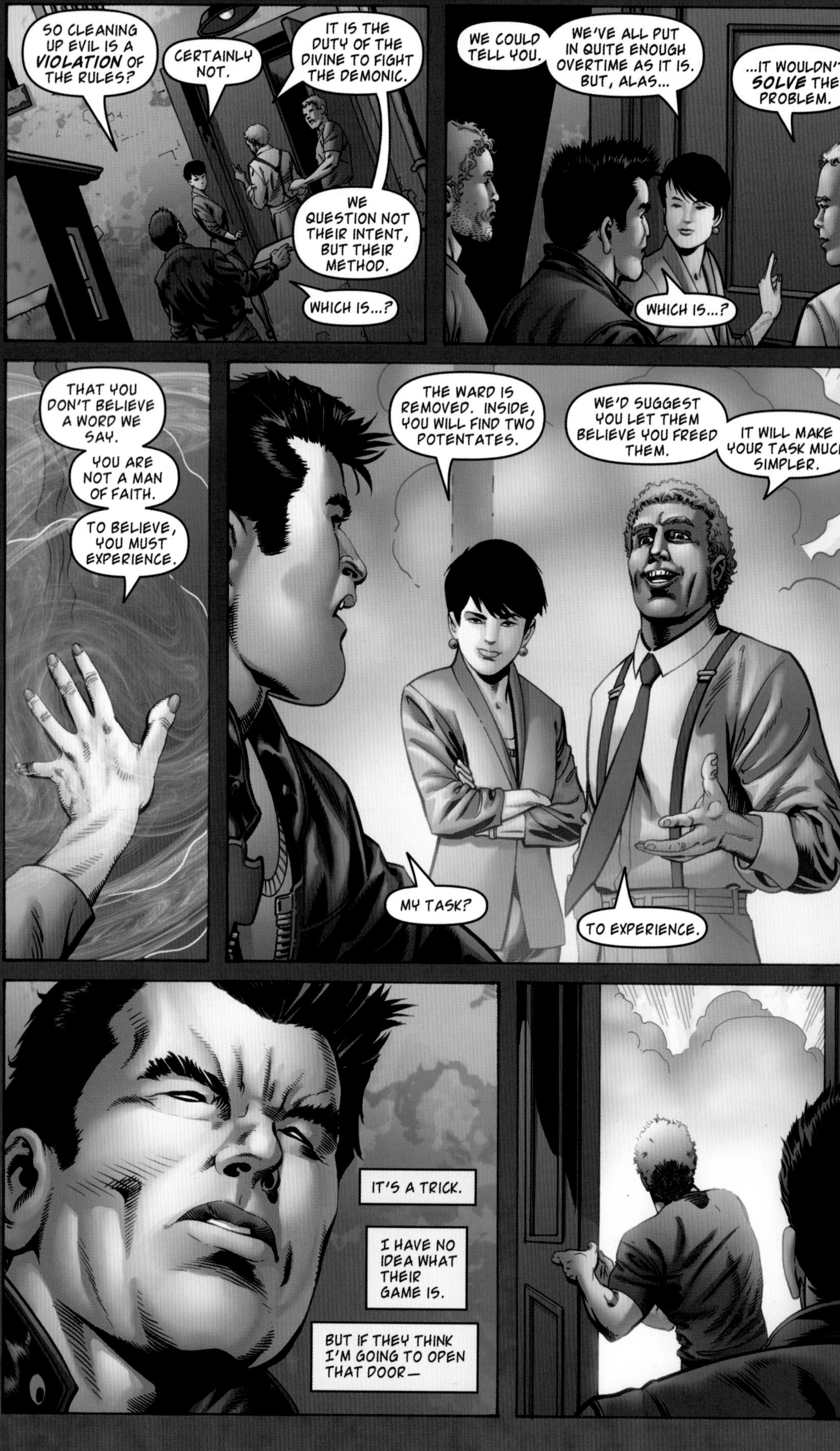
SO CLEANING UP EVIL IS A VIOLATION OF THE RULES?
CERTAINLY NOT.
IT IS THE DUTY OF THE DIVINE TO FIGHT THE DEMONIC.
WE QUESTION NOT THEIR INTENT, BUT THEIR METHOD.
WHICH IS...?
WE COULD TELL YOU.
WE'VE ALL PUT IN QUITE ENOUGH OVERTIME AS IT IS. BUT, ALAS...
...IT WOULDN'T SOLVE THE PROBLEM.
WHICH IS...?
THAT YOU DON'T BELIEVE A WORD WE SAY.
YOU ARE NOT A MAN OF FAITH.
TO BELIEVE, YOU MUST EXPERIENCE.
THE WARD IS REMOVED. INSIDE, YOU WILL FIND TWO POTENTATES.
WE'D SUGGEST YOU LET THEM BELIEVE YOU FREED THEM.
IT WILL MAKE YOUR TASK MUCH SIMPLER.
MY TASK?
TO EXPERIENCE.
IT'S A TRICK.
I HAVE NO IDEA WHAT THEIR GAME IS.
BUT IF THEY THINK I'M GOING TO OPEN THAT DOOR—

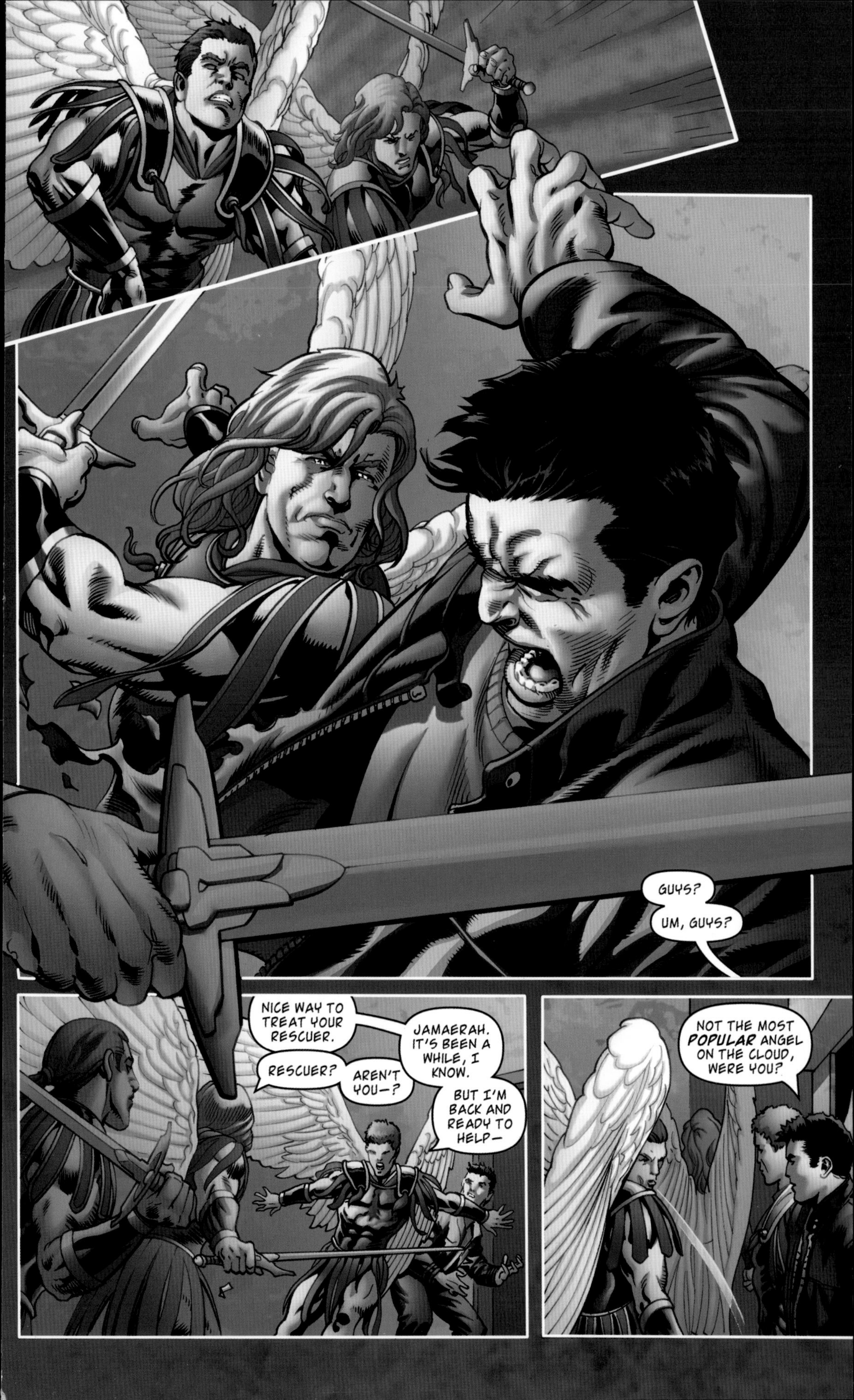
GUYS?
UM, GUYS?
NICE WAY TO TREAT YOUR RESCUER.
RESCUER?
AREN'T YOU—?
JAMAERAH. IT'S BEEN A WHILE, I KNOW.
BUT I'M BACK AND READY TO HELP—
NOT THE MOST POPULAR ANGEL ON THE CLOUD, WERE YOU?

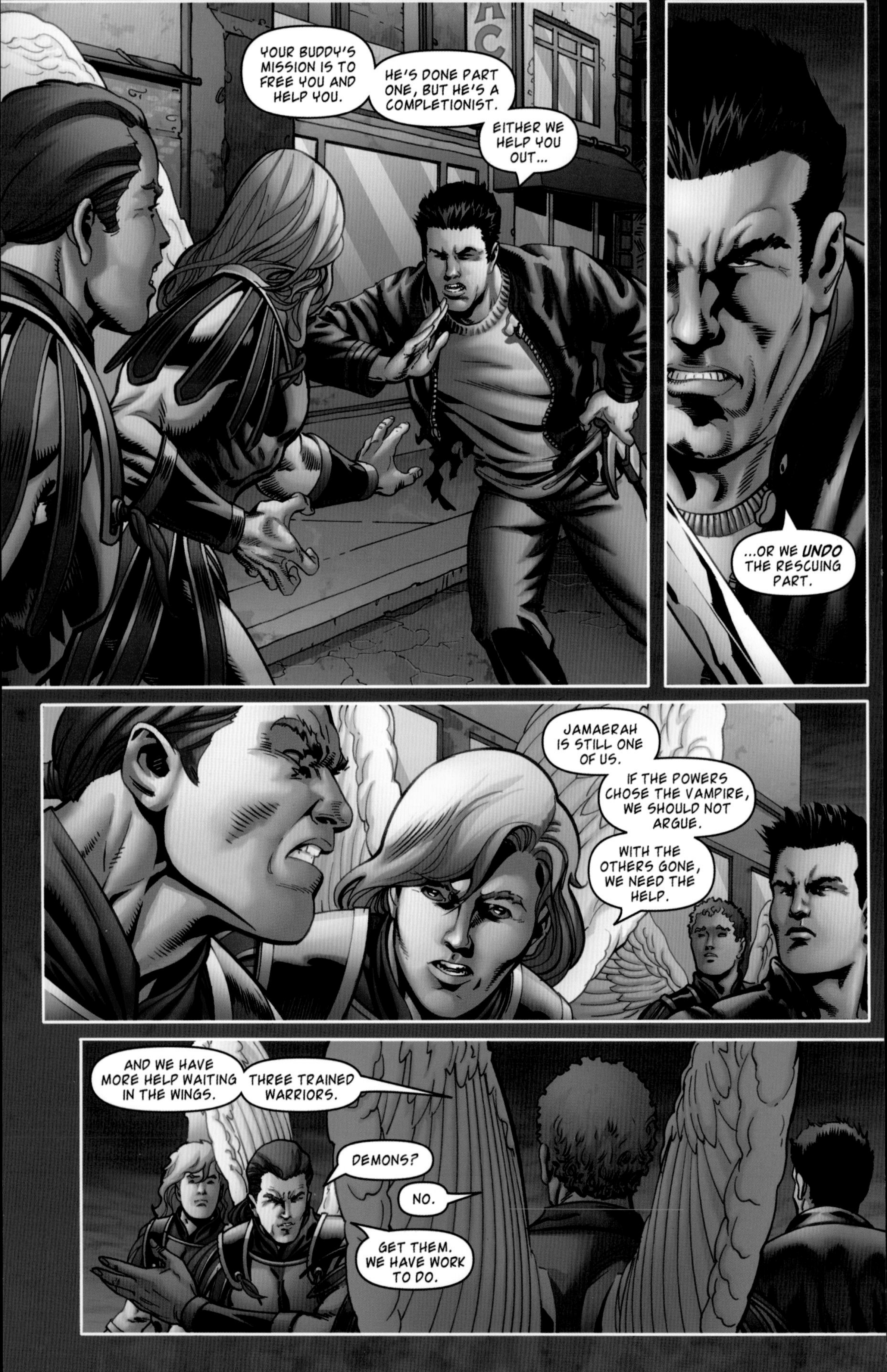

YOUR BUDDY'S MISSION IS TO FREE YOU AND HELP YOU.
HE'S DONE PART ONE, BUT HE'S A COMPLETIONIST.
EITHER WE HELP YOU OUT...
...OR WE *UNDO* THE RESCUING PART.
JAMAERAH IS STILL ONE OF US.
IF THE POWERS CHOSE THE VAMPIRE, WE SHOULD NOT ARGUE.
WITH THE OTHERS GONE, WE NEED THE HELP.
AND WE HAVE MORE HELP WAITING IN THE WINGS.
THREE TRAINED WARRIORS.
DEMONS?
NO.
GET THEM. WE HAVE WORK TO DO.

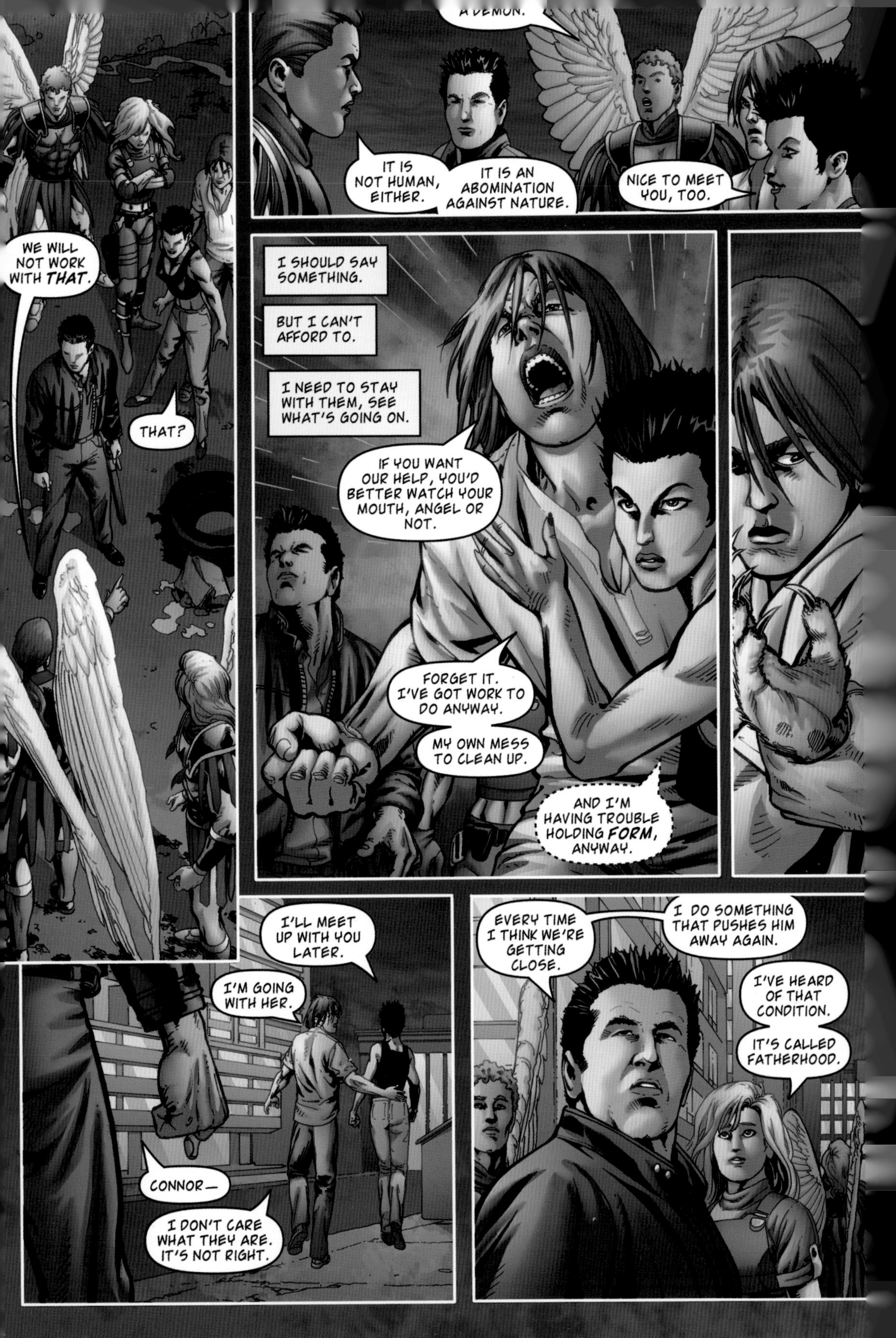

WE WILL NOT WORK WITH *THAT*.
THAT?
A DEMON.
IT IS NOT HUMAN, EITHER.
IT IS AN ABOMINATION AGAINST NATURE.
NICE TO MEET YOU, TOO.
I SHOULD SAY SOMETHING.
BUT I CAN'T AFFORD TO.
I NEED TO STAY WITH THEM, SEE WHAT'S GOING ON.
IF YOU WANT OUR HELP, YOU'D BETTER WATCH YOUR MOUTH, ANGEL OR NOT.
FORGET IT. I'VE GOT WORK TO DO ANYWAY.
MY OWN MESS TO CLEAN UP.
AND I'M HAVING TROUBLE HOLDING *FORM*, ANYWAY.
I'LL MEET UP WITH YOU LATER.
I'M GOING WITH HER.
CONNOR—
I DON'T CARE WHAT THEY ARE. IT'S NOT RIGHT.
EVERY TIME I THINK WE'RE GETTING CLOSE.
I DO SOMETHING THAT PUSHES HIM AWAY AGAIN.
I'VE HEARD OF THAT CONDITION.
IT'S CALLED FATHERHOOD.

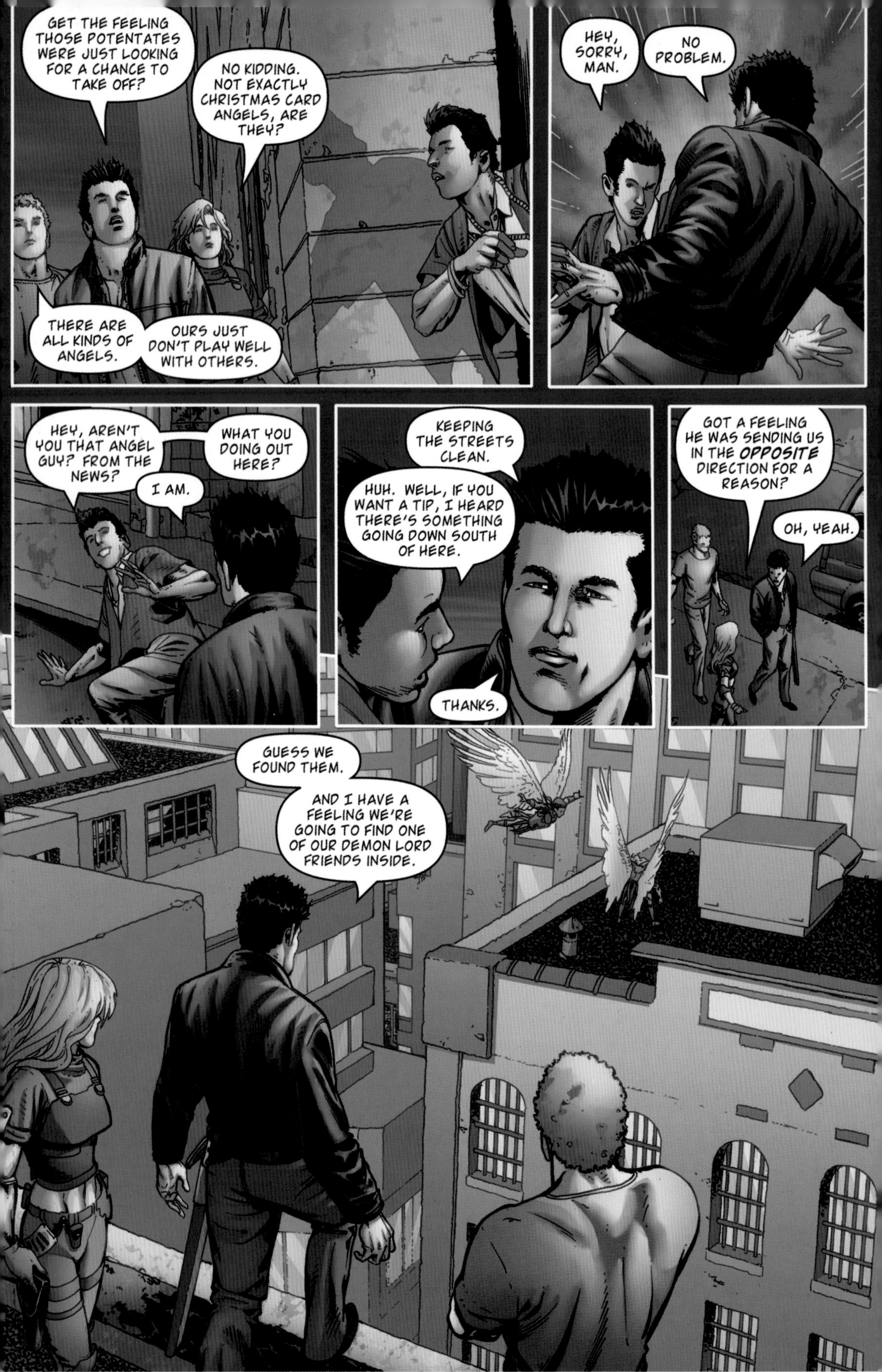
GET THE FEELING THOSE POTENTATES WERE JUST LOOKING FOR A CHANCE TO TAKE OFF?
NO KIDDING. NOT EXACTLY CHRISTMAS CARD ANGELS, ARE THEY?
THERE ARE ALL KINDS OF ANGELS.
OURS JUST DON'T PLAY WELL WITH OTHERS.
HEY, SORRY, MAN.
NO PROBLEM.
HEY, AREN'T YOU THAT ANGEL GUY? FROM THE NEWS?
I AM.
WHAT YOU DOING OUT HERE?
KEEPING THE STREETS CLEAN.
HUH. WELL, IF YOU WANT A TIP, I HEARD THERE'S SOMETHING GOING DOWN SOUTH OF HERE.
THANKS.
GOT A FEELING HE WAS SENDING US IN THE *OPPOSITE* DIRECTION FOR A REASON?
OH, YEAH.
GUESS WE FOUND THEM.
AND I HAVE A FEELING WE'RE GOING TO FIND ONE OF OUR DEMON LORD FRIENDS INSIDE.

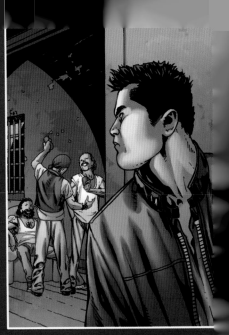

IF THERE'S A DEMON HERE, I'M NOT SEEING HIM.

VAMPIRE MAYBE?

NO. I CAN DETECT DEMONS, AND THERE AREN'T ANY HERE.

SO WE'RE IN THE WRONG PLACE?

ARE YOU READY?

FOR WHAT? WHERE'S THE—?

FOLLOW OUR LEAD.

OR STAY OUT OF OUR WAY.

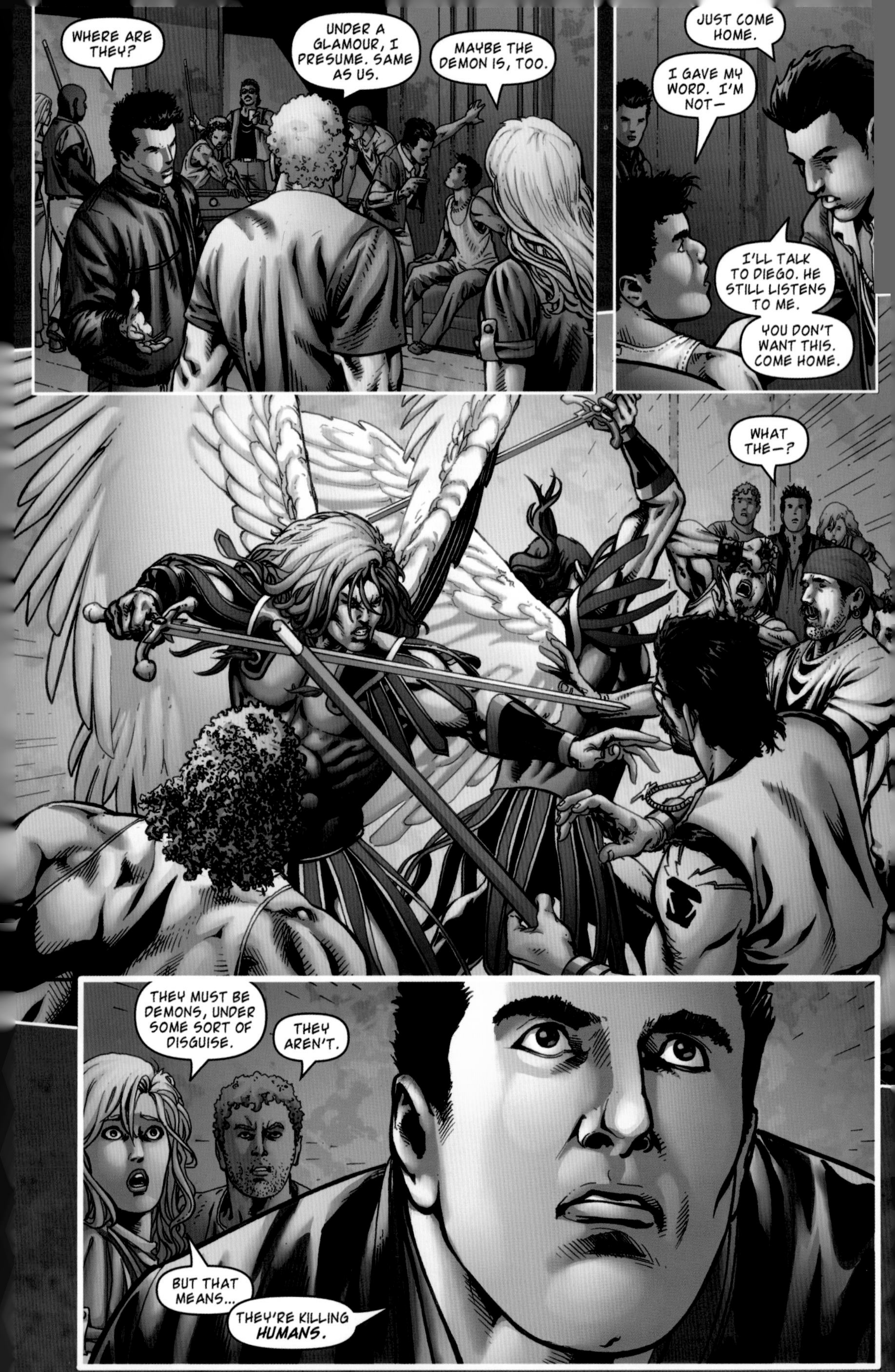
WHERE ARE THEY?
UNDER A GLAMOUR, I PRESUME. SAME AS US.
MAYBE THE DEMON IS, TOO.
JUST COME HOME.
I GAVE MY WORD. I'M NOT—
I'LL TALK TO DIEGO. HE STILL LISTENS TO ME.
YOU DON'T WANT THIS. COME HOME.
WHAT THE—?
THEY MUST BE DEMONS, UNDER SOME SORT OF DISGUISE.
THEY AREN'T.
BUT THAT MEANS...
THEY'RE KILLING *HUMANS*.

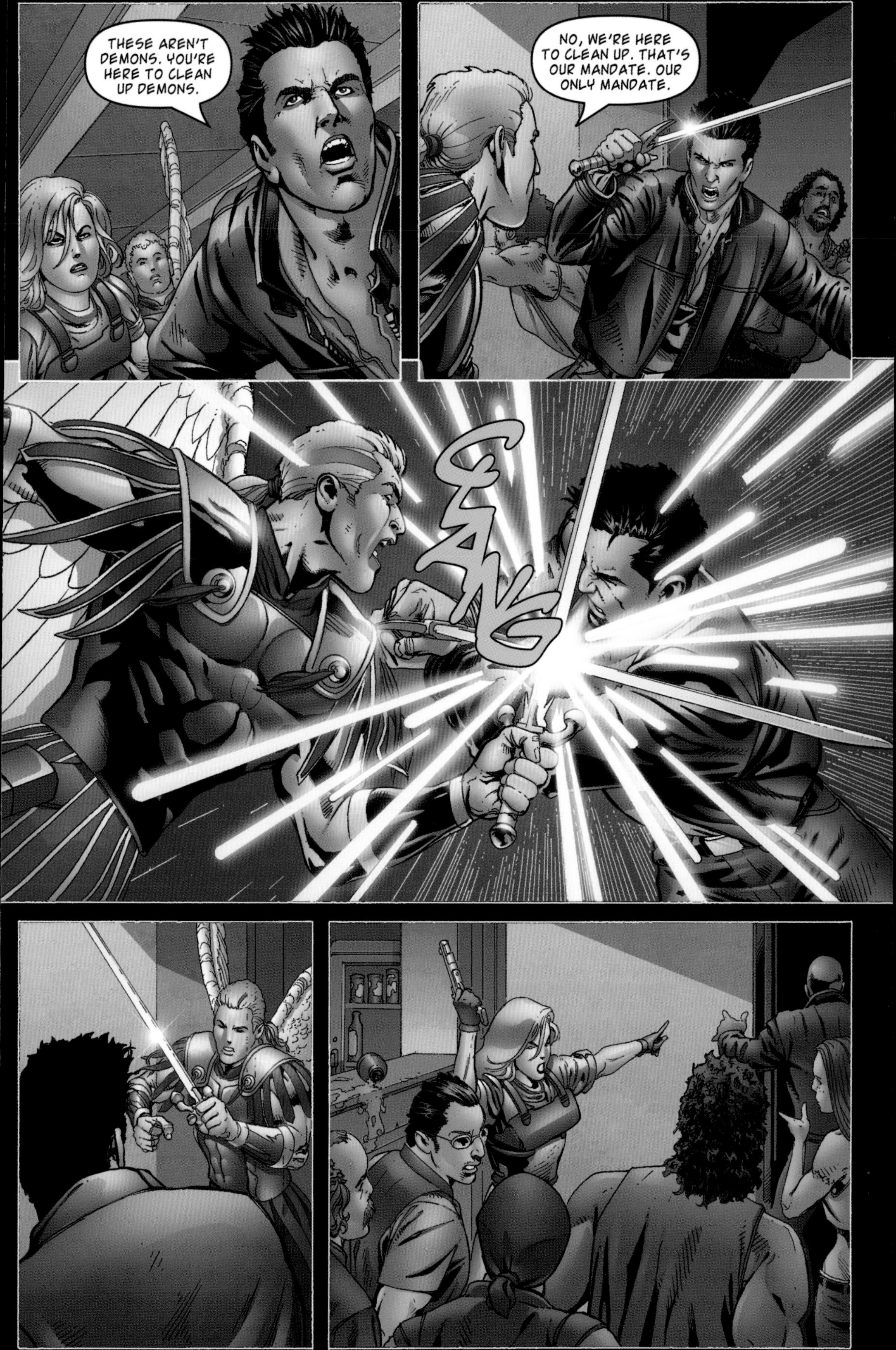
THESE AREN'T DEMONS. YOU'RE HERE TO CLEAN UP DEMONS.
NO, WE'RE HERE TO CLEAN UP. THAT'S OUR MANDATE. OUR ONLY MANDATE.
CLANG

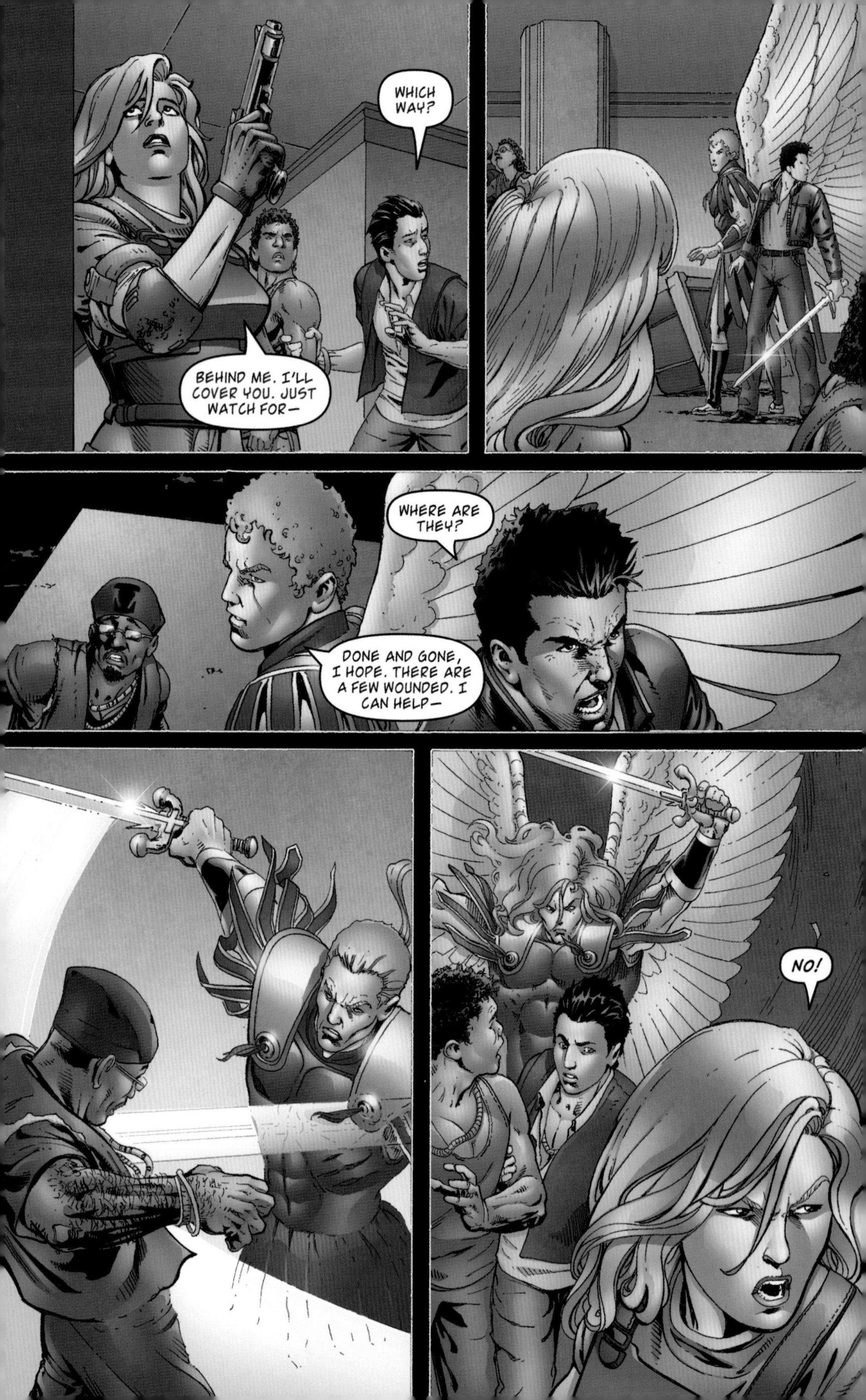
WHICH WAY?
BEHIND ME. I'LL COVER YOU. JUST WATCH FOR—
WHERE ARE THEY?
DONE AND GONE, I HOPE. THERE ARE A FEW WOUNDED. I CAN HELP—
NO!

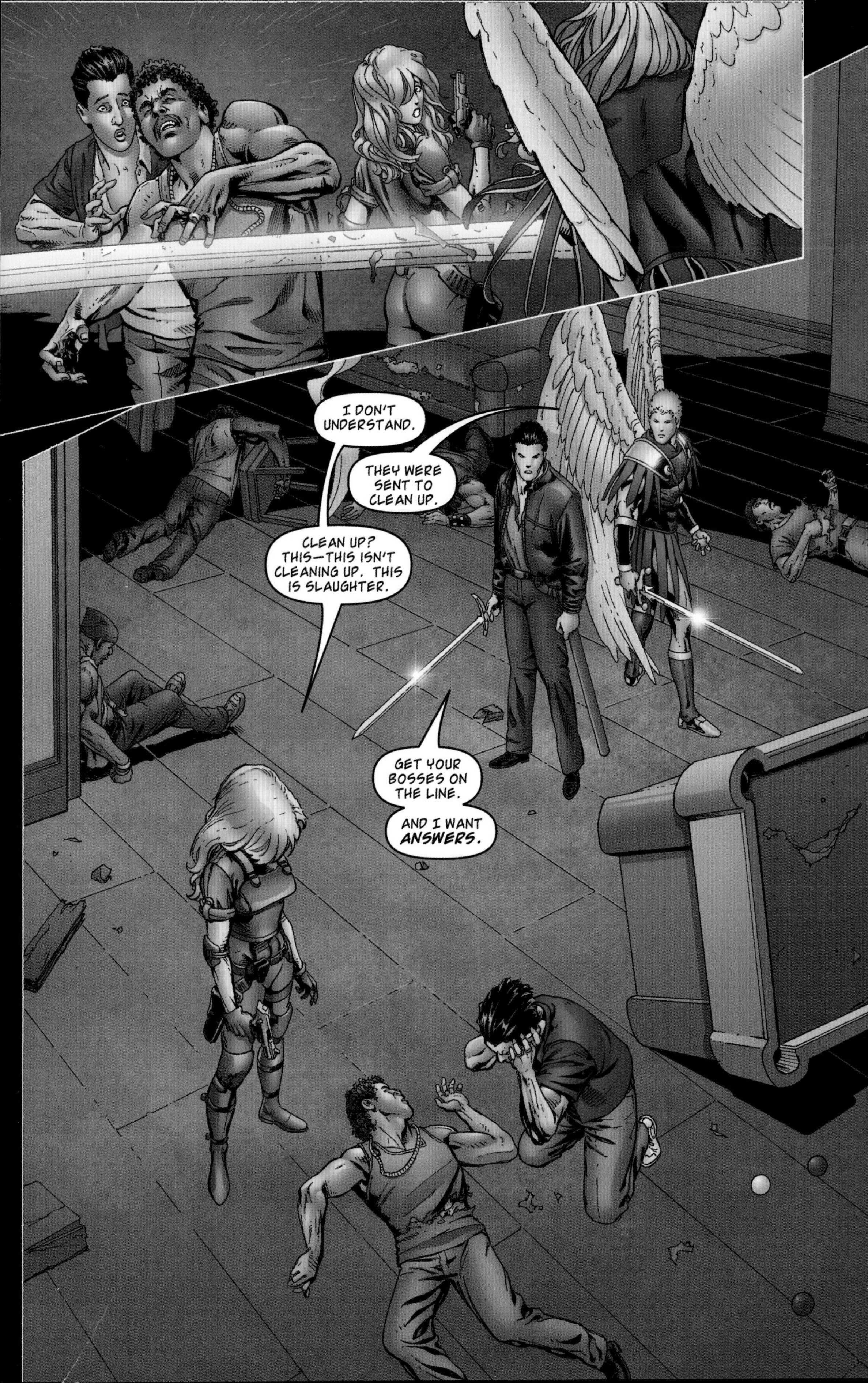
I DON'T UNDERSTAND.
THEY WERE SENT TO CLEAN UP.
CLEAN UP? THIS—THIS ISN'T CLEANING UP. THIS IS SLAUGHTER.
GET YOUR BOSSES ON THE LINE.
AND I WANT ANSWERS.

YOU SHOULDN'T HAVE LET THEM TALK TO YOU THAT WAY.

MY SKIN IS THICKER THAN THAT.

ANGEL SHOULDN'T HAVE LET THEM TALK TO YOU THAT WAY.

IT'S NOT FAIR.

LOTS OF THINGS AREN'T.

I CAN'T HOLD FORM MUCH LONGER. GIVE ME A MINUTE TO CHANGE.

HOW OLD ARE YOU ANYWAY?

TOO OLD FOR YOU.

I WASN'T—

SURE YOU WERE. HAVE YOU EVER WORKED WITH A WOMAN YOU DIDN'T WANT TO BED?

HEY!

JUST AN OBSERVATION.

I'M 19. I HAVE AN EXCUSE.

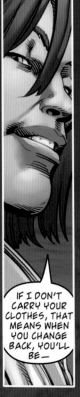

IF I DON'T CARRY YOUR CLOTHES, THAT MEANS WHEN YOU CHANGE BACK, YOU'LL BE—

OWW!

THERE'S NO ONE HERE. LET'S HIT THE STREET. I KNOW A PLACE.

MRR-OWW.

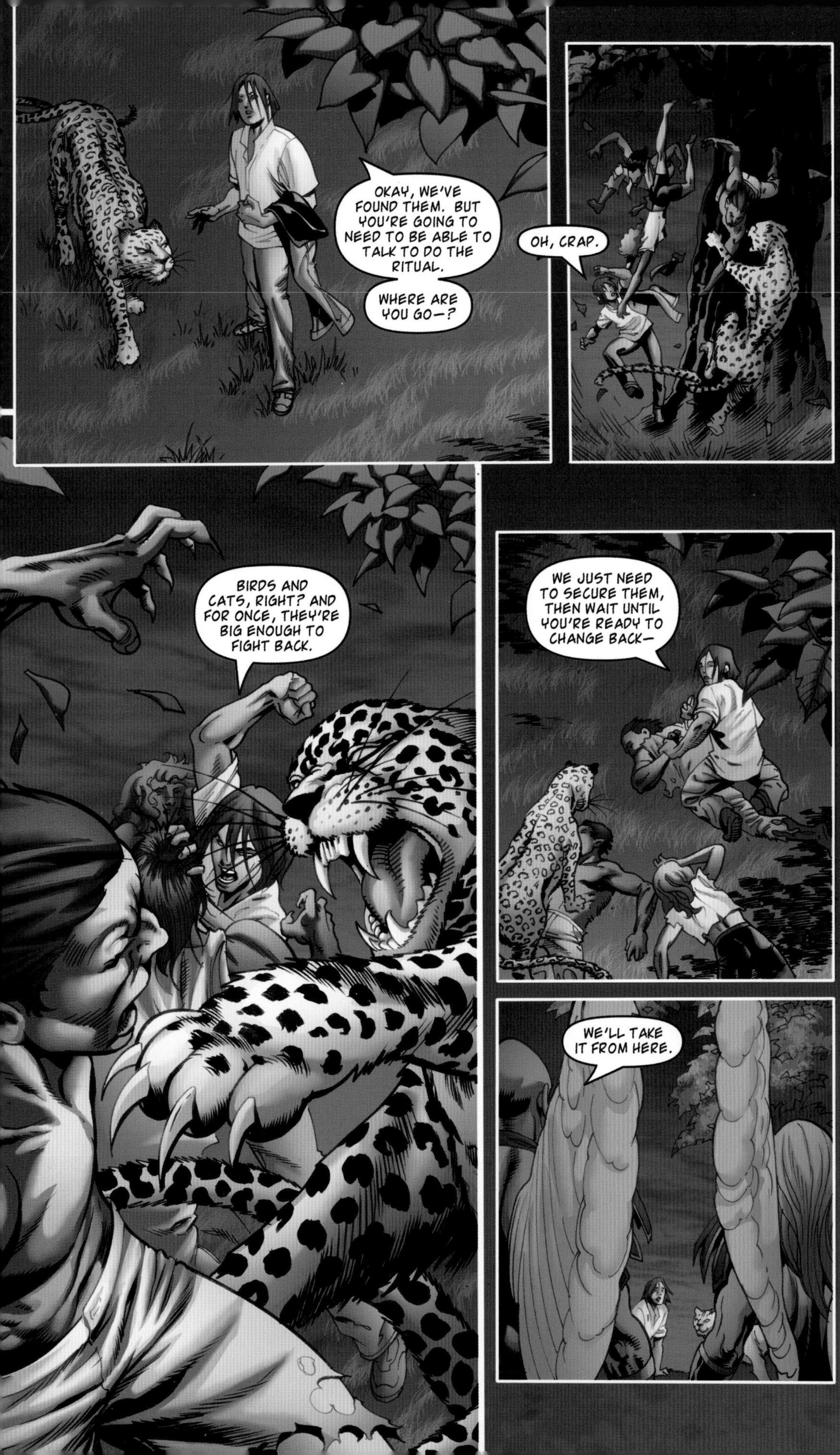
OKAY, WE'VE FOUND THEM. BUT YOU'RE GOING TO NEED TO BE ABLE TO TALK TO DO THE RITUAL.
WHERE ARE YOU GO—?
OH, CRAP.
BIRDS AND CATS, RIGHT? AND FOR ONCE, THEY'RE BIG ENOUGH TO FIGHT BACK.
WE JUST NEED TO SECURE THEM, THEN WAIT UNTIL YOU'RE READY TO CHANGE BACK—
WE'LL TAKE IT FROM HERE.

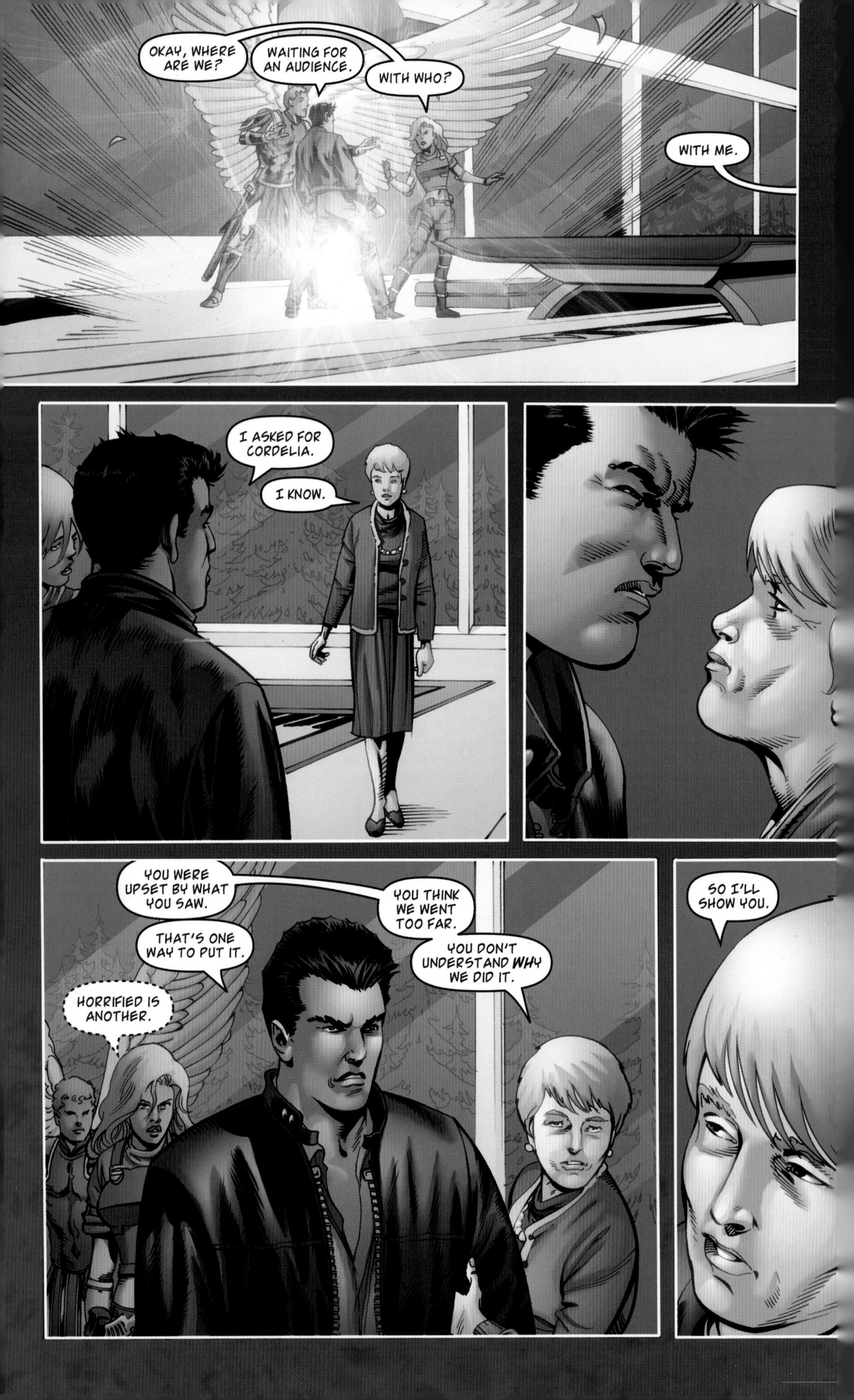
OKAY, WHERE ARE WE?
WAITING FOR AN AUDIENCE.
WITH WHO?
WITH ME.
I ASKED FOR CORDELIA.
I KNOW.
YOU WERE UPSET BY WHAT YOU SAW.
THAT'S ONE WAY TO PUT IT.
HORRIFIED IS ANOTHER.
YOU THINK WE WENT TOO FAR.
YOU DON'T UNDERSTAND WHY WE DID IT.
SO I'LL SHOW YOU.

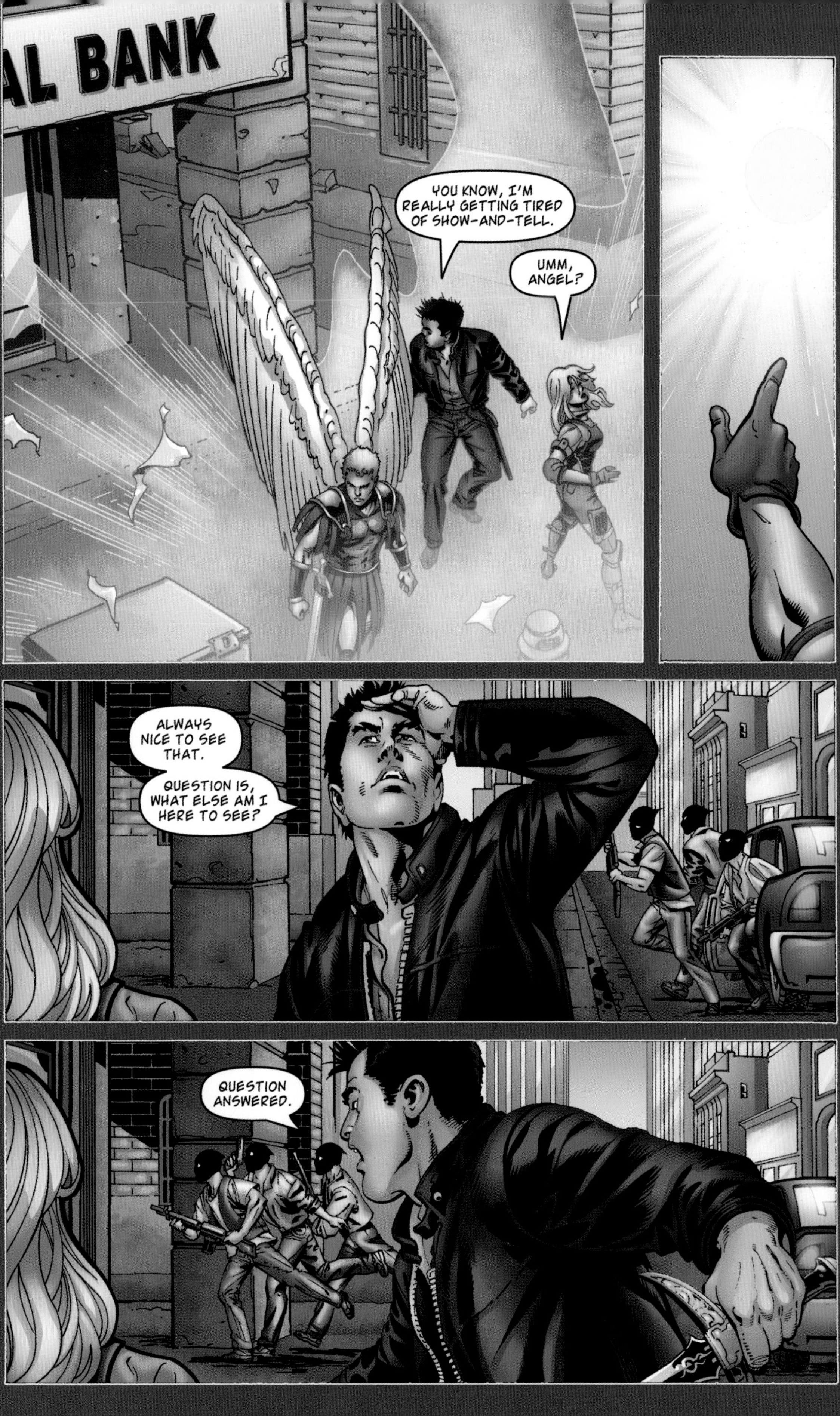
AL BANK
YOU KNOW, I'M REALLY GETTING TIRED OF SHOW-AND-TELL.
UMM, ANGEL?
ALWAYS NICE TO SEE THAT.
QUESTION IS, WHAT ELSE AM I HERE TO SEE?
QUESTION ANSWERED.

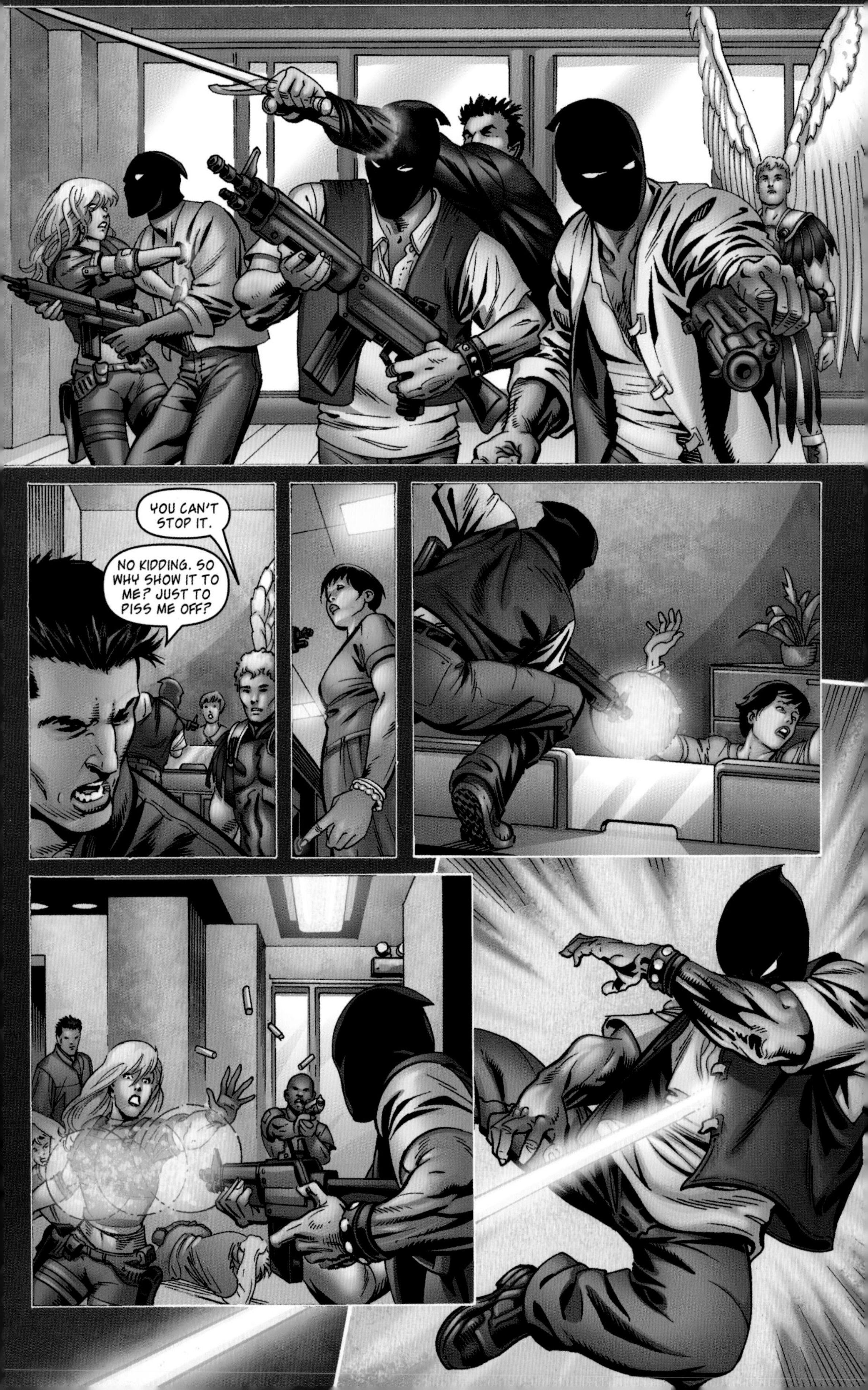
YOU CAN'T STOP IT.
NO KIDDING. SO WHY SHOW IT TO ME? JUST TO PISS ME OFF?

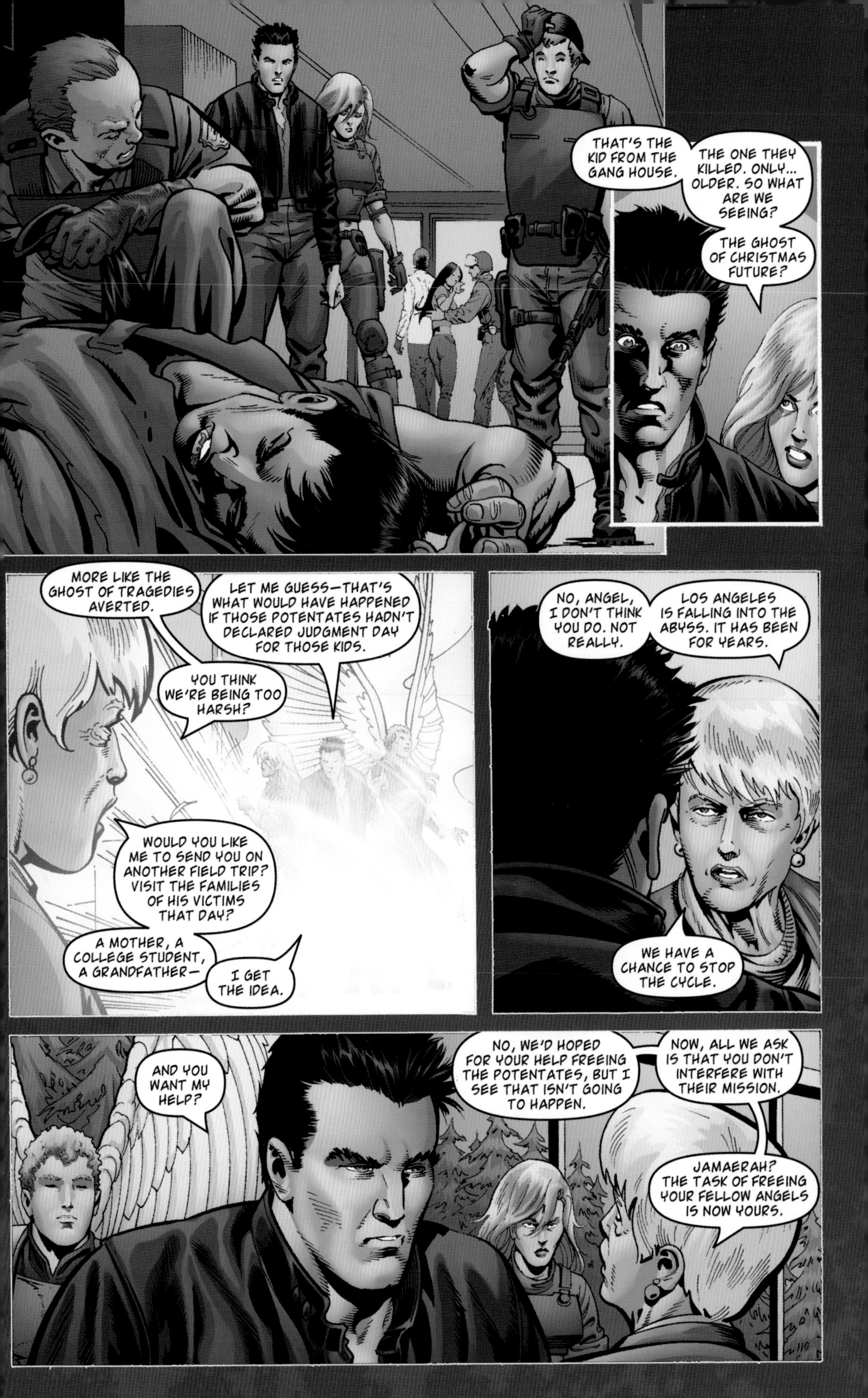
THAT'S THE KID FROM THE GANG HOUSE.
THE ONE THEY KILLED. ONLY... OLDER. SO WHAT ARE WE SEEING?
THE GHOST OF CHRISTMAS FUTURE?
MORE LIKE THE GHOST OF TRAGEDIES AVERTED.
LET ME GUESS—THAT'S WHAT WOULD HAVE HAPPENED IF THOSE POTENTATES HADN'T DECLARED JUDGMENT DAY FOR THOSE KIDS.
YOU THINK WE'RE BEING TOO HARSH?
WOULD YOU LIKE ME TO SEND YOU ON ANOTHER FIELD TRIP? VISIT THE FAMILIES OF HIS VICTIMS THAT DAY?
A MOTHER, A COLLEGE STUDENT, A GRANDFATHER—
I GET THE IDEA.
NO, ANGEL, I DON'T THINK YOU DO. NOT REALLY.
LOS ANGELES IS FALLING INTO THE ABYSS. IT HAS BEEN FOR YEARS.
WE HAVE A CHANCE TO STOP THE CYCLE.
AND YOU WANT MY HELP?
NO, WE'D HOPED FOR YOUR HELP FREEING THE POTENTATES, BUT I SEE THAT ISN'T GOING TO HAPPEN.
NOW, ALL WE ASK IS THAT YOU DON'T INTERFERE WITH THEIR MISSION.
JAMAERAH? THE TASK OF FREEING YOUR FELLOW ANGELS IS NOW YOURS.

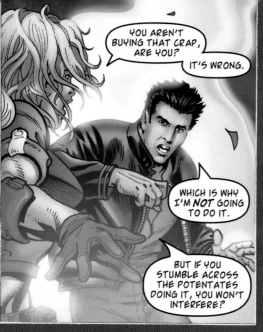

YOU AREN'T BUYING THAT CRAP, ARE YOU?

IT'S WRONG.

WHICH IS WHY I'M *NOT* GOING TO DO IT.

BUT IF YOU STUMBLE ACROSS THE POTENTATES DOING IT, YOU WON'T INTERFERE?

KATE...

I WON'T HUNT THEM DOWN, BUT IF I SEE IT, I'LL STOP IT.

IF THAT MEANS I PISS OFF THE POWERS, THAT'S FINE.

I LEARNED MY LESSON. IF I THINK IT'S WRONG, THEN IT'S WRONG FOR ME. THAT'S ALL THAT COUNTS.

SO, JAMES, I TAKE IT—

WELL, THIS FEELS FAMILIAR.

GO ON, CONNOR. THIS IS *MY* FIGHT.

THERE'S NOT GOING TO BE A FIGHT. WE DIDN'T COME TO KILL YOU.

YOU MAY BE AN ABOMINATION, BUT IT ISN'T YOUR FAULT. YOU'RE A PAWN.

WE'RE GOING TO REMOVE THE CURSE. RETURN YOU TO YOUR NATURAL STATE.

AND IF *SHE* DOESN'T *WANT* THAT?

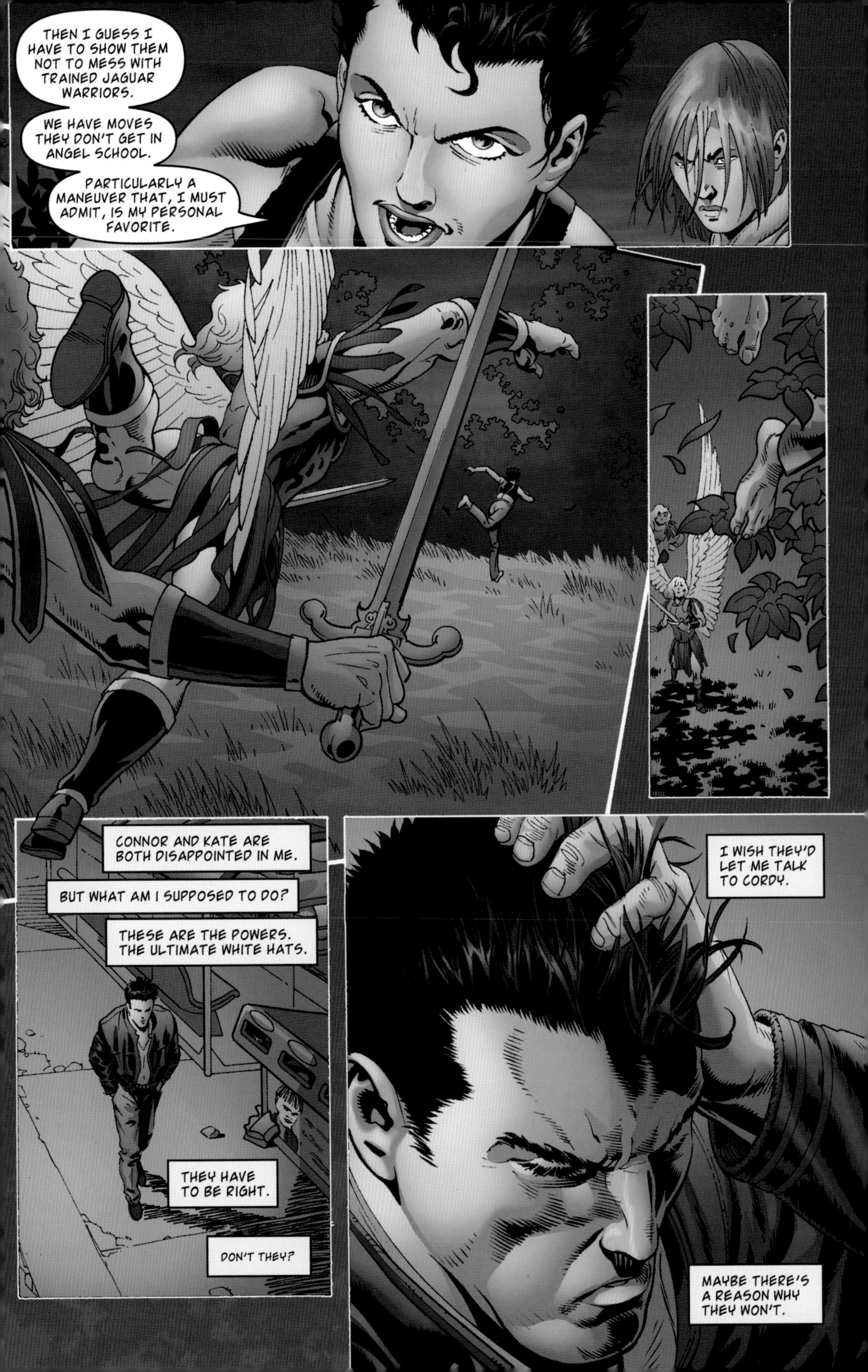
THEN I GUESS I HAVE TO SHOW THEM NOT TO MESS WITH TRAINED JAGUAR WARRIORS.
WE HAVE MOVES THEY DON'T GET IN ANGEL SCHOOL.
PARTICULARLY A MANEUVER THAT, I MUST ADMIT, IS MY PERSONAL FAVORITE.
CONNOR AND KATE ARE BOTH DISAPPOINTED IN ME.
BUT WHAT AM I SUPPOSED TO DO?
THESE ARE THE POWERS. THE ULTIMATE WHITE HATS.
THEY HAVE TO BE RIGHT.
DON'T THEY?
I WISH THEY'D LET ME TALK TO CORDY.
MAYBE THERE'S A REASON WHY THEY WON'T.

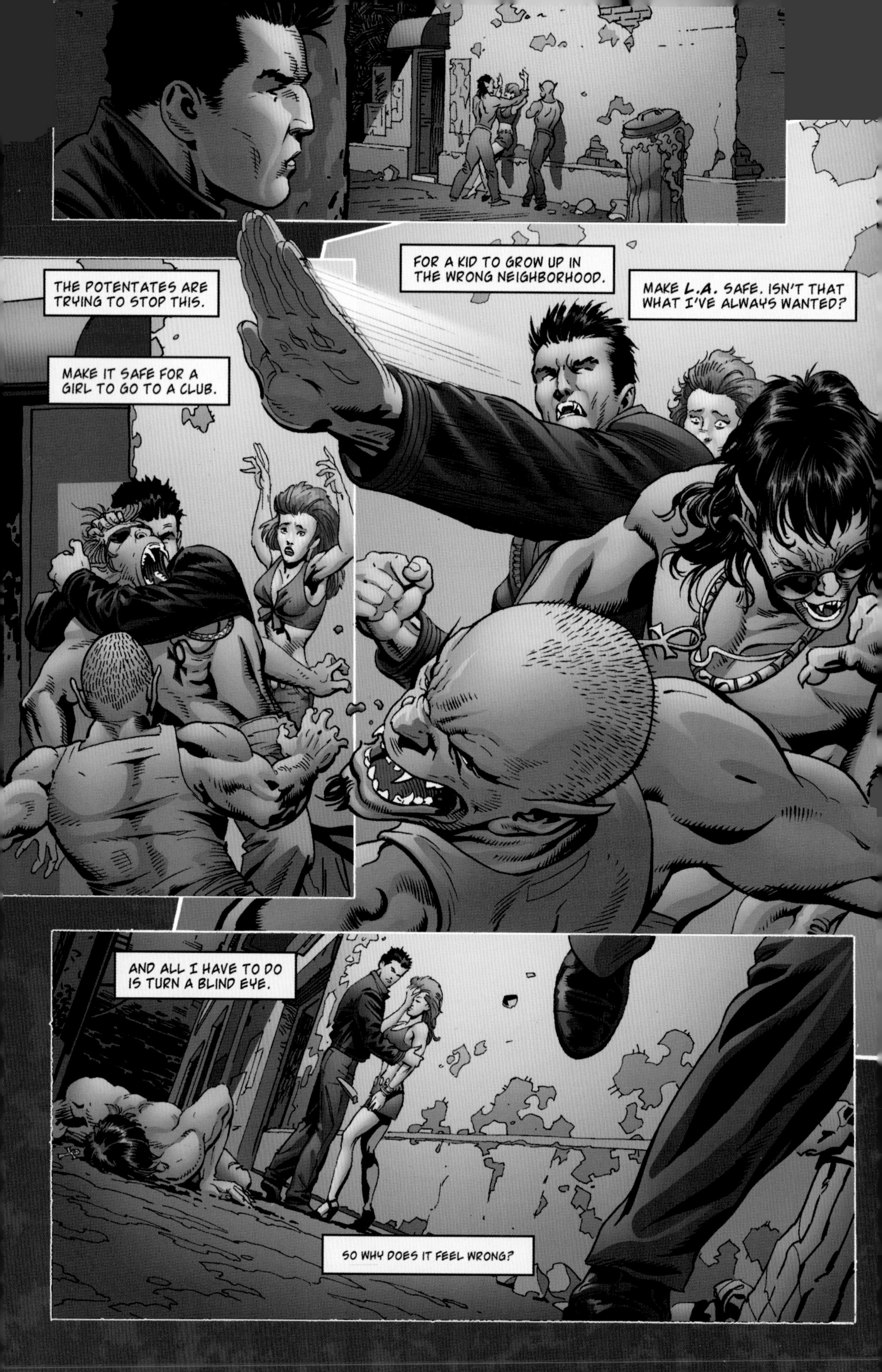
THE POTENTATES ARE TRYING TO STOP THIS.
MAKE IT SAFE FOR A GIRL TO GO TO A CLUB.
FOR A KID TO GROW UP IN THE WRONG NEIGHBORHOOD.
MAKE L.A. SAFE. ISN'T THAT WHAT I'VE ALWAYS WANTED?
AND ALL I HAVE TO DO IS TURN A BLIND EYE.
SO WHY DOES IT FEEL WRONG?

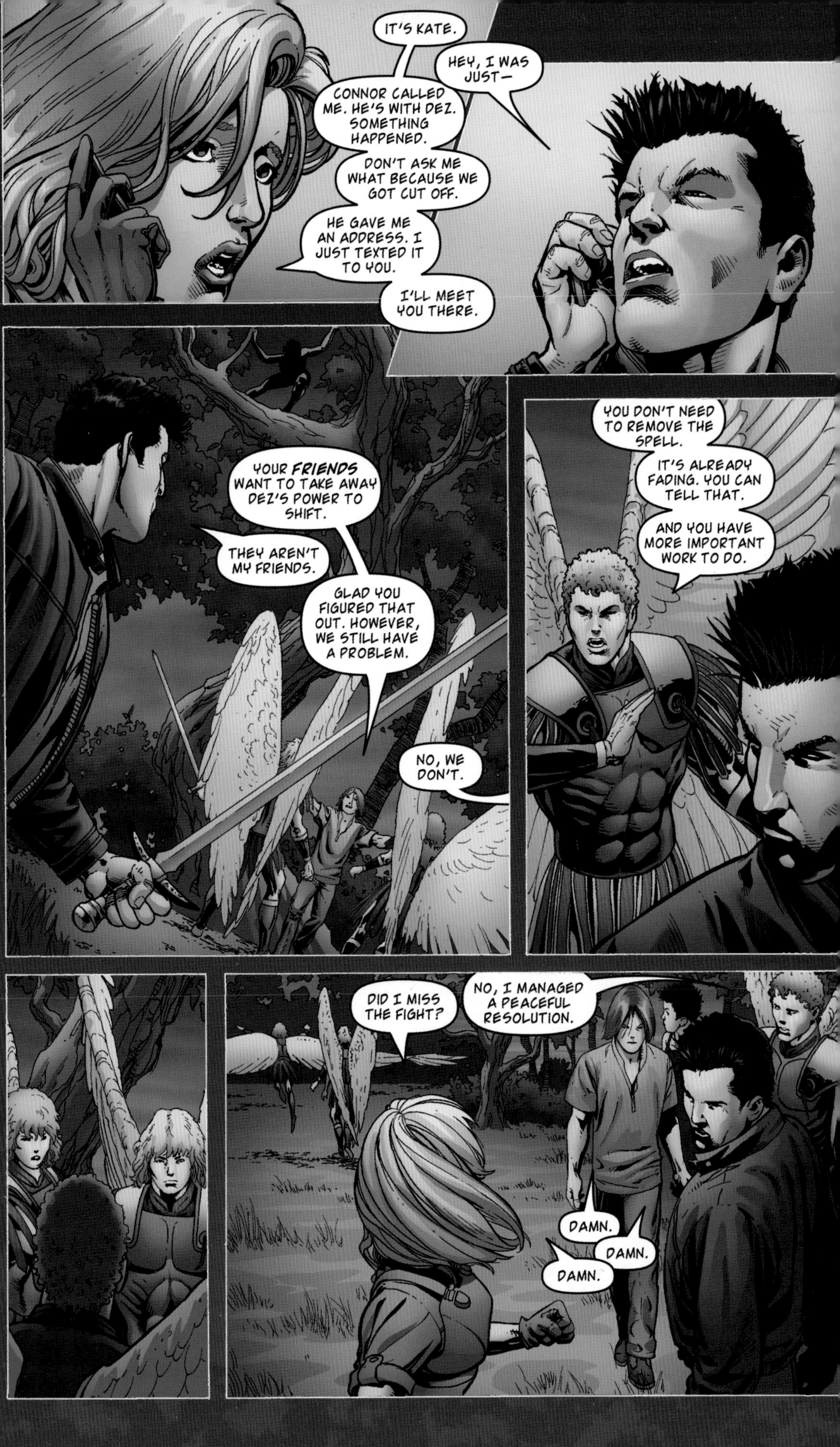
IT'S KATE.
HEY, I WAS JUST—
CONNOR CALLED ME. HE'S WITH DEZ. SOMETHING HAPPENED.
DON'T ASK ME WHAT BECAUSE WE GOT CUT OFF.
HE GAVE ME AN ADDRESS. I JUST TEXTED IT TO YOU.
I'LL MEET YOU THERE.
YOUR FRIENDS WANT TO TAKE AWAY DEZ'S POWER TO SHIFT.
THEY AREN'T MY FRIENDS.
GLAD YOU FIGURED THAT OUT. HOWEVER, WE STILL HAVE A PROBLEM.
NO, WE DON'T.
YOU DON'T NEED TO REMOVE THE SPELL.
IT'S ALREADY FADING. YOU CAN TELL THAT.
AND YOU HAVE MORE IMPORTANT WORK TO DO.
DID I MISS THE FIGHT?
NO, I MANAGED A PEACEFUL RESOLUTION.
DAMN.
DAMN.
DAMN.

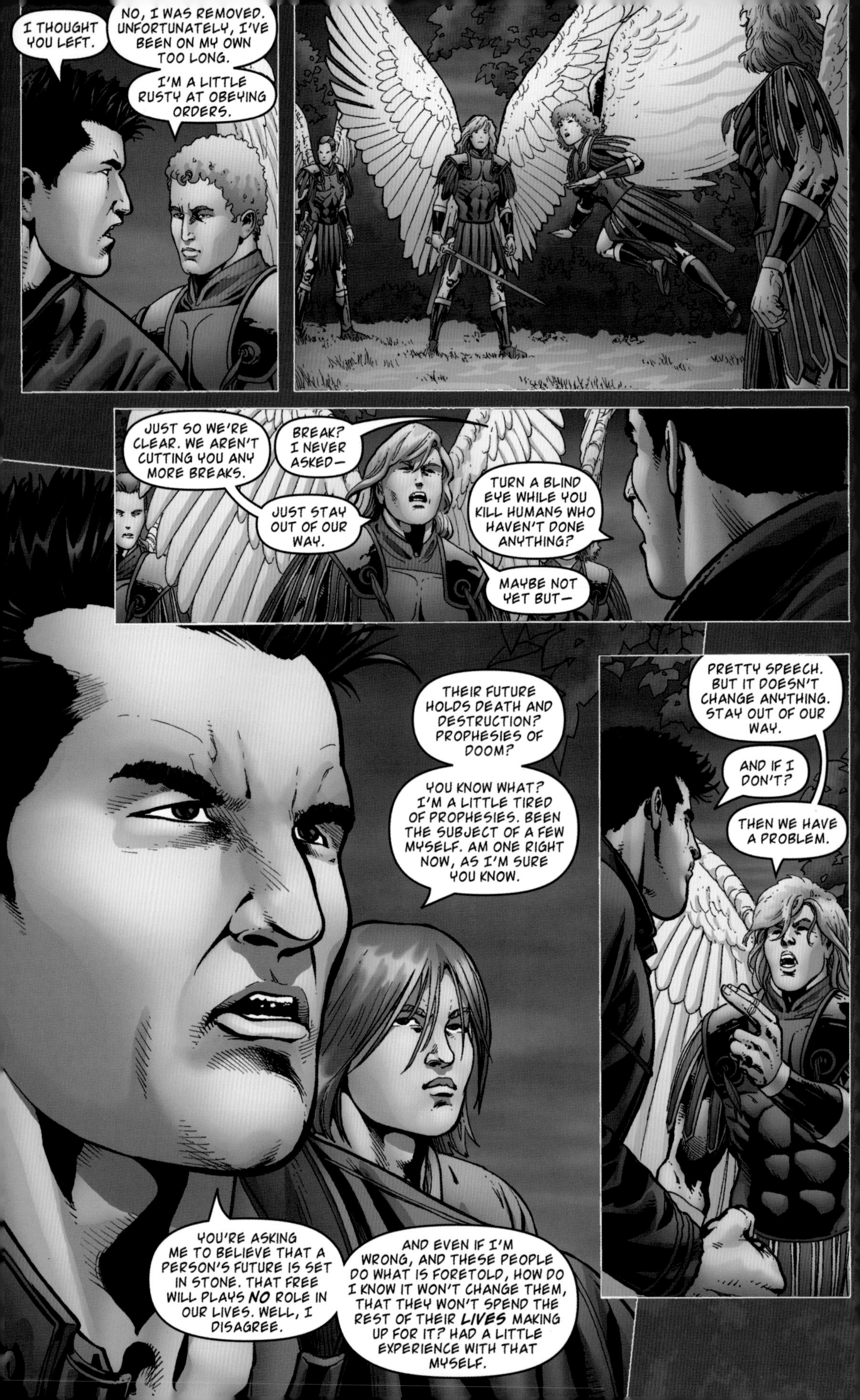
I THOUGHT YOU LEFT.
NO, I WAS REMOVED. UNFORTUNATELY, I'VE BEEN ON MY OWN TOO LONG.
I'M A LITTLE RUSTY AT OBEYING ORDERS.
JUST SO WE'RE CLEAR. WE AREN'T CUTTING YOU ANY MORE BREAKS.
BREAK? I NEVER ASKED—
JUST STAY OUT OF OUR WAY.
TURN A BLIND EYE WHILE YOU KILL HUMANS WHO HAVEN'T DONE ANYTHING?
MAYBE NOT YET BUT—
THEIR FUTURE HOLDS DEATH AND DESTRUCTION? PROPHESIES OF DOOM?
YOU KNOW WHAT? I'M A LITTLE TIRED OF PROPHESIES. BEEN THE SUBJECT OF A FEW MYSELF. AM ONE RIGHT NOW, AS I'M SURE YOU KNOW.
YOU'RE ASKING ME TO BELIEVE THAT A PERSON'S FUTURE IS SET IN STONE. THAT FREE WILL PLAYS NO ROLE IN OUR LIVES. WELL, I DISAGREE.
AND EVEN IF I'M WRONG, AND THESE PEOPLE DO WHAT IS FORETOLD, HOW DO I KNOW IT WON'T CHANGE THEM, THAT THEY WON'T SPEND THE REST OF THEIR LIVES MAKING UP FOR IT? HAD A LITTLE EXPERIENCE WITH THAT MYSELF.
PRETTY SPEECH. BUT IT DOESN'T CHANGE ANYTHING. STAY OUT OF OUR WAY.
AND IF I DON'T?
THEN WE HAVE A PROBLEM.

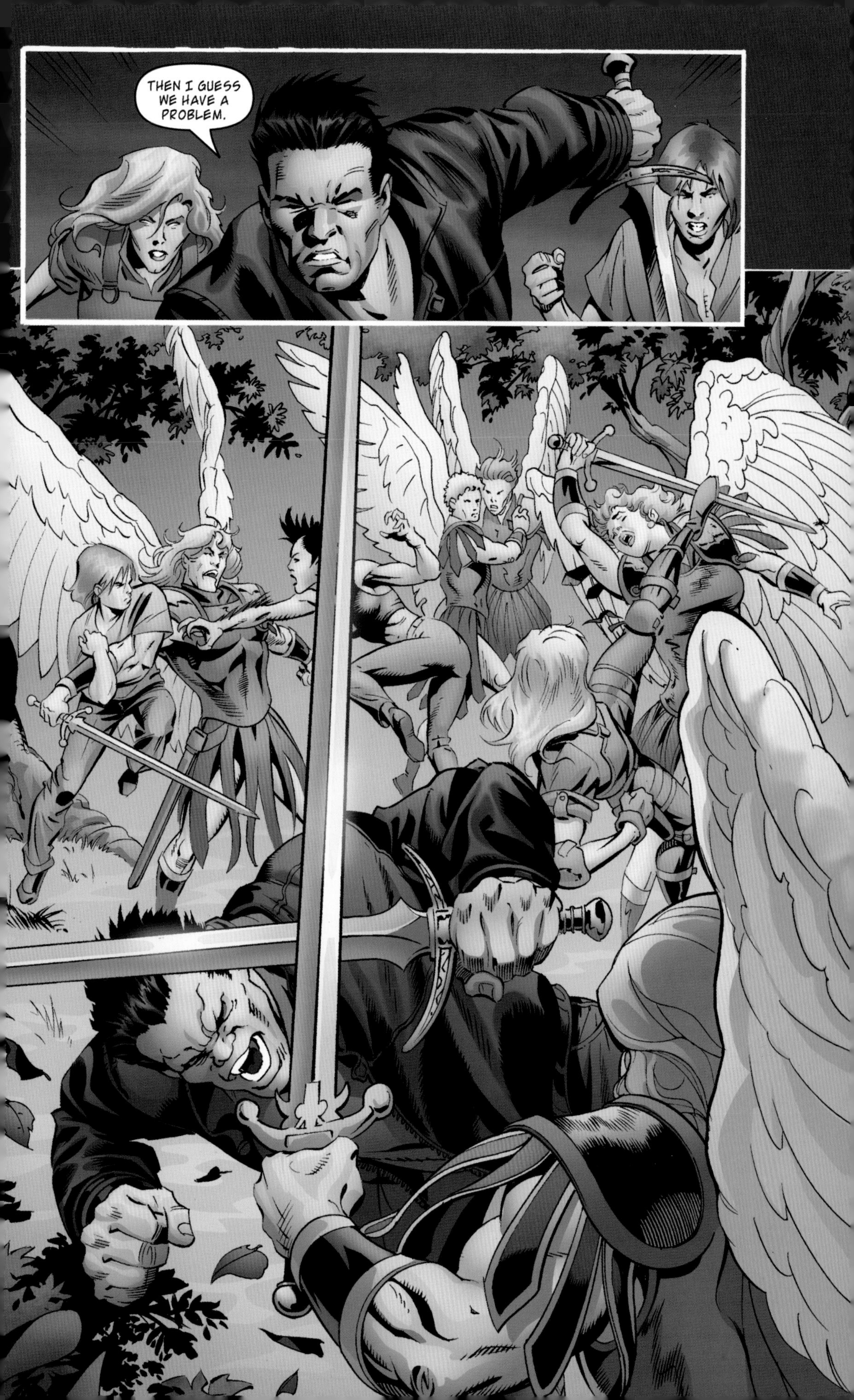
THEN I GUESS WE HAVE A PROBLEM.

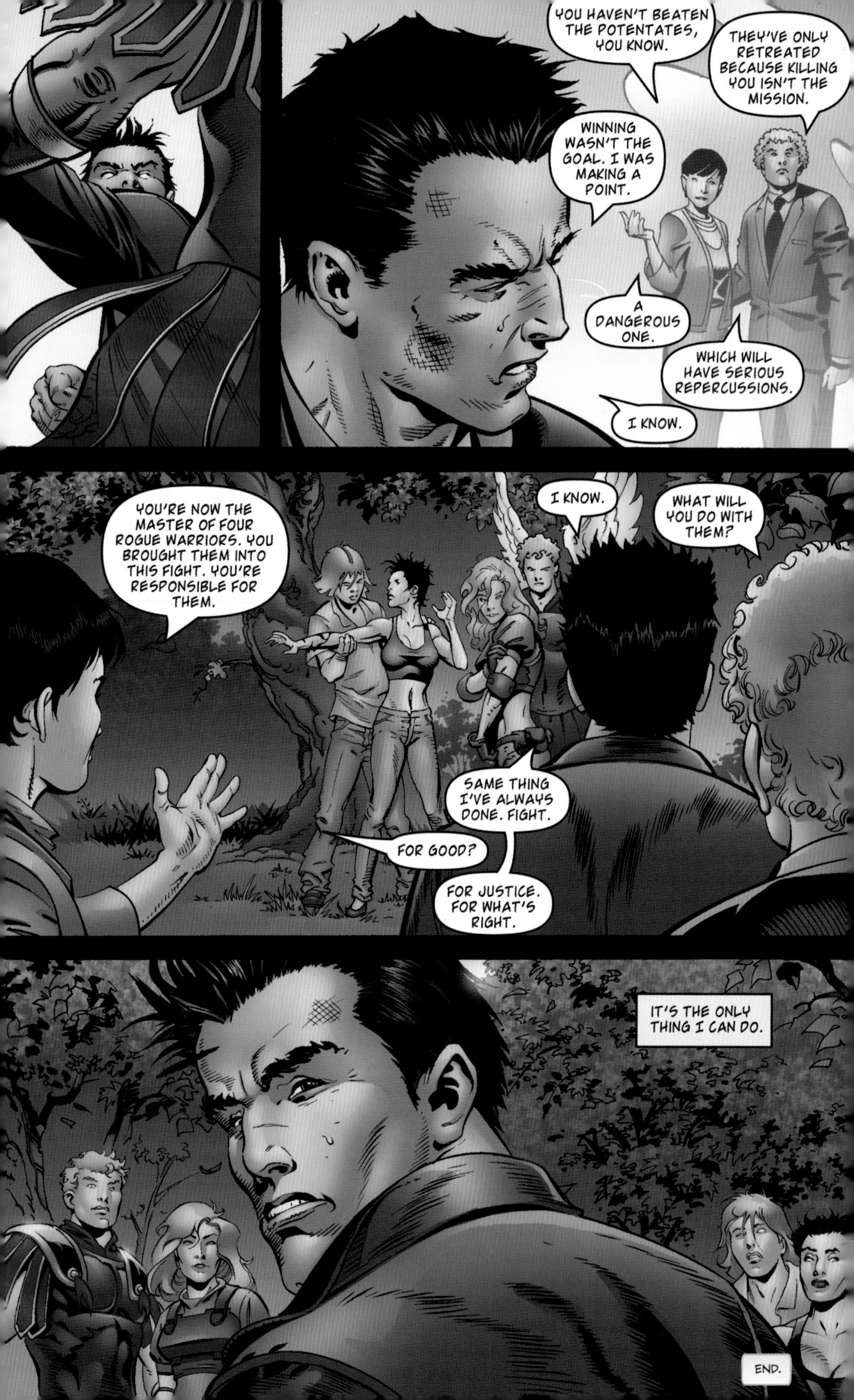

YOU HAVEN'T BEATEN THE POTENTATES, YOU KNOW.
THEY'VE ONLY RETREATED BECAUSE KILLING YOU ISN'T THE MISSION.
WINNING WASN'T THE GOAL. I WAS MAKING A POINT.
A DANGEROUS ONE.
WHICH WILL HAVE SERIOUS REPERCUSSIONS.
I KNOW.
YOU'RE NOW THE MASTER OF FOUR ROGUE WARRIORS. YOU BROUGHT THEM INTO THIS FIGHT. YOU'RE RESPONSIBLE FOR THEM.
I KNOW.
WHAT WILL YOU DO WITH THEM?
SAME THING I'VE ALWAYS DONE. FIGHT.
FOR GOOD?
FOR JUSTICE. FOR WHAT'S RIGHT.
IT'S THE ONLY THING I CAN DO.
END.

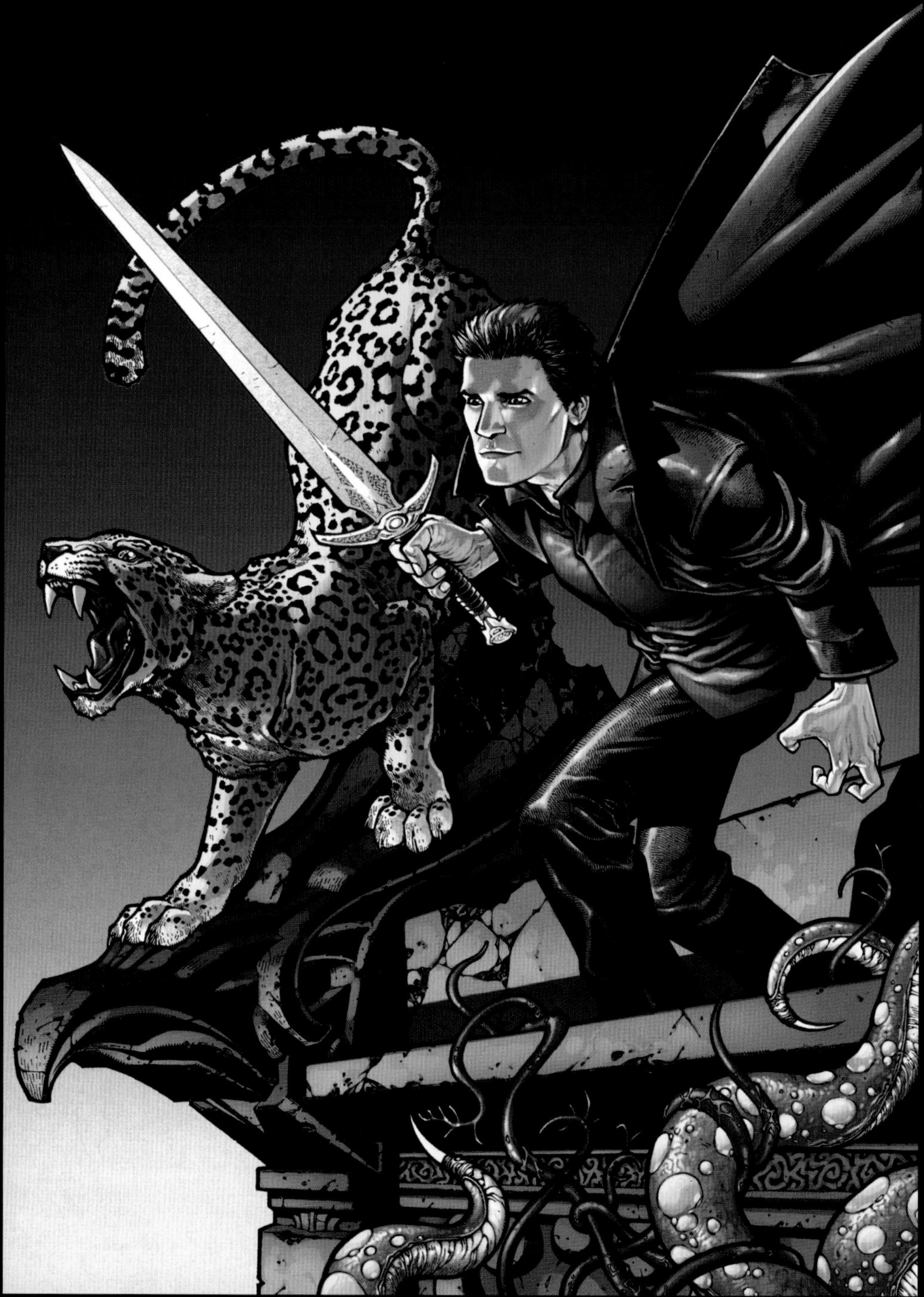

art gallery

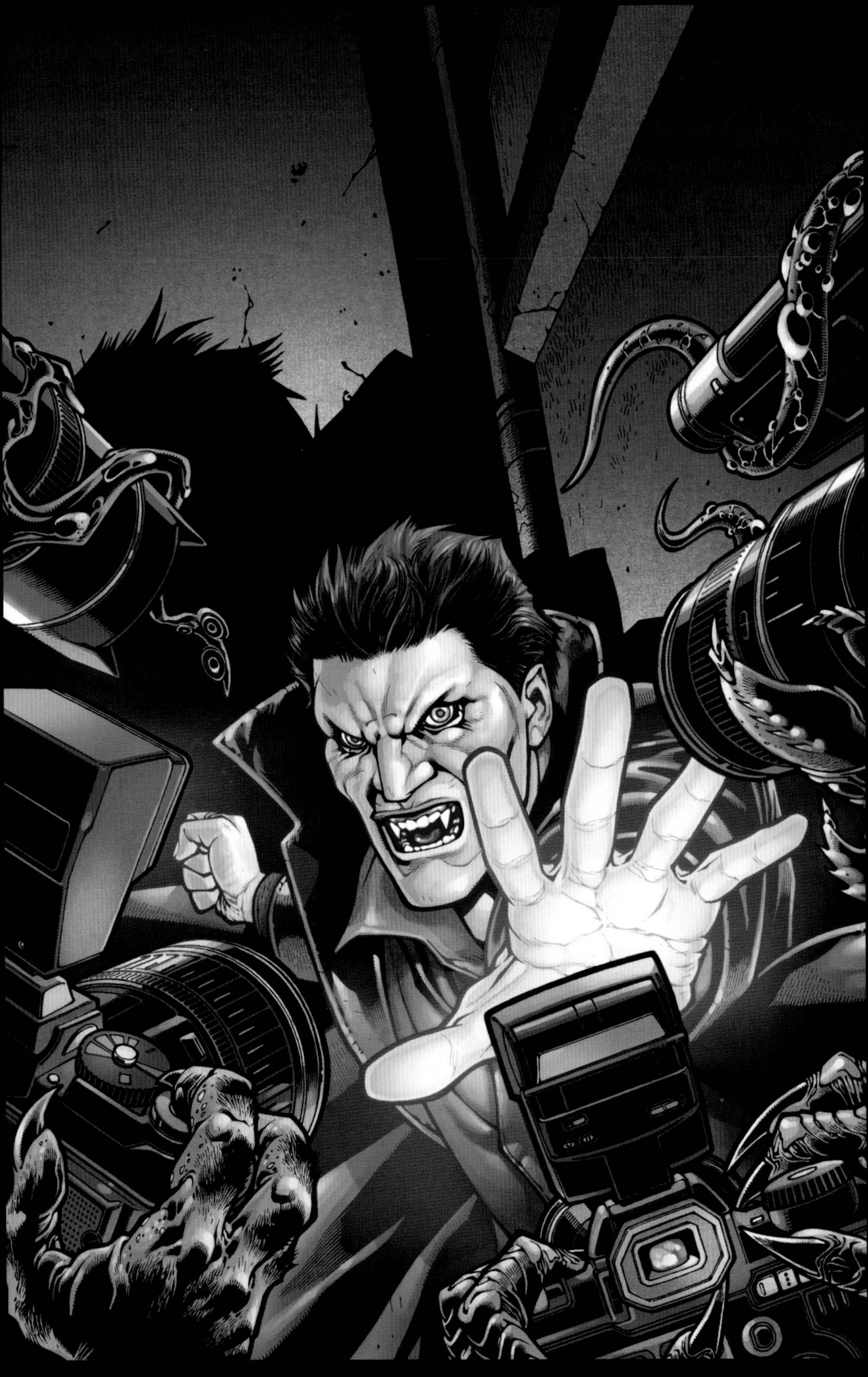

This Page: Art by Gabriel Rodriguez

Previous Page: Art by Gabriel Rodriguez

Opposite Page: Art by Nick Runge

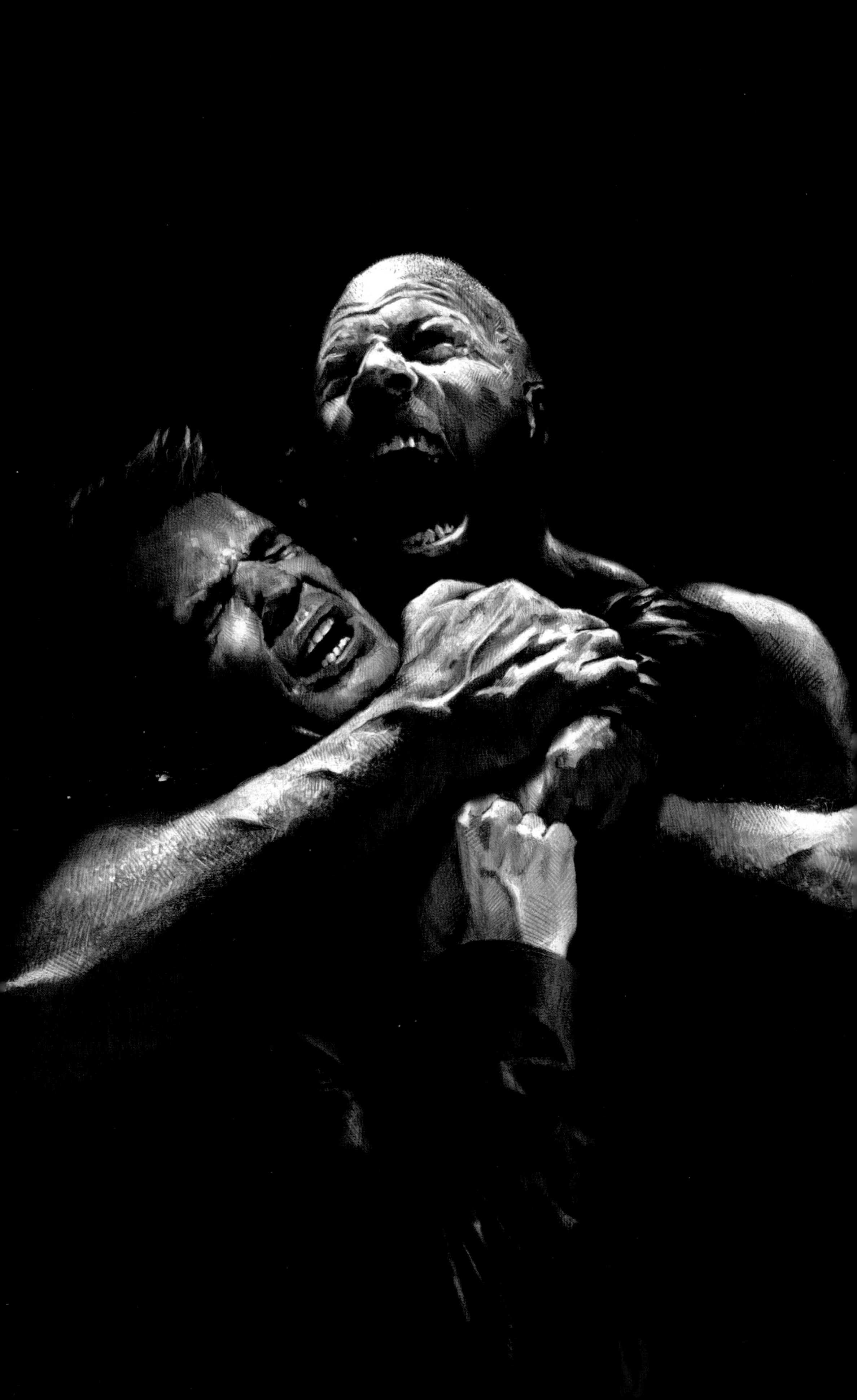

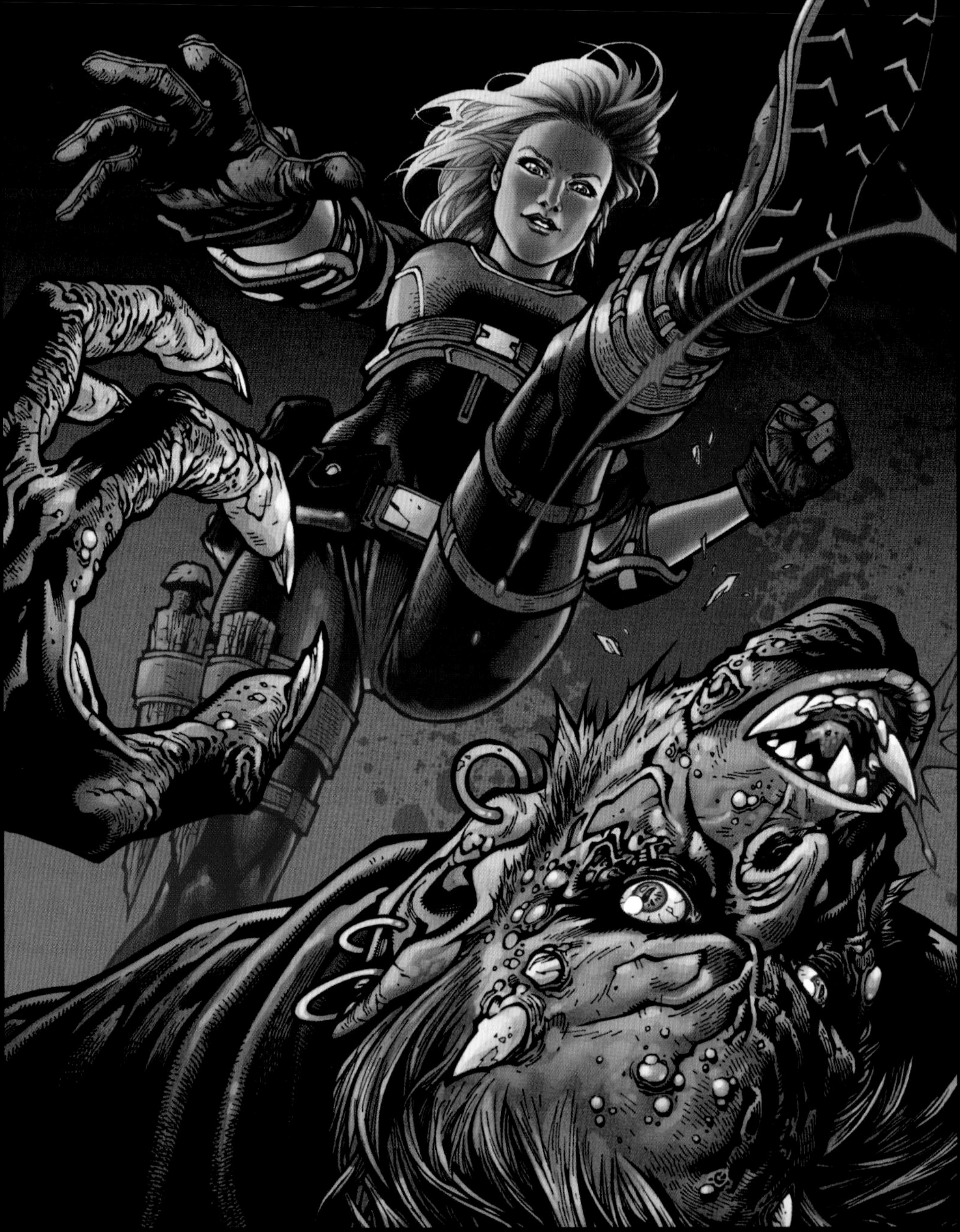

This Page: Art by Gabriel Rodriguez Opposite Page: Art by Nick Runge

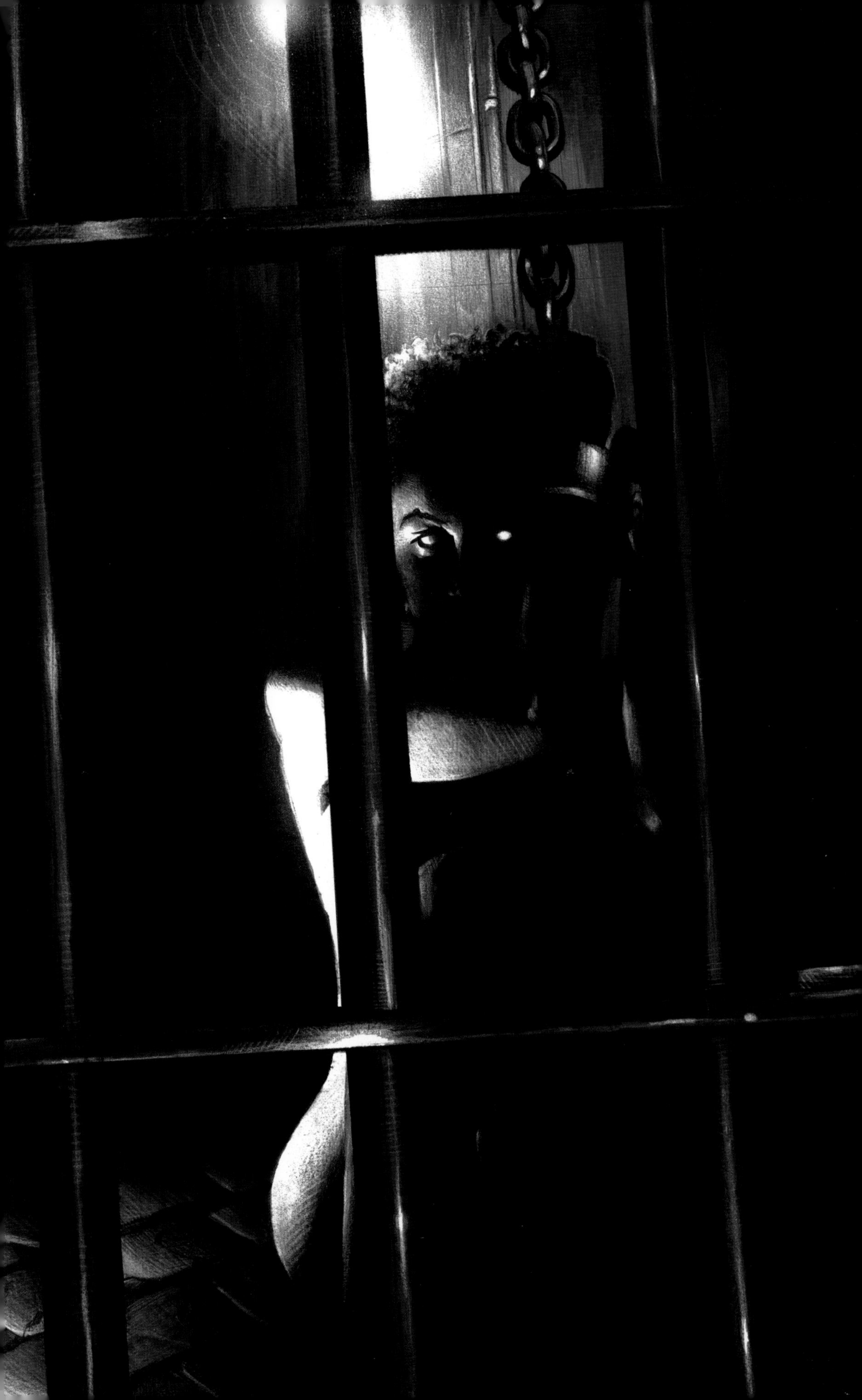

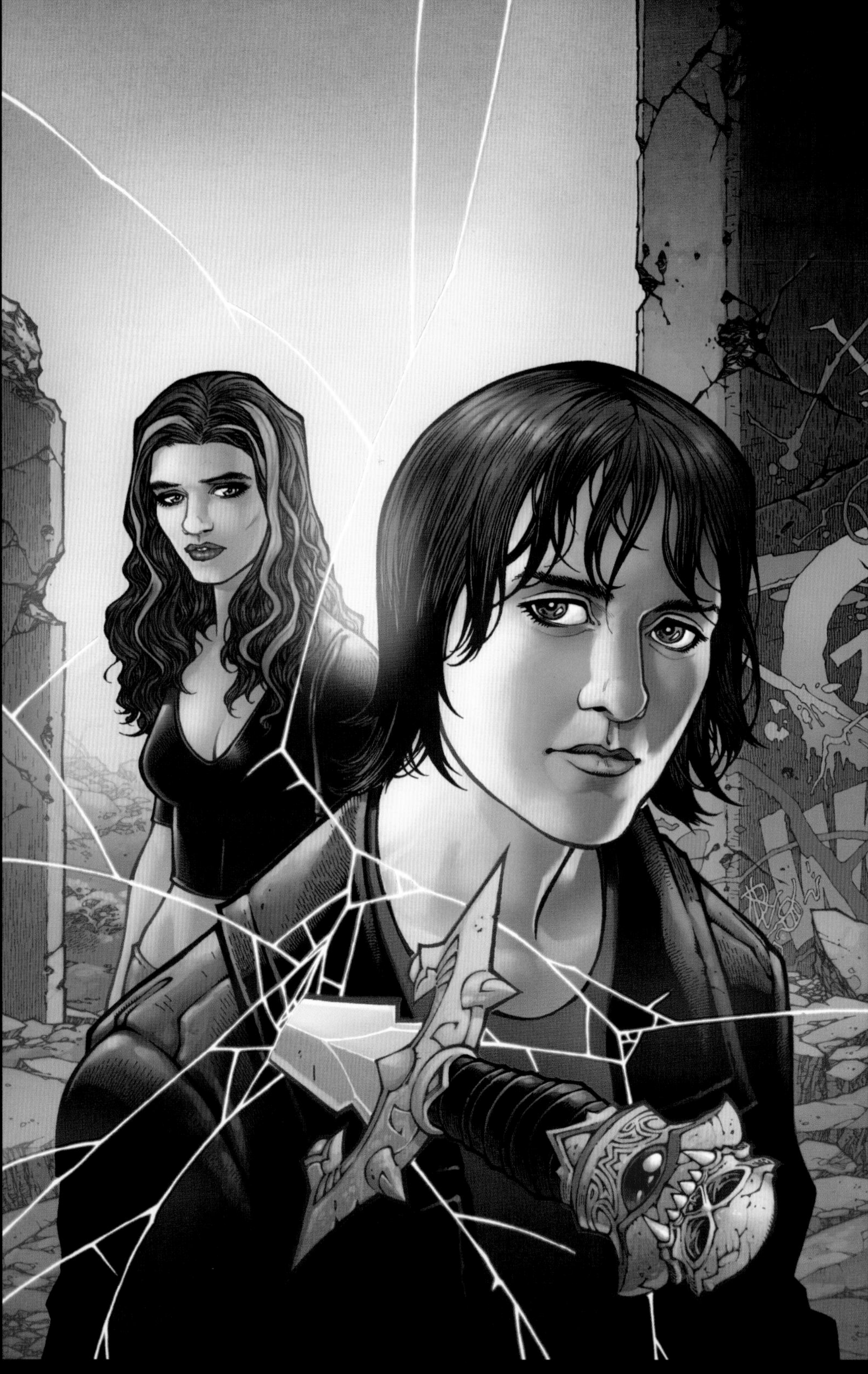

This Page: Art by Gabriel Rodriguez

Opposite Page: Art by Nick Runge

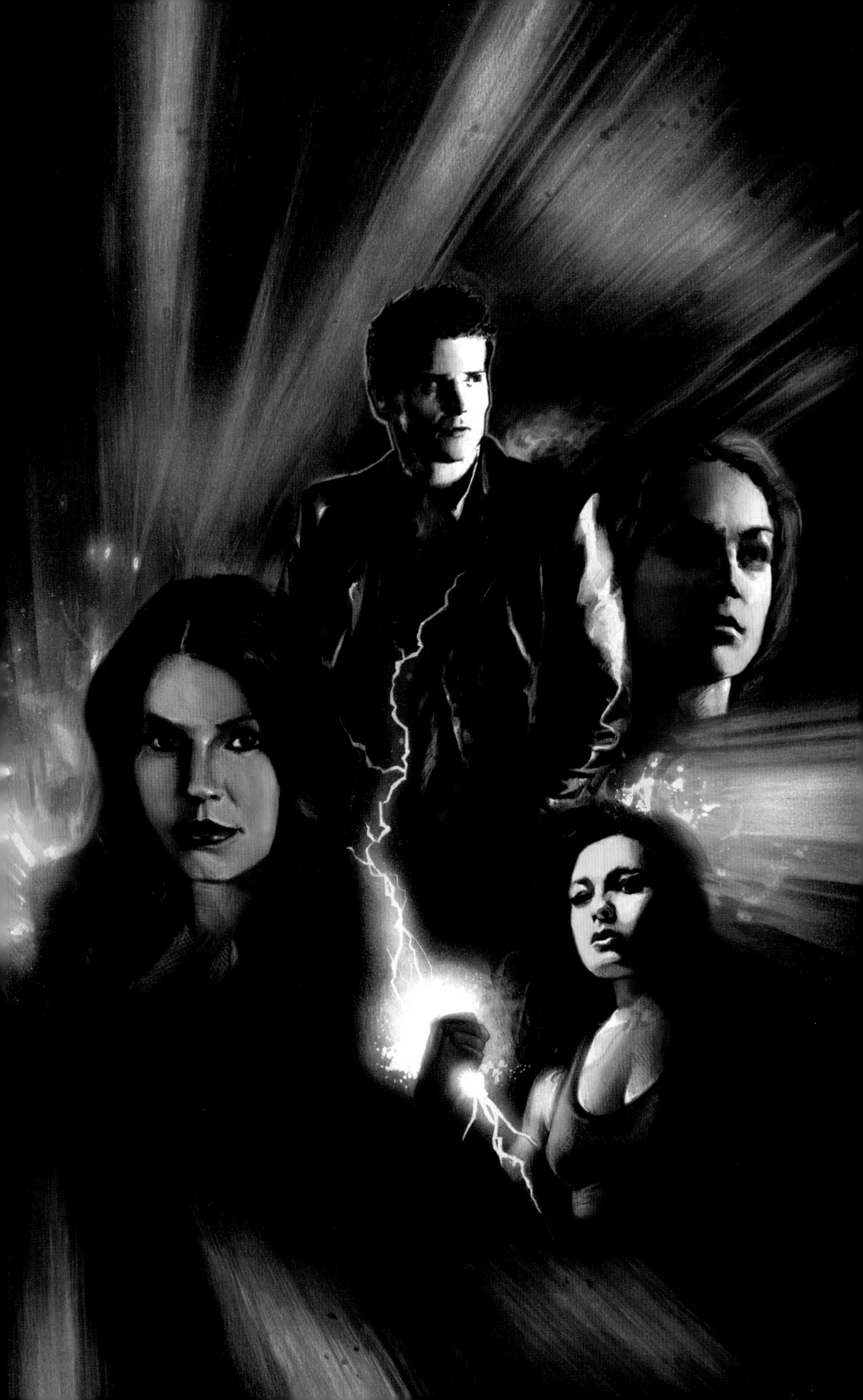

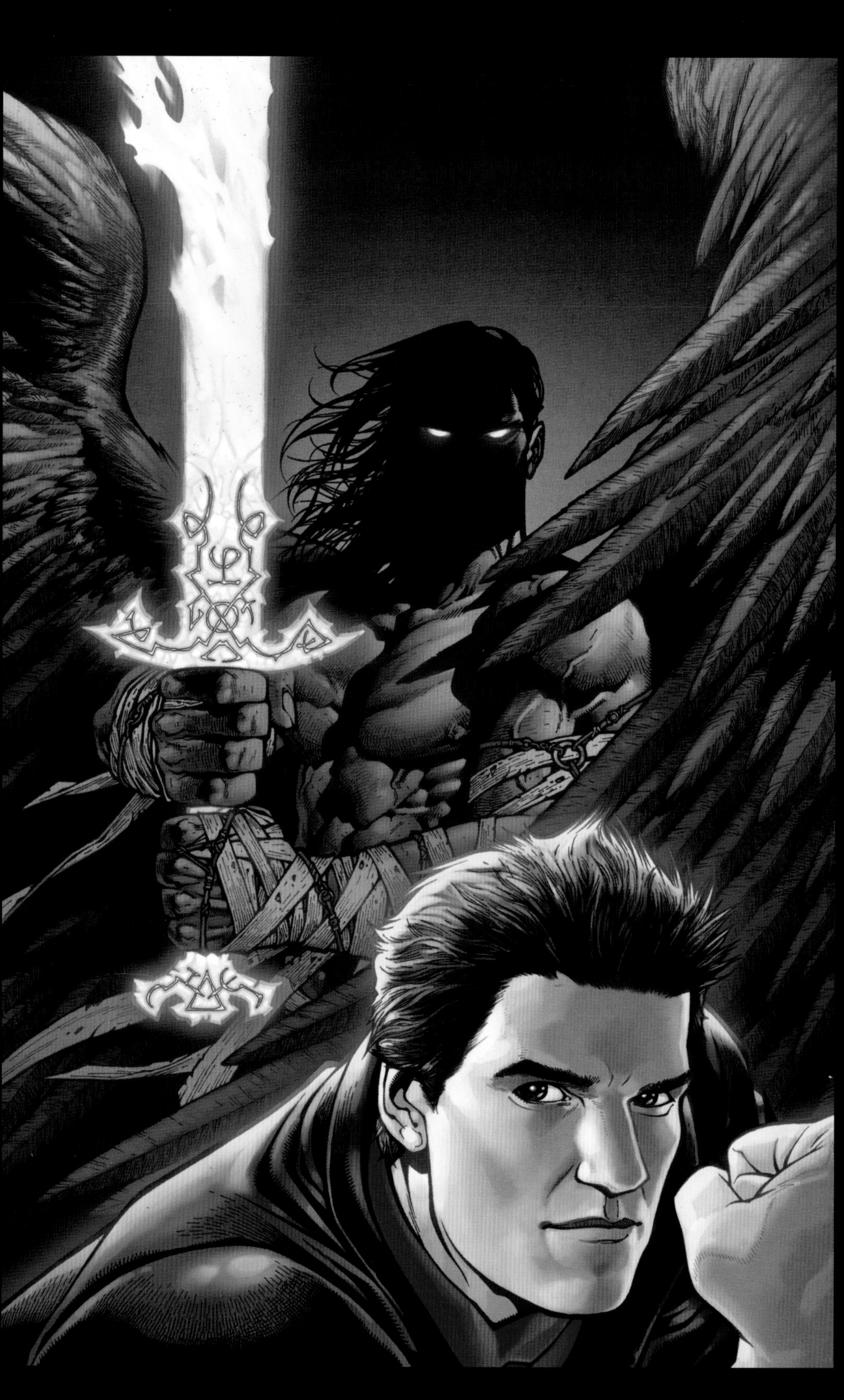

This Page: Art by Gabriel Rodriguez

Opposite Page: Art by Nick Runge

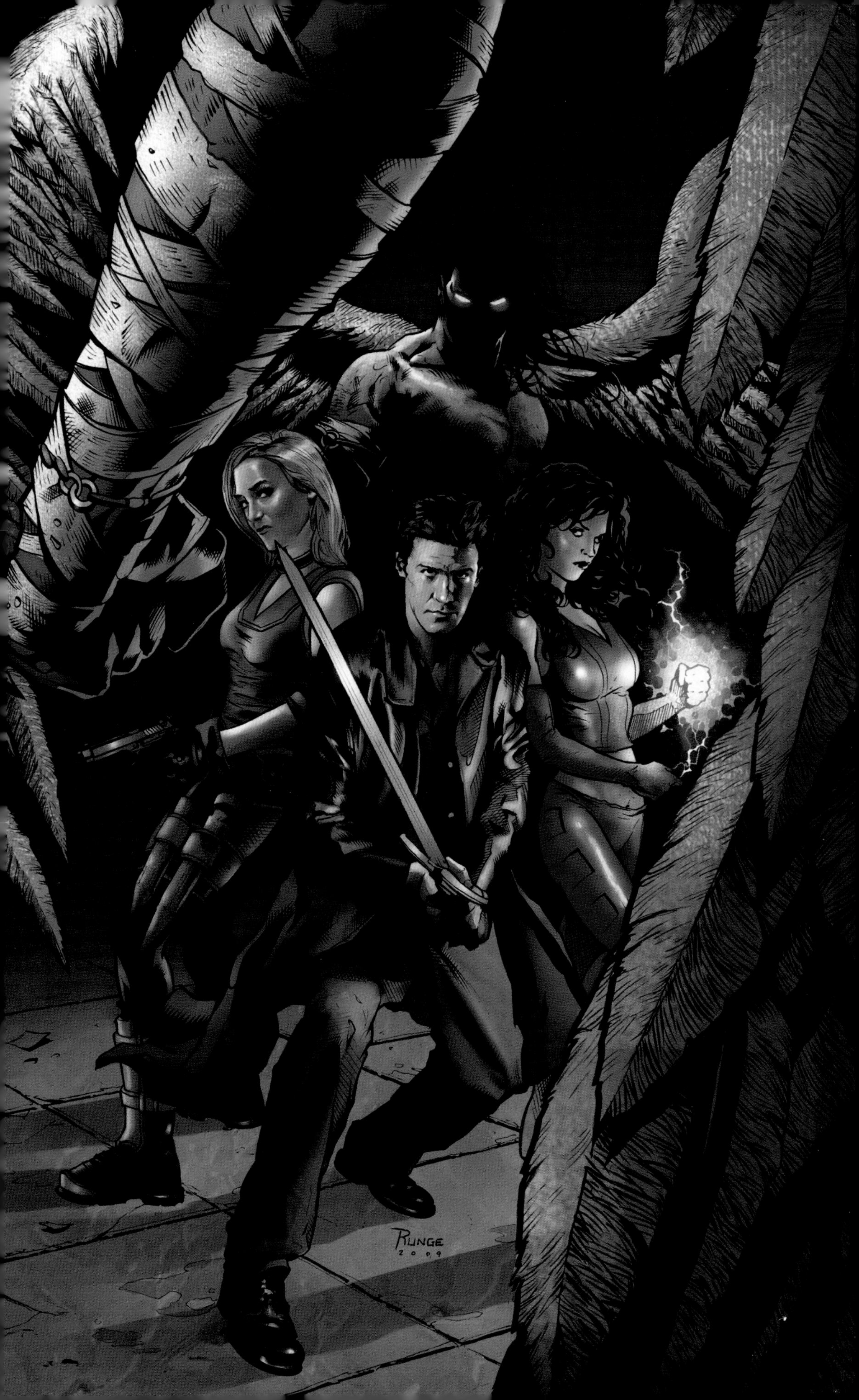
RUNGE
2009

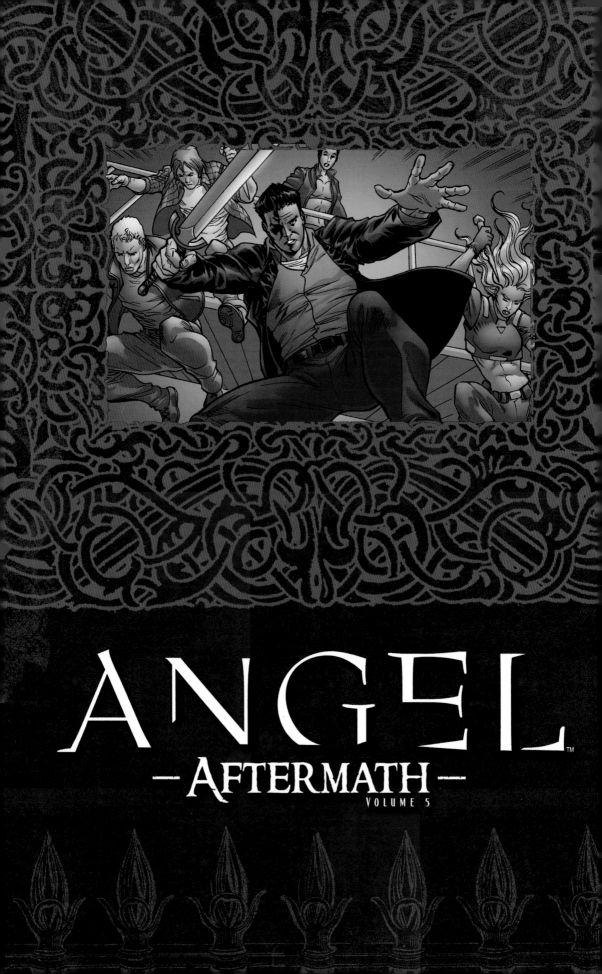

ANGEL
-AFTERMATH-
VOLUME 5